LOVE AND FRIENDSHIP

LOVE AND FRIENDSHIP

Maritain and the Tradition

EDITED BY MONTAGUE BROWN

AMERICAN MARITAIN ASSOCIATION

Distributed by

THE CATHOLIC UNIVERSITY
OF AMERICA PRESS
Washington, D.C.

Manufactured in the United States of America

Distributed by the Catholic Univesity of America Press
620 Michigan Avenue, N.E., 240 Leahy Hall
Washington, D.C. 20064

Library of Congress Cataloging-in-Publication Data
Love and friendship : Maritain and the tradition /
edited by Montague Brown.
pages cm
1. Maritain, Jacques, 1882-1973.
I. Brown, Montague, editor of compilation.
B2430.M34L68 2013
177′.62092—dc23
2013025501

ISBN 978-0-9827119-3-4

CONTENTS

IV. LOVE, FRIENDSHIP, AND THE POLITICAL COMMUNITY

V. THE LOVE OF BEING AND THE BEING OF LOVE

VI. THEOLOGICAL FOUNDATIONS: LITURGY, MARRIAGE, AND THE COVENANT

MONTAGUE BROWN

Introduction

The Analogy of Love

When it comes to matters of love and friendship, Jacques Maritain had wide-ranging interests, from particular relationships in the world to mystical experience, from marriage to political community, from natural law and natural rights to God's revealed covenantal relationship with us. So, of course, does the Catholic Church and the intellectual tradition it inspires and protects. Love and friendship are analogical terms, the first being applicable to all things: from activities of elements and cosmological structures (Dante's "the love that moves the sun and the other stars") to human motivations, from instincts and sensual desires to the search for wisdom, goodness, and beauty, and from all human loves to the God who is Love. The analogy of friendship includes all relationships between persons, from casual acquaintances to those based on virtue and duty, from the human bonds produced by creativity and kindness to divine creation and salvation, from the city of man to the City of God, from spousal love to the interior life of the Trinity. This volume touches on all these topics to some degree, and as such, is a reflection of Maritain's intellectual life as well as of the Catholic intellectual tradition in which he worked.

Analogy is the bastion against all forms of reductionism, whether material or formal. Material reductionism tries to explain all things in terms of more basic building blocks. Consider an act of free choice, which is among the most obvious and certain facts of our existence. If I am certain of anything, I am certain that "I" am certain; but this judgment of selfhood is inconceivable without freedom. My judgment is freely mine or it is not mine at all. In any case, this judgment about free choice, without which there can be no love or friendship, is the first casualty of reductionism. To explain free choice on other terms is to explain it away. Psychology would try to explain it, not with reference to free responsibility, but merely in terms of psychological drives or needs. Biology, putting aside the psychological account, would try to explain the action merely in terms of living adaptation to environment, or operations of organs, or cell structure. Chemistry would ignore all these biologically formal (living) explanations and concentrate on the chemical compounds and reactions which occur as the choice is made. Physics would dig even deeper into the material conditions of the act, trying to explain it in terms of the most basic material building blocks and energy. Each reduction is methodologically legitimate, and each allows for real discoveries about the way things are. But none of them explains the moral act, for a moral act that is not free is not a moral act; it could not be my act or yours.

Reductionism as the intentional ignoring of complex unities in favor of an analysis of parts is simply the method proper to scientific method (hypothesis and verification). The problem arises when one claims that the methodological limitation to measurable material conditions is, in fact, no limitation at all, that is, when one claims that the methodological limitations of scientific explanation explain free choice without remainder. Accepting this claim destroys the fullness of the reality to be explained and so also the basis and occasion for the scientific analysis in the first place.

But reductionism can also be formal in the sense of explaining the multiplicity of things in terms of some ultimate immaterial unity. This is a reductionism to which metaphysics and theology are prone. To understand things as sharing something in common is to recognize the presence of some universal and unifying cause. Taking again the example of a free choice, one might say that, since all human beings who are mature enough to have moral freedom are accountable for their actions, there is something the same about all human beings. And indeed it is legitimate to point this out; just as scientific analysis is legitimate, so is metaphysical synthesis. The problem arises when one claims that the more universal, unifying explanation is really the entire explanation, when multiplicity is reduced to unity. As Thomas Aquinas is famous for saying, from our experience of creatures and our attempt to explain them, we know that there is a Creator. However, as he is also ever careful to point out, we do not know what the Creator is, and therefore we are unable to deduce information about creatures from the Creator. In other words, knowledge of unity will never give us knowledge of multiplicity. Knowing that there is a single cause of all things is not the key to knowing what they are or why they exist. More than that, the insight into unity only arises from the experience of multiplicity: we see that things (plural) share something in common and thus have a single ultimate cause. To deny the multiplicity of things based on the unity of their cause is to deny the foundation for the metaphysical synthesis in the first place. Reducing human beings to their cause and human actions to the cause of those actions is simply to destroy humanity and human responsibility. This formal reductionism is quite as pernicious as the material kind.

The only way to preserve the true insights about the many and the one is to preserve the many and the one; and this can only be done by invoking analogy—insisting that things (and explanations of things) are really alike but never identical. Human love is, for example, something like gravity, but it is never reducible to gravity. Likewise, human love is unified like divine unity, but it is never reducible to divine unity. However, analogy is only really helpful if one invokes the proper prime analogate. To choose an inadequate prime analogate is to fall into reductionism of one kind or the other. If things are like each other, then they must be alike according to some one thing. Aristotle's famous example of the analogy of health is helpful here. We call many things healthy: we call animals healthy; we call medicine healthy; we call blood or urine healthy. Among these analogates, the prime analogate is the healthy animal, which alone is called healthy without reference to something else. Medicine is said to be healthy because it causes health in the animal; and urine or blood is said to be healthy because it is a sign of the health of the animal.

The analogy of love is different insofar as we are trying to explain an activity (love), not a characteristic (healthy). However, there is the same need for a prime analogate. Thus, if we are concerned to find among creatures the prime analogate for love, it can only be the free human act of selfless giving. It alone is capable of being the ground for what is alike in all the analogical cases. None of the other analogical loves can account for this act, just as no scientific explanation can account for moral choice. As Aristotle points out, essential friendship is that which is freely established between people, each of whom loves the other for that other's sake, and thus it is found only among human beings. Just as the term "healthy" has no meaning except in reference to animal, so "love" has no meaning except in reference to the free giving of self; that is, love in this primary sense enters into the definition of all the other instances. Yet the analogical instances are not to be reduced to this prime meaning in the sense of emptying them of their reality. Just as medicine is a real contributing (though secondary) cause of the healthy animal, so also the "love" at work in electrons or gravity is a real contributing cause of human love.

Of human friendships, the prime analogate would seem to be that between husband and wife, where each gives to another who is other (sexually differentiated), for the sake of the other, in an ongoing attempt to understand and care for what must remain free and undigested. The two are one, but not at the expense of their individuality. From this mutual devotion issues the family, the first community. In the family are found those relations which form the foundation for all community, extending to local groups, states, nations, and all humankind.

However, the analogy of love (and the attendant one of friendship) cannot be confined to creatures, for that would be to ignore the reality of the Creator, a reality implied metaphysically by creatures. Just as God is the cause of all being and goodness and beauty, so is God the cause of all love. If we are to fill out the analogy, then, no creature can suffice for the prime analogate; for just as no created thing can sufficiently explain the free act of the human being (and so in the creaturely analogy of freedom and love, the human act must be the prime analogate), so no creature—not even the human being—can sufficiently explain the Creator and the act of creation.

But here we come to a puzzle; for if we take the notion of the Creator derived from creatures, we must fail to have a working analogy. Natural theology or philosophical metaphysics can establish the existence of a first cause of everything, but it cannot establish the grounds for the relation between that first cause and creatures. As Thomas Aquinas puts it, creatures are really related to God, but God is not really but only rationally related to creatures. Creatures contribute nothing to the perfection of God; God is not made more perfect through creating. If there is no mutual relation, then there is really no analogy. Just as to deny that the "love" that is instinct or desire contributes to the free human love of the other as other is to deny the analogy, so to deny that the love that is in creatures contributes at all to divine free love is to deny the analogy. If the prime analogate destroys the possibility of the analogy, then it is clearly inadequate. God freely creates free creatures. Thus there must be some free intending of the freedom of the creature by God, or there is no sufficient explanation of the reality of human freedom. The model of God as self-thinking thought (whether Aristotelian of Neo-Platonic), unconcerned for and even unaware of creatures, cannot suffice.

That there is a mutual relation is the good news of revelation, revealed in the Old Testament stories of God's intervention in the world and of His covenant with humanity, and in the New Testament in the person of Jesus Christ, God and man, one and the same. Thus any intelligible account of love and friendship must have reference ultimately to the divine, but not the false god of pure unity removed from all multiplicity (and thus from all creatures), but the Trinity revealed to us by and in Jesus. God as a community of three persons mutually related in love is the authentic and adequate cause of human community—from the first community that is marriage with its trinity of husband, wife, and the free covenant between them (blossoming, hopefully, into the family trinity of love binding father, mother, and child) to the many concentric circles of real political community, from extended family to local organizations to the state, and even to the community that is all humankind.

The one and the many, the creator and creatures, the divine and the human are together. This cannot be understood on our terms, whether scientific or metaphysical. Our systematization of reality moves to one pole or the other, to material reduction or formal reduction, and both spell the destruction of the freedom of love and friendship. The only prime analogate that preserves this freedom is the Trinitarian God revealed in the free covenant of love given in creation, confirmed in the life, death, and resurrection of Jesus, and present to us in the Eucharistic liturgy of the Church.

This volume reflects this analogy of love, stretching from the physical, instinctive, and emotional through the aesthetic, moral, and political, to the metaphysical, both philosophical and theological. In this volume are celebrated love and friendship in historical relations, in art and literature, in moral and political life, in metaphysics, and in theology. These are the riches of the tradition, recognized and promoted by Jacques Maritain.

Although I have grouped the papers in categories relating to the analogy of love and friendship, the papers are far from defined by these categories. Given the nature of love and friendship, this is bound to be the case. Thus, each paper should be read in its own right; none can be nor should be read merely in terms of its category. On the other hand, the categories are instructive both as to the breadth of the presentations at the 2008 Maritain Conference, and as to the rich range of the analogy of love and friendship. Let us sketch out briefly the analogy as indicated by the six sections of the volume, as each emphasizes an aspect of the analogy of love and friendship.

Love and friendship are grounded in particular people, places, and times. As Aristotle says, one of the prime characteristics of friendship is that people like spending time and doing things together. Thus, the papers in the first section "Jacques, Raïssa, and Friends" set before us some particular, historical friendships in which Jacques Maritain participated and on which he reflected. Particular friendships are precious in themselves, to be valued for their own sakes, and should never be reduced to more universal categories or merely sublimated to higher kinds of love.

Love, which blossoms into a variety of friendships, begins with feelings and impressions, with delight in the world and in those around us. Thus, in the second section "Beauty, Art, and Love," human sensations, aesthetic experiences, desires, and emotions are appreciated as integral to the love of beauty and art for their own sakes, and for how beauty and art—and all forms of creativity—contribute to human relationships and community.

Human relationships include, of course, more than just instinctive, impressionistic, and emotional responses; we must intend love if it is to be adequate to lives of reasoned responsibility. Friendships in the fullest sense do not just happen to us: we choose our friends, and we intend the continuing perfecting of their well-being. Thus, in the third section, "Friendship, Virtue, and Duty," the foundations for friendship in virtue, duty, and the moral law are explored.

Human relationships are found to be ordered, as John Paul II said, by a living subsidiarity. Family relations form the foundations for community relations and ultimately for the political structures adequate to human dignity and individual freedom. This expanding circle of love and friendship from family to political community is the theme of the fourth section "Love, Friendship, and the Political Community."

But love and friendship are things we try to understand theoretically as well as live aesthetically, emotionally, and morally. There are many kinds of love to be distinguished, each with its own distinctiveness, not to be absorbed into the others. Thus, section five "The Love of Being and the Being of Love," contains reflections on the metaphysics of love.

Finally, as we said above, there is no analogy without the prime analogate of love and friendship, which for a Christian thinker must be the God of revelation, the historical incarnate Word, the Eucharistic Christ—God with us. The papers in section six "Theological Foundations: Liturgy, Marriage, and the Covenant" reflect on the revealed truths without which the analogy of love and friendship would collapse into irrelevancy.

It is this theological dimension, more than any other, on which virtually all the papers touch. Thus, in closing, let me emphasize once more that, just as love and friendship are analogical, so the papers are not defined by the sections in which they are placed. In virtually every case, they bring up points related to the themes of the other sections.

Along with the many fine papers from the 2008 Maritain Conference, I have included in this volume an invited piece by the theologian Fr. Donald Keefe, SJ, whose work on the meaning of covenant, considered morally, metaphysically, and spiritually, is truly monumental. I am grateful for his willingness to contribute to the collection.

≈ I ≈

JACQUES, RAISSA, AND FRIENDS

BROOKE WILLIAMS DEELY

Contemplation Overflowing the Roads of the World

Love and Friendship in the Lives of Jacques and Raïssa Maritain

I. Introduction

I went to France in the summer of 2007 to teach a course on Jacques and Raïssa Maritain and Thérèse of Lisieux. I desired to pass on to our students my own love of these three companion figures, and what better place than on the soil of France! We began the course with Raïssa Maritain's memoirs, *We have Been Friends Together,* all about the quest of youth, and we ended with a little-known work Jacques wrote in his very old age to the Little Brothers of Jesus concerning their vocation. Edward Baenziger, CSB, in command of this sojourn, had completed his translation and bi-lingual edition of this work just in time for my class to read.[1] These young Americans soon became devoted to the Maritains. One student wrote, "Oh to be in the beloved land of our friends Jacques and Raïssa! I will be reading Maritain for the rest of my life."

1. After Jacques' death, the Little Brothers printed this letter (dated December 14, 1964), in the form of a booklet (see note #33), a copy of which belonged to John Deely, as I here recount. With a letter of introduction from Maritain's friend, John Howard Griffin, John, as a young American, met Maritain at Kolbsheim, France, on July 20, 1972, in the company of Frère Heinz Schmitz (Maritain's secretary in his last years). On this occasion, John, who had finished his first book (dedicated to his Dominican mentor Ralph Austin Powell, OP, and to Jacques and Raïssa Maritain), delivered the book in person to Maritain. Next July, after Maritain's death in April of 1973, John stayed at the Hermitage of the Little Brothers in Toulouse, where Heinz gave him a copy of this booklet.

Before examining this particular text in Part IV, I pose some questions, as a historian of Maritain's work, which address the new relevance of this text within the context of the Maritains lived experience. How did Jacques Maritain embody the so-called "two Frances," revolutionary and Catholic? How did his work overflow from contemplation, beyond the boundaries of national identity, in the universal sense of Catholicism? What was the influence of contemplative traditions, and especially the Carmelite tradition, on both Raïssa and Jacques, which inspired Maritain's own work? Since the Maritains themselves tell us that their three favorite saints were St. Thomas and the Carmelites St. John of the Cross and St. Thérèse of Lisieux, all three now Doctors of the Church, this last question needs to be further explored.

I offer my random reflections, in the personal mode of writing of Maritain in *Reflections on America*. To me the marvel is how Maritain, through the agonizing struggle attributable to his own integrity, integrated the best of the "two Frances," secular republican and Catholic, in a way that transcended their historically presupposed opposition and indeed overflows from contemplation beyond national and religious identity. The contemplative tradition itself inspired Maritain's vocation both as a person and as a philosopher. Raïssa wrote, in 1934, "Everything that is in Jacques work we first lived in the form of a vital difficulty, in the form of experience—problems of art and morality, of philosophy, of faith, of prayer, of contemplation."[2]

Later in life, Jacques reflected: "The aid and inspiration of my beloved Raïssa have penetrated all my life and all my work. If there is something good I have done, it is to her, after God, that I owe it.... My beloved Raïssa! Only in Paradise will I know what I owe her."[3] We know Jacques relied deeply on Raïssa's experience of mystical contemplation, so we need take into account the spiritual sources of Raïssa's own witness. The Maritains did not go it alone, even in their writings. Their friend Thomas Merton points out: "Almost all their works were written to some extent in collaboration."[4]

2. Raïssa Maritain, *Journal de Raïssa* (Paris: Desclée de Brouwer, 1963); English: *Raissa's Journal*, with a preface by René Voillaume (Albany, New York: Magi Books, 1974), 235.

3. Raïssa Maritain, *Notes on the Lord's Prayer*, trans. Thomas Merton (New York: P.J. Kennedy & Sons, 1963), 12.

4. Thomas Merton, "Forward," in R. Maritain, *Notes*, 8.

II. A Look at the Mystery of History

Let's turn now, in my spiral interweave of future and past, to that mystery of how Maritain eventually reconciled in a higher synthesis both the France of the Revolution and the France of Roman Catholicism. That transformation is what we see, from our vantage point in history, as the outcome of how he once agonized within himself, true to his inner vocation, in developing his integral humanism as new to his time. Maritain was always controversial with the right or the left (a good sign of his own integrity), depending on what particular crisis at what particular time he took his stance. But, as always, he founded his work on the primacy of the *spiritual*, even when Catholics protested his championing of the temporal mission of the Christian on the roads of the world.

How could Jacques Maritain himself embody both Frances at once, through and beyond the impasse of binary logic: *either* he was a liberal republican Protestant, if he had any fidelity to his famous grandfather, Jules Favre, a founder of the Third Republic; *or* he was a Roman Catholic, in support of the restoration of monarchy and against the common people, against his own family heritage? Maritain once said, "History is not a problem to be solved, but a mystery to be looked at."[5] No historian or psychologist or philosopher can tell us precisely how Maritain got to where he was going; nor could he himself always have known, since he had to struggle through life to trail-blaze, finding his own way sometimes in the dark, by way of the mode of knowing through love, following John of the Cross, as we see in his concluding section on mystical contemplation in *Degrees of Knowledge.*

What we do know is that he went the very way St. Teresa of Avila speaks of in her book *Way of Perfection.* In any era, that way is "a hard act to follow," because it requires what St. Teresa called "a rough and uneven path,"[6] exemplifying a living tradition that forges new pathways in the spirit of the Gospel. One always risks censor for that, as Maritain's own life of controversy, even within the Catholic world, so well exemplifies.

5. Jacques Maritain, *On the Philosophy of History*, ed. Joseph W. Evans (New York: Charles Scribner's Sons, 1957), 31–32.

6. Teresa of Avila, *The Way of Perfection.* Vol. III, in *The Collected Works of St. Teresa of Avila*, trans. Kieran Kavanaugh and Otilio Rodriguez (Washington, D.C.: ICS Publications, 1985), Ch. 18, 102.

In his developing philosophy of history we can see, in retrospect, an integral relation between Maritain's profound influence on the Second Vatican Council and what he distinguished as not a new *type* but new *style* of sanctity in the world. While we know that the Maritains steeped themselves in the Christian contemplative tradition and were oblates in the order of St. Benedict, we need, further, to deepen our understanding of the role of the Carmelite tradition in the lives of Jacques and Raïssa and Vera (as the most hidden). In the world, but not of the world, each had a unique vocation; yet together they formed a union of religious community. In Jacques words, "I do not think there was ever a closer and more profound union between three human beings than that which existed between us.... What a mystery!"[7]

In considering the development of Maritain's own life from youth to old age, in relation to key friendships, we can see that the starting point of all Jacques' work was contemplation itself, as the mode of knowing through love that is the wisdom of the saints. He lived among non-believers or non-Christians with fraternal love. He knew first-hand from his youth what it was like to model the world from the absolute presuppositions of a free-thinker: and with maturity Maritain would deepen understanding of an apostolate wherein one existed among non-Christians and suffered with them, without trying actively to convert them but simply loving them. He had once felt at home among family and friends who were free thinkers—why not feel at home with *humanity*, while being in the world but not of it? Converting to Catholicism would ultimately not narrow Maritain's horizons but widen them.

At the time of his conversion, however, Jacques' mother, Genevieve Favre, had good reason to grieve over the profound influence of Léon Bloy. Bloy signified, within that historically steeped dichotomous logic of choosing between the "two Frances," an anathema to her deepest sympathies and highest hopes for Jacques. The Church in her *mystical life* the Maritains found "infinitely lovable," but the mediocrity of the Catholic world "strangely hateful." One can appreciate why they did not tell Jacques' mother of their conversion. She found out anyway. She wrote, "A source of anxiety tortured me ever since my son became so enthusiastic over the writings

7. Jacques Maritain, *Notebooks*, trans. Joseph Evans (Albany, New York: Magi Books, 1984), 73–74.

of Leon Bloy."[8] As for Jacques' conversion, she writes, "I shrank from believing it, I was indignant, convinced that it could not be."[9]

Indeed, Bloy would present to the Maritains what I call a semiotic anomaly. He was neither a right-thinking Catholic nor a free thinker. Nor had he tried to convert the Maritains. He simply read to them from the lives of the saints. And that was enough for the Maritains, in their own lives, to search for the source of such a mystery as the saints signify in any time.

Maritain eventually took the lead in shaping a contemporary culture that not only integrated revolutionary and Catholic France, but offered a practical model of cooperation for the common good, rooted not in abstract principles philosophers could agree upon, but in fraternal love. Actually, as a co-author of the United Nations Declaration of the Rights of Man, Maritain attracted others by his very attitude. Thus, over time he fulfilled his family heritage in its central intuition of fraternal love for the people. He paved the way for lay spirituality and dialogue with the world.

Hence, Maritain's future indeed bestows new relevance on his past. A few examples of people who were close to him illustrate how they contributed to his own development over time. At age sixteen, Jacques eagerly awaited the daily arrival of the socialist newspaper of the husband of the family cook. His home was other than Thérèse of Lisieux's sheltered home, where she was forbidden to read even the Catholic newspaper *La Croix*. Yet Thérèse's home was far removed from that bourgeois spirit Maritain identified as militating against the poor; so there were both discontinuities and continuities that will one day meet in a new synthesis in the mature work of Maritain.

Ernest Psichari, grandson of the renowned freethinker Ernest Renan, and Jacques were such close friends that Maritain thought of themselves as one; and his mother, too, thought of Ernest as a son. These two families, joined in this great friendship, represented the intellectual and politically-minded elite of liberal and republican France. At Psichari's house, as Jacques put it, "One did not fight Christianity. One was deeply persuaded at having assimilated and outgrown it."[10] When Psichari, who also converted to Catholicism, was

8. Raïssa Maritain, *We Have Been Friends Together*, trans. Julie Kernan (New York: Doubleday and Co., 1961), 224.

9. Raïssa Maritain, *We Have Been Friends*, 224.

10. Jacques and Raïssa Maritain, *Prayer and Intelligence*, trans. Algar Thorold (New York: Sheed and Ward, 1929), 208–09.

killed as a soldier during World War I, Jacques felt he had his friend's vocation, too, to fulfill in his own life.

His older friend of his youth, Charles Péguy, gave Maritain his understanding of the temporal vocation of the Christian at a time the Catholic Church was only beginning to rally in support of the working person's rights. Maritain later deepened his historical consciousness from his friendship with Péguy, who had exclaimed, "If Catholics only knew!.... They could take the lead in temporal history, nothing could stand against them; but they are too dumb for that!"[11] Maritain would creatively resolve, rather than replicate, those aspects of the intransigent opposition between Catholic France and liberal republican France that were potentially reconcilable, given a new historical climate. For Maritain, as for Péguy, the social revolution will be rooted in love, or it will come to nothing. On this point Maritain quotes St. John of the Cross as applied to civilizations: "By love shall you be judged."[12]

Jacques and Raïssa's earlier friendship with Bloy continued to be the vital source, the living example, of how mystical contemplation overflows the roads of the world, given that in this experience social action is rooted in what is most revolutionary, Gospel love. "For the first time," Raïssa later reflected, "we found ourselves before the reality of Christianity." They experienced directly, through their friendship with Bloy, the "immensity of his soul, his burning zeal for justice. Faith, poverty, and sanctity were all equally exalted and united."[13]

There is a striking continuity, as we will see in Part IV, between the Maritains' experience of Bloy and Jacques' vocation in old age with the Little Brothers of Jesus. Bloy offered them the example of how he lived his own life—not by theological discourse but by the experience itself of the nonrational mode of knowing through love, a purely contemplative apostolate. He realized his calling of simply being with the suffering poor in the world, as witness of contemplative love for a person.

Yet as a young philosopher Maritain became embroiled with the *Action Française*. He was a founder and editor of a journal associated with this movement to get rid of the Third French Republic, which Maritain's own grandfather had helped found, with its French revolutionary principles of

11. Raïssa Maritain, *We Have Been Friends*, 229.

12. Jacques Maritain, "A Note on the Bourgeois World," *The Commonwealth, XVIII*, June 2, 1933: 119–20, at 120.

13. Raïssa Maritain, *We Have Been Friends*, 88.

Liberty, Equality and Fraternity, in order to restore monarchy, based on conservative Catholicism. Maritain focused on speculative philosophy, and wrote as a Catholic disengaged from the liberal politics of his family tradition. But, to his surprise, in 1926, Pius XI condemned the *Action Française*. Maritain personally experienced such intervention as deliverance, as an opening toward what would eventually become his integral humanism, which would profoundly influence the Second Vatican Council.

In 1936, Maritain's *Integral Humanism* established him as a giant in the Catholic world. His good friend Giovanni Montini, later Pope Paul VI, wrote the introduction to the Italain version. In this book, Maritain transcends the binary logic of the principles of liberty, equality and fraternity as militating against Christianity itself. Christians must take social justice seriously, but more than just that. In bringing into integral relation contemplation and social action in a secular world, Maritain reconciles seemingly opposed truths from his youth:

> A vitally Christian renewal will be a work of sanctity or it will be nothing: sanctity turned toward the temporal, the secular, the profane. Has not the world known leaders of the people who were saints? If a new Christendom arises in history, it will be the work of such a kind of sanctity.[14]

Furthermore, Maritain points the way to a new style of sanctity that he will further delineate in his work to the Little Brothers of Jesus. Already in *Integral Humanism* he transcends the older distinction of religious life as perfect and lay life as imperfect in insisting on what he calls "simplicity, or the value of ordinary ways," which he notes began to appear in "certain souls hidden from the world" in the most purely contemplative orders.[15] He points out that this new style has spread into secular life. Implicit here is the simplicity of St. Thérèse's ordinary, hidden life in the cloister—a simplicity Maritain always held to be marvelously suitable to lay life in the world.

III. Maritain's Reflections on America

After the Maritains came to America, Raïssa pressed Jacques to write *Reflections on America*, and he tells us she collaborated in it. He tells us of

14. Jacques Maritain, *Integral Humanism*, trans. Joseph W. Evans (South Bend, Indiana: University of Notre Dame Press, 1973), 122.

15. Maritain, *Integral Humanism*, 125.

his love at first sight, realizing that first impressions contain an element of chance; yet whatever the margin of error, he was confident that "at the core" of his reflections there nonetheless were what he calls "true insights."[16]

Unlike Tocqueville, Maritain, with more historical hindsight, also lauds what he calls America's "great thirst for knowledge,"[17] as exemplified by the great American philosopher Charles Sanders Peirce. Maritain muses that only in America does he find to be so appreciated the seventeenth-century master of the Western philosophical tradition who inspired Jacques and Raïssa, John of St. Thomas. Maritain himself tells us in his *Reflections on America*, that he and his friends "dearly loved" and "worshipped" this Latin genius, now known more widely by his family name, John Poinsot.[18] Maritain cites a translation in America, by his former student and close friend Yves R. Simon, of this philosopher's *Material Logic*.[19]

America's interest in this Latin-age genius led, in 1985, to the University of California Press bi-lingual edition of Poinsot's 1632 *Treatise on Signs*, translated and arranged by John Deely in consultation with Ralph Austin Powell. On Easter Sunday of 1986 this edition received the feature review in the *New York Times Book Review*. I muse that Maritain himself would further marvel that both Poinsot and Peirce are now co-recognized worldwide as founders of the philosophical tradition in semiotics, and that Maritain himself is a recognized figure in this transdisciplinary field.

While Maritain considers the autonomy of reason and free inquiry into truth essential for a civilization, he clarifies that in no way does he privilege the rational mode of knowing as the highest degree of knowledge. The mode of knowing Maritain *does* privilege—as did Poinsot—is the suprarational one of mystical contemplation by way of love. Maritain's *Reflections on America* further testify to his ever-developing philosophy of history, which, as we have seen, embraces the modern principles of liberty, equality and fraternity as, in themselves, Gospel-inspired. He saw in America, in spite of the work ethic, a quest for wisdom in "great reserves for love and contemplation."[20] His hope for America was its infusing the secular gov-

16. Jacques Maritain, *Reflections on America* (New York: Charles Scribner's Sons, 1958), 17.
17. Maritain, *Reflections*, 39.
18. Ibid., 151–52.
19. John Poinsot, *The Material Logic of John of St. Thomas—Basic Treatises*, trans. Yves R. Simon, John J. Glanville, and G. Donald Hollenhorst (Chicago: University of Chicago Press, 1955).
20. Maritain, *Reflections*, 71.

ernment with the primacy of love and friendship, as inspired by Christianity. He admired America not for its defects, but for its self-criticism of such defects, as well as for its evangelical compassion and responsibility for those in distress.

Maritain is attuned especially to the "invisible" manifestation of Gospel-inspired values in America. In his words, "This spark of the Gospel lying deep in people who more often than not do not think of the Gospel" is a "hidden" disposition for fraternal love "active in the great mass of the nation." A visible sign of that expression of love in the American people is what he calls their "symbolic smile."[21] In his later work on the vocation of the Little Brothers of Jesus, he will again refer to a smile as an unconscious sign of evangelical compassion overflowing the roads of the world.

Maritain was at ease in uniting his love for America with his love for France. Even though their national identities are "profoundly different," he sees a "mysterious affinity, a strange and deep-seated congeniality, which make their historical destinies convergent."[22] Whereas in the French revolution the adversaries of Christianity led the way to historical progress in the revered formula "Liberty, Equality, Fraternity," America signifies to him "yet more deeply the spirit of this formula in the concrete sense of trying to realize it."[23]

For Maritain, the Catholic Worker movement in America well illustrates this mysterious affinity, this convergence, between these two nationalities. This movement was itself founded on friendships in France. In the early 1930s, the Frenchman Peter Maurin (a friend of Maritain's) and the American Dorothy Day together turned from the intellectual and spiritual foundations of the Catholic Worker movement to the writings of Jacques Maritain, above all, as well as to others who had met at the Maritains' home in Meudon. We see a convergence of intellectual and spiritual roots, as evidenced by Day's own reading of Bloy and Péguy, both of whom profoundly inspired her. When Day read her friend Raïssa's memoirs, she tells us that she carried this work with her, refusing to loan it, for a long while. She, like Raïssa, was fond of Bloy's moving words: "There is only one sadness, not to be among the saints." In his *Reflections on America,* Maritain cites the Catholic Worker movement as exemplifying such fraternal love.[24]

21. Ibid., 89–92.
22. Ibid., 11–12.
23. Ibid., 15.
24. Ibid., 96.

There is a convergence, too, especially in tapping the deep roots of Carmelite spirituality. Jacques, Raïssa, and Dorothy chose in particular the *Way of Perfection* by Teresa of Avila. This type of sanctity is predicated on practicing the sister virtues of humility, detachment, and love, in relation to an overflow of the gift of contemplation into fraternal love and good works. Given the deep influence of Carmelite spirituality in the lives of these friends in America, I note that Dorothy Day named her daughter after Teresa of Avila, and Day also wrote a book on Thérèse of Lisieux.

To give a token sign of Jacques' own effect on America, I won't take us to Princeton but to prison. There a young American read Maritain and, after leaving prison, changed his name from Jack to Jacques, volunteered at the Catholic Worker headquarters, and started reading philosophy. This example is a grain of sand that reveals the universe of contemplation overflowing the roads of the world.

IV. Roots of the Vocations of Jacques and Raïssa

My underlying point about the source of spiritual inspiration among these French and American friendships is that we can well verify the type of mystical contemplation that both Jacques and Raïssa represent. True, Raïssa's own experience provided direct inspiration for Jacques in daily life. True, too, that however ordinary or extraordinary in its states of consciousness, this call to contemplation is grounded in the humanity of Jesus, in the way of the Cross. That is why, of course, this type of sanctify has never been fashionable, whatever its specific style.

Fully to appreciate Maritain as a philosopher, we need to look at the *sources* of Raïssa's own spirituality. Attempts to evaluate Raïssa's mystical experience, as evidenced especially by her journal, are remarkably varied.[25] We know how greatly Jacques valued her contemplative experiences. Nor did it hinder her performance in daily life. When we consider that Raïssa collaborated in most of Jacques' writing, authored works herself, and hosted so many gatherings in their home, I say, "Give her a break." Even if frail in health, she had plenty to do. The Trappist monk Thomas Merton, an-

25. See Ralph McInerny, *The Very Rich Hours of Jacques Maritain: A Spiritual Life* (Notre Dame, Indiana: University of Notre Dame Press, 2003), 13.

other friend of theirs in America, champions her as "perhaps one of the great contemplatives of our time."[26] He viewed her journal as contributing to the tradition of Christian mysticism "a doctrine of special interest and rare beauty."

The objection sometimes arises that Maritain himself relied more on Raïssa's own testimony than on any of the saints. One scholar suggests that Jacques was just too devoted to Raïssa not to see that her experience was often enough mystical in the sense of being out of touch with bodily reality.[27] Recall that the same was said of Teresa of Avila in her day. And she, too, had her champions. Teresa's way of perfection was actually quite down to earth. Raïssa's spirituality, a living witness to Jacques, eventually flowed outward, and she, not Jacques, was the first to encourage Jacques' calling as a philosopher in the world. Yves R. Simon reminds us that "from the beginning Maritain had the soul of a contemplative and that of an artist."[28]

The Prior of the Little Brother of Jesus, Fr. René Voillaume, wrote the preface to Raïssa's controversial journal. His testimony confirms my own interpretation, as a historian, that we cannot talk about the influence on Jacques of Raïssa's living testimony as a contemplative without acknowledging the profound influence, implicit and explicit, in the pages of her journal—and in Jacques own work—of St. Thérèse of Lisieux. The Prior emphasizes that what is most "striking" is "the marked parallel" between Raïssa's spiritual way and that of the Little Brothers of Jesus, given the "source" of such "certainty" in the teaching of St. Thérèse of Lisieux.[29]

For further evidence of Carmelite influence, we can read Raïssa's *Notes on the Lord's Prayer*. Both Jacques and Raïssa immersed themselves in St. Teresa of Avila's *Way of Perfection* as an instruction on prayer and contemplation, based on the Lord's Prayer and centered on the humanity of Jesus, as was the spirituality of St. Thérèse of Lisieux. Both these Carmelite saints kept close *The Imitation of Christ* as a key guide. Such *intertexuality* itself showcases the centrality of the Carmelite tradition in the Maritains' lives. Maritain devoted the last chapter of his *Degrees of Knowledge* to mystical

26. Merton, "Forward," in R. Maritain, *Notes*, 10.

27. William Bush, "Raïssa Maritain ... et Jacques," in *Understanding Maritain: Philosopher and Friend*, ed. Deal W. Hudson (Macon, Georgia: Mercer University Press, 1987), 65–70.

28. Yves R. Simon, "Jacques Maritain: the Growth of a Christian Philosopher," in *Jacques Maritain. The Man and His Achievement*, ed. with an intro. by Joseph W. Evans (New York: Sheed and Ward, 1963), 3–24, at 7.

29. René Voillaume, "Foreword" to *Raïssa's Journal*, xiv–v.

contemplation, with special attention to John of the Cross and, in concluding the *Peasant of the Garonne*, he emphasized "the importance of the witness and mission of Thérèse of Lisieux" as a model for lay spirituality.[30] We see such influence as well in their co-authored books on prayer and contemplation, *Prayer and Intelligence* and *Liturgy and Contemplation*.[31]

Thus, in order historically to situate the influence of Raïssa's witness on Jacques, the question to ask is not whether Jacques relied more on Raïssa for testimony than on the canonized saints, but rather on whom did Raïssa herself rely in her own spiritual development. Although the objection sometimes arises that Raïssa's experience of contemplation was too reclusive and out of touch with reality for Jacques to have taken it so seriously as witness, at one time Teresa of Avila received far worse criticism for her withdrawal from social life in order to experience the deepened solitude of prayer that eventually overflowed the roads of Spain in her founding of reform monasteries. So, too, we can ultimately say the same of Raïssa's own unique call to contemplation on the roads of the world.

Teresa of Avila herself duly weighs and considers the effects—as indexical signs—of contemplative experience. In the case of Raïssa, we see, as a mystery to look at, her life-long effect on Jacques's own work as a philosopher. Is that effect not a good sign?

V. Jacques and the Little Brothers of Jesus

Jacques came to the Little Brothers in Toulouse a few months after Raïssa's death, with "a great thirst for silence."[32] Disconsolate to be without Raïssa's physical presence, he reflected on how pleased Raïssa would be that he was with the Little Brothers of Jesus, that new order that had so deeply moved her. Although he had returned to France not to do something, but rather to prepare to die, nonetheless he wrote several more books, among them the best-selling *Peasant of the Garonne*.

In view of his own contemplative vocation, influenced deeply by the

30. Jacques Maritain, *The Peasant of the Garonne*, trans. Michael Cuddihy and Elizabeth Hughes (New York: Holt Rinehart and Winston, 1968), 235.

31. Jacques and Raïssa Maritain, *Liturgy and Contemplation*, trans. Joseph W. Evans (New York: P.J. Kennedy and Sons, 1960). (For *Prayer and Intelligence*, see note #10.)

32. Kenneth L. Woodward, "Jacques Maritain and American Intellectual Life," *Critic* (March 1963): 30–34, at 34.

Carmelite tradition, especially Thérèse of Lisieux's Little Way, the question arises: What was Jacques now like to live with? Now Jacques would be living not with two women who nurtured his work, each in her own incomparable way, but in a new environment, in his old age, with young men.

Since no religious superior ordered him to write the story of his soul, let's glimpse what the Prior of the Little Brothers, Fr. René Page, has to say, after Jacques died, in his introductory comments to Jacques' 1964 writing on the vocation of the Little Brothers. Fr. Page says that what holds the Little Brothers' deepest attention is what he himself "held dearest in his heart and expressed in his life's work." Approaching Jacques through his works is "the only way to go."[33]

But still we desire to know what Jacques was like to live with, because the man is the sign of his work. The Prior begins pointing out a more intimate knowledge of someone that daily life and written work cannot adequately show. Jacques preferred to be hidden in the world. So, at an admitted loss of what to say, the Prior speaks simply about Jacques' extraordinary ordinariness in these telling words:

> One can say, as was said about Thérèse of the Child Jesus, that there is not much that can be told. Because his life among the brothers was just ordinary, he lived the life of the Fraternity and the brotherhood of the brothers without fanfare. And that already shows something of the quality of the man, because believe me, not many 90 year-olds are capable of living in community with youngsters of 25–30 years without being a heavy burden on them, nor getting tired of them or finding them a pain. With Jacques, even with the serious bodily pains he had in the last weeks, everything seemed natural, as if there was never a problem. He just *naturally* got up early every morning to *work*.[34]

After living with the Little Brothers nine years, Jacques asked to be admitted to their Fraternity. This vocation gets to the heart of the matter, the spiritual source of Maritain's life work. As a Little Brother, he exemplifies, to the end, how he integrated throughout his life deep love for the com-

33. René Page, "Introduction" to the fascicule published shortly after the death of Maritain (April 28, 1973), consisting of the following: Page's introduction, "Frère Jacques Maritain"; remarks by Fr. Marie Michel Labourdette, OP, from a conference at the Institut Catholique de Toulouse, dated June 13, 1973; a "Lettre de Jacques aux Frères" on the occasion of becoming himself one of the Little Brothers, dated July, 1970; "Un mot du prieur, Frère René Page," accompanying the letter; and concluding with Jacques' writing "A Propos de la Vocation des Petites Frères de Jesus," December 14, 1964.

34. Ibid., 2.

mon people and the poor, from his upbringing in youth to his sense of the temporal mission of a lay Christian in the world, which Bloy and Péguy awakened both in him and in Raïssa.

In his reflections on the vocation of the Little Brothers of Jesus, in 1964, Maritain *distinguishes two* meanings of the word "apostolic": first, the signification of the word in *common usage*, and second the *reality* to which that word refers. The *recognized* meaning of the word, he says, does not entirely contain the *reality* to which it refers.[35]

Maritain drives home this point as foundational to understanding the vocation of the Little Brothers of Jesus as apostolic. The reality, he says, "overflows" the sense of the mere word "apostolic," when people talk about "an apostolic order of religious, or apostolic life." The accepted signification is that a person lives an apostolic calling when the purpose is to announce the Word of God or to convert souls, to guide them toward the Kingdom of God. According to this definition, such a life is at once contemplative and active, a mixed life, according to the teaching of St. Thomas, as opposed to the purely contemplative life. In relation to the Little Brothers of Jesus, in this restricted usage of the word "apostolic," the Little Brothers' life is, in Maritain's words, "purely contemplative and *not an apostolic* calling" (emphasis mine).

Next, Maritain points to the reality *beyond* the customary limited signification of the word "apostolic." In reality, the apostolate is, he says, "something supernatural, transcendent, infinitely more mysterious than we thought—just like the Gospel itself." In this extended sense, the apostolate is no longer reduced to transmitting the spoken word, to announcing the Word of God, to teaching and preaching, let alone to proselytizing. I am reminded of the example of how Bloy lived his own life as an influence on the Maritains' conversion. Bloy's example was apostolic only in Maritain's suggested "new" or extended sense of the term.

In this sense, *every* Christian is called to participate in this reality. The heart of the matter, to Maritain, is "living the truth and by this fact helping others to do it too." Certainly all varieties of vocations are proper to religious life in general, in order to give real breadth to what Maritain calls "apostolic functionality." But in previous centuries Christians conceived of this appointed work of apostolic functionality, witnessing to love, as an *ex-*

35. Jacques Maritain, "A Propos de la Vocation des Petites Frères de Jesus" (December 14, 1964), printed in Page, Fascicule (see note #33), 11–24.

terior manifestation, through works of fraternal charity—as, for example, St. Vincent de Paul, whose active life overflowed from contemplation.

In reaffirming that, in any age, the cloister remain cloistered, Maritain addresses directly the question of those who are in vows in monasteries seeking unity with God, such as Benedictines, Trappists, Carthusians, and cloistered Carmelites. Clearly, these vocations are exclusively contemplative. Just as clearly, they are apostolic through their prayer and witness to the Gospel. So there is no doubt here that a purely contemplative vocation is also apostolic. Yet the anomaly that Maritain showcases is that these great orders are in no way apostolic in the *restricted* signification of the term—"apostolic" as generally understood. Maritain further develops this point in showing how our historical consciousness itself must be raised in order properly to understand what is new about the vocation of the Little Brothers. In past centuries, Christians conceived of the witness given to the love of Jesus as a *visible* sign, as shown through works of charity, or large monastic institutions.

Maritain asks, "What is the prophetic role but to make an existential affirmation for the primordial value of the witness of Jesus' love for men and women?" This affirmation takes place not through the mediation of visible signs, but rather through the "invisible or nearly invisible" mediation of fraternal presence among the poor and abandoned. "Your vocation," he concludes to the Little Brothers, "is to bear witness to evangelical love knowingly." He puts his finger on what people want in the first place, in saying: "They need to be loved: to be known; to be treated as human beings; to feel that they are valued and respected for themselves." That's all. But that is a lot of work in itself. One must pass one's *existence* with people, not simply *say* one loves them or "do a good deed" for them.

Here we can look back at the mystery of Jacques' youth, when he identified with the people and wanted to be one with them. In his old age, he is still the same Jacques, but now he is *consciously* tapping the roots of Christian mysticism, in his distinction between the temporal and spiritual orders that he unites in his integral humanism.

Such contemplation overflowing the roads of the world comes about through the action of micro-signs, of "passing, imperceptible things which are written on the subconscious more than on the conscious mind." These micro-signs include "a look, a gesture, a friendly smile." And what is even less visible, or more hidden, is, in Jacques' words, "a certain manner of listening or of paying attention to this or that, what we could call micro-signs." As the agent, the soul, "without knowing it, sends out micro-signs." In such action of signs, the person does not even imagine whether or not they are received by the other person. What is absolutely essential is that these micro-signs not be willed or intentional. Indeed, Maritain cautions that it would be "catastrophic to seek them out deliberately." Maritain goes deeper: "For those souls consecrated to the deepest love of the Lord, there is all around them a sort of *aura* of contemplative love, for they see Jesus in their neighbor." This aura "creates micro-signs of redemptive love."

On one level, therefore, the Little Brothers of Jesus are in precisely the same category as is, say, a Carmelite, "for whom contemplation ... brings about invisible witness ... and nearly visible witness of the Lord's love for men." But, on another level, in a state of life, there is a world of difference in these historically diverse vocations. As Maritain puts it, "The Little Brothers of Jesus do not cut themselves off from the world but, to the contrary, throw themselves into its misery, where there are no more monastic walls for protection. They wear no distinct garb. Their visibility is their very presence itself among ordinary people, working among them as one of them in their poverty of means."

Maritain gives an example of a Little Brother living among non-Christians without an attempt to convert them:

> Nothing seems to me more beautiful for a Little Brother of Jesus than to be an instrument that God uses so that a Muslim, for example, live in the grace of Christ and die in Christ without ceasing to be Muslim. In just such a case, there has not been a transmission of the gospel message by words; no *conversion* has taken place, the Church foundation is not visibly extended in the mystical Body, the Kingdom of God. But that Muslim saved by the grace of Christ, that's enough to fulfill the Little Brother's vocation.[36]

Maritain tells us, "I have insisted on this example because I really wanted to point out that the *love* of neighbor, in a contemplative vocation lived in the midst of the world, is not a trick for *taming* the neighbor and preparing him to welcome a parish priest or a missionary. Fraternal love of Jesus, by and through Him is not a means for anything beyond itself." He emphasizes, "I need to underline that their vocation ... is essentially hidden, hidden in God."

36. Maritain, "A Propos de la Vocation des Petites Frères de Jesus," 20.

Thus, we can deepen understanding of St. Thérèse's influence on the Maritains' theme of contemplation on the roads of the world. We can deepen understanding, too, of Maritain's claim that, in the face of diverse historic or cultural conditions, within and beyond the Catholic world, the vocation of the Little Brother bears witness to the Church's universality. Reflection on the *sources* in which Raïssa steeped herself goes to the roots of spirituality upon which the Maritains both so deeply drew throughout their lives.

I conclude with the words of another young American student, who read this letter for my course in France:

> In the Little Brothers Maritain could pursue a contemplative life without having to abandon the people he valued so much throughout his life. His act of contemplation could now be lived and God's love could radiate through him to others, despite any racial, religious, or philosophical differences.... He understood that this apostolic mode was universal—the mode of love.

CATHERINE M. A. MCCAULIFF

The Friendship of Pope Paul VI and Jacques Maritain*

In *Friendship: The Art of Happiness*, John Cuddeback suggests that good conversation is essential to philosophy and that friends are most capable of good conversation. Furthermore, friends desire to pursue the virtuous life together. For Giovanni Battista Montini (1897–1978) and Jacques Maritain (1882–1973), this friendship centered on Maritain's thoughts about Christian life and Christians in society as expressed in several of Maritain's books. Montini was himself a philosopher. He began to read Maritain very early on in life. Maritain's books spoke to the central concerns of Montini's life and ministry from the start. Maritain's ideas came to fruition as Montini's ecclesiastical influence grew, as archbishop of Milan, as a diplomat in Rome, still later as a strong and major leader at the Second Vatican Council, and finally during the later sessions as Pope Paul VI, the head of the Council.[1] How did the ideas in Jacques Maritain's books work in the life

*This essay, first given to the AMA (in 2008), was developed into a larger article published (in 2011) as "Jacques Maritain's Embrace of Religious Pluralism and the Declaration on Religious Freedom," *Seton Hall Law Review*, Vol. 41 (Iss. 2., Art. 4): 593–624 (available at http://erepository.law.shu.edu/shlr/vol41/iss2/4). The author wishes to thank John Trapani, Angela Carmella, Patrick Brennan, John Desiderio, and Kyle Grimm. Cornelia Borgerhoff, formerly an administrative dean at Princeton University, translator of Jacques Maritain's work into English, and personal assistant and friend of Jacques Maritain, was a constant source of inspiration. Ms. Borgerhoff died Dec. 19, 2011.

1. The Second Vatican Council (1962–1965) was concerned with the role of the Church in the world, as well as internal renewal and reform. See, generally, Gerhard B. Ladner, *The Idea of Reform: Its Impact on Christian Thought and Action in the Age of the Fathers* (Cambridge: Harvard University Press, 1959) (discussing concepts involved in calling the Council and noting, at ix,

and actions of Giovanni Battista Montini? In directing the philosophy of the Church at the Council, Paul VI drew on the ideas of human dignity, society, and the state that he developed through his friendship with Jacques Maritain and used them in his great support for the *Declaration on Religious Freedom* (*Dignitatis Humanae*), promulgated at the end of the Council.[2]

This paper treats the intellectual friendship between Montini and Maritain in terms of the concept of human dignity underlying both Jacques Maritain's work and the *Declaration on Religious Freedom*. It then sets forth the vision of society and the state that human dignity both demands and requires.

I. Christianizing the Enlightenment Legacy: The Selfish Individual Actor Personalized

The Roman Catholic Church, which had been estranged from modern governmental developments prior to the Council because of determined and hostile continental government secularity, responded favorably to the possibilities for cooperation between modern liberal states and the church. Montini was among those who approved of such a rapprochement. It was Maritain's writing that, at least in part, contributed to this positive response. Maritain looked at the whole person, not the individual acting only for himself and his own self-interest, and examined rights in the context of the community. Jacques Maritain's *Integral Humanism* put the values of the Enlightenment and the French revolution into a Christian framework of human personality, much the same as Thomas Aquinas had interpreted Aristotelian principles in a Christian way.[3]

Maritain's works on philosophy were actively read in seminaries. It

---

that Jacques Maritain offered comments on portions of the draft dealing with the history of philosophy and theology).

2. Vatican II, *Declaration on Religious Freedom* [*Dignitatis Humanae*], available online at http://www.vatican.va/archive/hist_councils/ii_vatican_council/documents/vat-ii_decl_19651207_dignitatis-humanae_en.html. In *Dignitatis Humanae* 1, the Council fathers "affirmed the link" between "a sense of the dignity of the human person" and the right to the "free exercise of religion."

3. Jacques Maritain, *Humanisme intégral: Problemes temporels et spirituels d'une nouvelle chrétienté* (Paris: Aubier, Editions Montaigne, 1936); *Integral Humanism*, trans. Joseph Evans (New York: Charles Scribner's Sons, 1968). See also, *Scholasticism and Politics*, ed. Mortimer J. Adler (New York: Macmillan, 1940), 70–88, where Maritain writes of personalist democracy, not the individualist [self-interested] democracy of the Enlightenment.

is no surprise that from his first foreign posting in Poland in September, 1923, young Father Montini sent home for, among other books, Maritain's *Introduction to Philosophy*.[4] Montini was deeply interested in art and "trying to develop an aesthetic based on Thomistic principles" when he read Maritain's *Art and Scholasticism*, written in 1927.[5] This mutual interest in art brought their parallel lives into closer conjunction, although Peter Hebblethwaite, the late Pope's biographer, does not mention when the two met and probably could not determine the date for lack of sources.[6] Meanwhile, Maritain's biographer says of this time period only that a friend of Jean Cocteau brought Montini to the Maritains' home in July 1924, and that Maritain had a private audience with Pope Pius XI on November 19, 1927.[7] Montini had translated Maritain's *Three Reformers* into Italian in 1928, and, in 1936, he wrote the introduction to the Italian version of Maritain's magisterial philosophy of history, entitled *True Humanism* in one translation and *Integral Humanism* in another.[8] Much later, as Pope Paul VI, Montini cited this book in his first social encyclical, *Populorum Progressio* (*On the Development of Peoples*).[9]

While the Maritains held salons and seminars on everything from art to Thomism in their home at Meudon, just outside Paris, Montini and his friends organized study weeks at Fiesole, just outside Florence, directed at leadership and democracy: "The common good was to be norm, genuine democracy the means, and Jacques Maritain the prophet."[10] Maritain en-

4. Peter Hebblethwaite, *Paul VI: The First Modern Pope* (London: Harper Collins, 1993), 75.

5. Hebblethwaite, *Paul VI*, 107.

6. Ibid., 83.

7. Jean-Luc Barré, *Jacques & Raïssa Maritain: Beggars for Heaven*, trans. Bernard E. Doering (Notre Dame: Notre Dame University Press, 2005), 176 and 186.

8. Giorgio Campanini, "Montini e Maritain," in *G.B. Montini e la Società Italiana 1919–39* (Brescia: Instituto Paolo VI, 1983), 83 and 92. In the preface to the Italian edition of *Three Reformers*, Montini underlined the importance of always uniting truth to charity, even in a polemical situation. Franco Molinari, "Le Letture del Giovane Montini," in *G.B. Montini e la Società Italiana 1919–39* (Brescia, 1983), 59 and 70, n. 32. Maritain's *Réligion et culture* (Paris: Desclée, 1930)—English: *Religion and Culture: Essays in Order*, trans. J.F. Scanlon (London: Sheed & Ward, 1931)—was therefore important to Montini and was already reviewed by the Federazione degli Universitari Cattolici Italiani in Azione Fucina in 1931. Montini, a Christian humanist and dedicated Thomist, was profoundly appreciative of the role of culture in Christian humanism. Bishop Carlo Manziana, "Intervento," in *G.B. Montini e la Società Italiana*, 209 and 211.

9. See below, note #33 and accompanying text.

10. Hebblethwaite, *Paul VI*, 121. Montini and his close associates had a "different" view of how Christians should relate to the secular world. "The Church for them was not a mass movement in which individuals were lost [in the crowd]. It was rather a community of common

gendered a hostile reaction from the Fascists in Italy. As a foreigner, Maritain could not return to Milan after lecturing there in 1930, or to Rome after he lectured on religion and culture there in 1934. These lectures provide an early blueprint of the themes developed more fully in *Integral Humanism*. According to Hebblethwaite, "Maritain provided Montini and his friends with a vision" of a new Christian civilization which was "lay rather than clerical, democratic rather than authoritarian, and capable of inspiring a mass political party in which all who shared 'Christian values' could participate. The Church's influence would be indirect rather than direct, accepting autonomous institutions (like political parties and trade unions) and imbuing them with a Christian spirit."[11] This book is seminal because it served both as a working document for Christian Democrats as they waited for the Fascists and Nazis to be thrown out of power and as a guideline for Christian Democratic parties after the war.

Integral Humanism deals with the "new Christianity" in the circumstances of the secular dictatorships of 20th-century Europe. In such circumstances, Christians had to be ecumenical and share their point of view indirectly through their memberships in social, political, and professional organizations. Christian Democratic parties in various European countries only had hopes for the future, after the dictators were defeated, since they could not oust the dictators politically. This new Christianity was designed to avoid the pitfalls of socialism, extreme capitalism (as we have been experiencing recently) and fascism. As Robert Song put it, Maritain argued that Catholics had to work with all people of good will to develop a Christian social order without, on the one hand, equivocating on eternal truths or, on the other, rigidly adhering to language which does not fit the times.[12] Maritain saw that society in the 20th century was to be led by lay people and oriented toward the common good.[13] The Church, political society, and the state had to cooperate. As Maritain contrasted the "new Christianity" with the middle ages, the medieval paradigm had been a German emperor

endeavour in the intellectual and spiritual sphere. Priests like Montini preferred to tutor talented individuals than to address vast crowds in demagogic fashion. *Witness* rather than *conquest* was their watchword" (Hebblethwaite, *Paul VI*, 243; emphasis in original).

11. Ibid., 122.

12. Robert Song, *Christianity and Liberal Society* (Oxford: Clarendon Press, 1997), 134.

13. Jacques Maritain, *Pour le bien Commun, Les Responsabilités du chretien et le moment présent* (Paris: Desclée de Brouwer, 1934), (pamphlet); Jacques Maritain, *The Person and the Common Good*, trans. John J. Fitzgerald (New York: Charles Scribner's Sons, 1947), 31–46.

seeking both secular and ecclesiastical power. Maritain envisioned the new temporal order as being held together by citizens who have learned that they must respect each other's rights. Therefore, political uniformity is neither a goal nor a necessity of society.

Instead, unity comes through sharing in the achievement of the common good. In effect, this means that pluralism will exist in religion, economic systems, and juridical structures and that conscience rather than doctrinal uniformity should be recognized. Temporal society and the state have authority in civic matters. Moral influence, rather than legal compulsion, characterizes Maritain's new Christianity, because the lay leader represents Christian values to the society at large. The state will be guided by democratic votes and popular consensus. Furthermore, the state itself can no longer afford to be so imperial. People of different views must work together to achieve governmental objectives. The value of religious freedom was centrally important in the struggle against both fascism and communism. The new Christianity depicted in *Integral Humanism*, in which the individual Christian acts in the immediate community and the larger society, contributing to the common good, was later reflected in the vision of society set forth in the *Declaration*.

During Maritain's ambassadorship to the Holy See beginning in 1945, Montini (working in the Vatican Secretariat of State) and Maritain had the opportunity to meet at dinner for conversation about the reconstitution of European society in the post-War period. Maritain found Montini's expansiveness congenial because of his openness "to all forms of renewal and progress."[14] Maritain was among those who approved of a rapprochement between the Church and the modern representative, if not democratic, state. The future pope and Jacques Maritain shared the same outlook on solving problems and expressing the role of the Christian in society and in the Church. In 1954, Monsignor Montini became archbishop of Milan (and during the papacy of John XXIII, Cardinal). As archbishop, Montini "undertook to put into practice much of Maritain's social philosophy as he devoted himself to the workers and the poor...."[15] Deeply interested in philosophy throughout his life, Montini favored "a school of mediation between the ancient and the modern, tradition and revolution, order and

14. Barré, *Jacques & Raïssa Maritain*, 397.

15. Julie Kernan, *Our Friend Jacques Maritain: A Personal Memoir* (New York: Doubleday, 1975), 170.

adventure."[16] The continuing evolution of Jacques Maritain's thought allowed his ideas to be particularly useful at the time of the Second Vatican Council. The shared outlook of Montini and Maritain was strong enough to forge bonds that facilitated the work of the Council in drawing up the *Constitution of the Church in the Modern World* (*Gaudium et Spes,* 1965) and other declarations.

After the death of Pope John XXIII, Cardinal Montini, now Pope Paul VI, presided over the Council and invoked Maritain's work. This was especially true with regard to *Gaudium et Spes,* which embodied some of these same principles, and in the dialogue within the Church leading to the *Declaration on Religious Freedom* (1965), which also had direct American input from the draftsmanship of John Courtney Murray.[17] *Gaudium et Spes* stated that the Church proclaims the rights of man "by virtue of the Gospel committed to her."[18] The government exists to promote the common good, which means the protection of the rights and performance of the duties of the human person. The government must not "hamper the development of family, social or cultural groups, nor that of intermediate bodies or organizations, and not deprive them of opportunities for lawful and constructive activity.... Citizens ... must be careful not to attribute excessive power to public authority...."[19] As the *Declaration on Religious Freedom* recognizes, government must act in accordance with human dignity and the common good. "The welfare of society ... consists chiefly in the protection of the rights, and in the performance of the duties, of the human good."[20] These are clear and recurrent themes in the thought of Jacques Maritain. The notions of the centrality of the lay person as a prime Christian actor in society, the dignity of the human person regardless of his or her personal

16. Barré, *Jacques & Raïssa Maritain,* 389. The words are from Chenaux's translation of Montini's preface to Maritain's *Trois Réformateurs.* Philippe Chenaux, *Paul VI et Maritain: Les Rapports du 'Montinianisme' et du 'Maritainisme'* (Brescia: Istituto Paolo VI, 1994).

17. Angela C. Carmella, *John Courtney Murray, S.J. (1904–1967),* in *The Teachings of Modern Christianity: On Law, Politics, and Human Nature,* ed. John Witte Jr. and Frank S. Alexander (New York: Columbia University Press, 2006), 115.

18. Vatican II, *Gaudium et Spes,* ¶41, where it is also written: "By no human law can the personal dignity and liberty of man be so aptly safeguarded as by the Gospel of Christ which has been entrusted to the church." This conciliar document is available online at http://www.vatican.va/archive/hist_councils/ii_vatican_council/documents/vat-ii_cons_19651207_gaudium-et-spes_en.html.

19. Vatican II, *Gaudium et Spes,* 75.

20. Vatican II, *Dignitatis Humanae,* 6.

merit (or lack of it), the person as the prime actor in society, pluralism in religion, and the limitation on the powers of the state to act in society and against individuals had long been explained and elaborated in Maritain's books. These ideas became a part of the mix that went into the inspiration for the Council.[21]

II. The Declaration and Human Dignity: Vision for the Person's Action in Society and the State

The *Declaration on Religious Freedom* itself eschews use of force in matters of conscience. Freedom of conscience in religious matters is central to the *Declaration.* Legally, the state protects public order and justice, including human rights. Thus, the person's freedom of conscience is recognized as something that cannot be interfered with; rather, the person must assume responsibility for his views. Jacques Maritain, with his commitment to a pluralist society, was uniquely positioned to interpret these ideals to the Church. According to some philosophers, bestowal of human rights is the right of the government, but, for Jacques Maritain, each person possesses an absolute dignity by virtue of being human.[22] Jacques Maritain contributed to this dialogue about freedom of religion over the years by thinking deeply about the problems of his time as he saw them and by developing a body of writings in response. Some of Maritain's topics that later proved important to the Council included "ecumenism and religious liberty, the dignity and rights of the human person, fraternal feeling for the Jewish people and their exculpation from the age-old charge of deicide, the highlighting of the status of the laity, [and] the recognition of the values of science, art and democracy."[23]

In October 1957, Msgr. Montini, the Archbishop of Milan, had invoked Maritain's *Integral Humanism* at the second World Congress for the Apostolate of the Laity, thus defending Maritain when he was under attack by important Italian prelates who did not like the vision of a new Christianity,

21. René Mougel, "Maritain et l'Église du Concile," in 40 *Cahiers Jacques Maritain* (2000), 21; Philippe Chenaux, "Paul VI et Maritain," in *Jacques Maritain et ses contemporains*, ed. B. Hubert Y. Floucat (Paris: Desclée, 1991), 323–42.

22. Jacques Maritain, *The Rights of Man and Natural Law*, trans. Doris C. Anson (New York: Charles Scribner's Sons, 1943), 65–66 and 89.

23. Kernan, *Our Friend Jacques Maritain*, 170.

based on the action of the individual Christian lay person in society.[24] At the conference, Montini had said that "the works of Catholic philosophers on Christian humanism, such as those of Maritain for example, can make a good contribution to our reflections and to our actions."[25] That remark continued to hurt Montini and in fact weakened Montini's position in the Roman Curia during the early years of the papacy of John XXIII, to whom Montini (but not Maritain) was close.[26]

Then, in 1960, Archbishop Montini again used Maritain's arguments in *Integral Humanism* in his presentation to the Commission preparing for the Council.[27] In his advice, Montini treated the most common questions and errors and urged:

> That the doctrine on the principal questions of relationships between the supernatural order and human realities ought to be put clearly and defined, that is, the human problems which anguish the people of today. It seems to me that in the Council sessions, the following subjects ought to be treated: a) the relationship between political life and religious life, affirming the accomplishments of the Church as well as its limits in order that a clear and worthwhile doctrine may be proposed to Christians; b) the value of temporal things and actions in their relationship with supernatural ends through which the true religious sense of all human temporal activities may be set forth; c) Christian charity and its logical consequences in social life so that Christian life may be presented as the true ferment of all good, even the temporal good, of the human being, a ferment which nothing can replace.[28]

As the above quotation demonstrates, the ideas publicized in *Integral Humanism* and Maritain's later works echo through Cardinal Montini's proposals for discussion during the Council.[29] Maritain was setting forth a vision for Christian society in an era of lay responsibility after reflecting on the history of the Church. At the same time, when Maritain published his

24. Jean-Dominique Durand, "Jacques Maritain et l'Italie," in *Jacques Maritain en Europe: la réception de sa pensée* (Paris: Beauchesne, 1996), 71.

25. Durand, "Jacques Maritain et l'Italie," 71.

26. Barré, *Jacques Raïssa Maritain*, 419.

27. Roberto Papini, "Jacques Maritain e il Concilio Vaticano II," paper presented at the Vatican City Conference, "The Call to Justice: The Legacy of *Gaudium et Spes* 40 Years Later" (March 2005), 2.

28. Papini, "Jacques Maritain e il Concilio Vaticano II," 2 (my translation); see also, Chenaux, "Paul VI et Maritain," 77–79.

29. Maritain's philosophy of history "deeply influenced the Pope." Compare Montini's views of pastoral work, which involves a "certain apostolic relativism" (Hebblethwaite, *Paul VI*, 257). Montini, too, recognized that Communists could have ideals and that "fraternal service between brothers is the only lever that can lift the world" (Ibid.).

visionary blueprint for a new Christianity in *Integral Humanism*, dictators were growing stronger from Spain to Germany to Russia. His work provided inspiration to those who envisioned the *Declaration*. When like-minded thinkers (such as Pope Paul VI) came to address the problems with solutions, Maritain's work stood as a perspective and resource for the fathers of the Council.[30]

On September 11, 1965, just before coming to New York to address the United Nations, Pope Paul VI received Maritain at Castelgandolfo. Furthermore, Maritain was given a special invitation to come to Rome for the closing day ceremonies of the Council in December when the Council's message to Seekers of Truth was presented to Jacques Maritain. It was appropriate that at the close of the Council the Pope "made a gesture of gratitude to the slight, elderly man in St. Peter's that day."[31] According to Brooke Williams Smith, "[m]ore than any other Catholic, it was Maritain who prepared the way for the Roman Catholic renewal. Following the lead of Pope Leo XIII, Maritain's social writings appeared to many, before the Council, to be revolutionary. He developed a philosophy of Christian openness to the world that was significant in creating the intellectual conditions that led to Vatican II. Indeed, if there be any point on which his critics agree, it is that the influence of his writing on Vatican II was overwhelming."[32]

Maritain's ideas very directly influenced Pope Paul VI. Maritain's philosophy was not only frequently invoked at the Council, but Pope Paul VI also credited him for his part in inspiring the encyclical *Populorum Progressio*, in 1967. In *Populorum Progressio*, the Pope wrote, "Each man is a member of society. He is part of the whole of mankind. It is not just certain individuals, but all men who are called to this fullness of development. Civilizations are born, develop and die. But humanity is advancing along the path of history like the waves of a rising tide encroaching gradually on the shore."[33] Furthermore, "development cannot be limited to mere eco-

30. Silvia Scatena, *La fatica della libertà: La elaborazione della Dichiarazione: Dignitatis humanae* (Bologna: Il Mulino, 2003), 12.

31. Brooke Williams Smith, *Jacques Maritain, Antimodern or Ultramodern? An historical Analysis of His Critics, His Thought, and His Life* (New York: Elsevier Science Ltd., 1976), 21 (noting that Maritain was "summoned to Rome in December 1965, at the close of the Second Vatican Council, to receive from Pope Paul VI unprecedented credit for his major rule in inspiring the reforms of the Council").

32. Smith, *Jacques Maritain, Antimodern or Ultramodern?*, 24–25.

33. Paul VI, *Populorum Progessio*, ¶ 17. One can find this encyclical on-line at http://www

nomic growth. In order to be authentic, it must be complete: *integral,* that is, it has to promote the good of every man and of the whole man."[34] He urges laymen "to take the initiative freely and to infuse a Christian spirit into the mentality, customs, laws and structure of the community in which they live." The resonance of Maritain's work for the Pope's vision is clear in this quotation. "I am a disciple of Maritain," the Pope said; "I will call him my teacher."[35] Clearly, Maritain's philosophy had deeply influenced Pope Paul VI.

Maritain's most important contribution was to link democracy and human rights to the Roman Catholic tradition, ending the hostility of Catholicism to liberal, individualist, and secular democracy in Europe and Latin America. His major contribution in political philosophy was to provide a religious and philosophical justification for liberalism, understood as the defense of human freedom:

> Maritain was responsible for a new development in Catholic political thought that had been anticipated but never articulated in terms of the Catholic tradition by earlier French and Italian writers—the argument that democracy was not simply one of several forms of government, all of which were acceptable provided that they promoted "the common good," but was the one form that was most in keeping with the nature of man and with Christian values.[36]

Maritain envisioned the Christian engaging in society and politics, acting as a leaven, and sharing Christian insights, persuading voters in a pluralist society with the rightness of his positions. What made Jacques Maritain's fluid yet timeless philosophy so useful to the spirit of Vatican II? His book entitled simply *Antimoderne*[37] explains the importance of the notion of keeping timeless truths in mind (*antimoderne*) in the atmosphere and

---

.vatican.va/holy_father/paul_vi/encyclicals/documents/hf_pvi_enc_2603197_populorum_en.html.

34. Ibid., ¶ 14. In *Populorum Progressio.* ¶ 20, the Pope went back over the theme of the primacy of the spiritual: "If development calls for an ever-growing number of technical experts, even more necessary still is the deep thought and reflection of wise men, in search of a new humanism, one which will enable our contemporaries to enjoy the higher values of love and friendship, of prayer and contemplation." In footnote 44, Paul cited *Integral Humanism* (*Populorum Progressio,* ¶ 42).

35. Joseph W. Evans, "Jacques Maritain: Philosopher Was Pope's Teacher," *National Catholic Reporter,* May 11, 1973, at 5.

36. Paul Sigmund, "The Catholic Tradition and Modern Democracy," in *Religion and Politics in the American Milieu,* ed. Leslie Griffin (Notre Dame: University of Notre Dame Press, 1986), 13.

37. Jacques Maritain, *Antimoderne* (Paris: Desclée, 1922).

language of the moment (*ultramoderne*).[38] The title *Antimoderne* responded to the then current cultural linking of modernism to the end of Christian influence.[39]

In Jacques Maritain's works, the rights of the Jews[40] and other human rights,[41] including freedom of religion through the juridical value of pluralism,[42] realigned the relationship of the state and the Church. Jacques Maritain, a refugee in the United States during and after World War II, in some senses interpreted the United States Constitution in reference to the Church.[43] The democratic rights of individuals in the United States were not divorced from religious exercise as they had been in European Enlightenment philosophy.[44] The Church profited from this knowledge when writing its own constitution, *Gaudium et Spes*. Jacques Maritain reflected on human rights and realigned the relationship of the state and the Church. Maritain's reflections played a significant role when the Roman Catholic Church came to accept ideas of human rights, recognize the contribution of the republican form of government, and value freedom of conscience.

III. The Fruit of the Friendship: A Better Vision of Christianity Able to Claim Rights for Itself because It Respects the Right of Conscience

As we approach a half century of familiarity with the *Declaration*, the vision for religious freedom and confessional pluralism juridically recognized

38. "[A]*nti-modern* might just as well be called *ultra-modern*": Stephen Schloesser, *Jazz Age Catholicism: Mystic Modernism in Postwar Paris, 1919–1933* (Toronto: University of Toronto Press, 2005), 163.

39. According to Ezra Pound, 1922 started the new calendar of the post-Christian era (Schloesser, *Jazz Age Catholicism*, 162).

40. See Jacques Maritain, *Les Juifs parmi les nations* (Paris: Les Editions du Cerf, 1938), translated as *A Christian Looks at the Jewish Question* (New York: Longmans, Green, 1939) and Jacques Maritain, *Le Mystère d'Israel* (Paris: Desclée de Brouwer, 1965).

41. See Maritain, *The Rights of Man*. For Maritain's role in promoting the Universal Declaration of Human Rights, see my article "Cognition and Consensus in the Natural Law Tradition and in Neuroscience: Jacques Maritain and The Universal Declaration of Human Rights," *Villanova Law Review* 54 (2009): 435.

42. See Maritain, *Integral Humanism*.

43. See Jacques Maritain, *Reflections on America* (New York: Charles Scribner's Sons, 1958).

44. "Congress shall make no law respecting an establishment of religion ... or prohibiting the free exercise thereof" (U.S. Constitution, Amendment I).

by governments is becoming clearer. The use of the *Declaration* in examining the role of government in society is exactly what its inspirers (Maritain and many others) and sponsors (Pope Paul VI, John Courtney Murray and many others) would have wished for the integration of these principles in daily life. Schloesser attributes Maritain's ability to introduce this balance into the discussion to his insight that timeless ideas are expressed in terms of each generation's circumstance. This perspective allowed Thomistic philosophy to be a vital force in the 1920s.[45] Furthermore, Maritain did not neglect theology, the sacraments, and manifestations of the incarnation. Maritain welcomed the new and saw that philosophy is "as much a thing of today as it is of yesterday."[46] Theologically speaking, Maritain used "the analogy of the Incarnation: the divine was capable of becoming something else without replacing it or destroying it, even as it remained itself without confusion."[47] According to Schloesser, Maritain looked at the modern world as the essential constancy of dialectical images reprising eternal themes. If "Maritain's transformation of Thomists into ultramodernists was one of the most important catalysts for the 1920s neo-Thomistic revival,"[48] his political philosophy (which remained true to the essentials of Christianity) formed part of the groundwork making the Council possible and contributed to the positions taken during the course of the Council itself.

The Roman Catholic conception of human rights developed from looking at foundational truths in the light of new democratic political possibilities.[49] The human person at the center of Church doctrine provided the focus of interpretation of these political conditions assessing the temporal role of the state and the securing of religious freedom, particularly freedom for the church itself in its relations with political society and not just its individual members. In other words, the internalization and assimilation of these political conditions arose from an undertaking as extensive and fundamental as Aquinas's absorption of Aristotelian principles, which resulted in a transformation of our understanding of Aristotle as well. This renewal of Christianity took place over many years in many different Christian circles, culminating in the Second Vatican Council. Maritain's philosophical

45. Schloesser, *Jazz Age Catholicism*, 163.

46. Ibid., 165.

47. Ibid., 165.

48. Ibid., *Jazz Age Catholicism*, 163.

49. Kenneth L. Grasso, "Beyond Liberal," in *Catholicism, Liberalism, and Communitarianism: The Catholic Intellectual Tradition and the Moral Foundations of Democracy* ed. Kenneth L. Grasso, Gerard B. Bradley, and Robert P. Hunt (Lanham, Maryland: Rowman and Littlefield, 1995), 50–51.

thought was influential both during the Council's debates and in the Council's documents on the relationships between the Church and the world, the Church and the state, and religious liberty, with its recognition of religious pluralism. Friendships like those between Jacques Maritain and Paul VI proved crucial.

When Jacques Maritain died on April 28, 1973, Paul VI sent his secretary Msgr. Pasquale Macchi as his special delegate for the funeral and burial at Kolbsheim, near Strasbourg.[50] On the 29th, the Pope himself, in St. Peter's Square for the feast of St. Catherine of Siena, remembered Maritain's life in the following way:

> And the other voice which today draws our attention says this, in an unedited fragment: "Each professor seeks to be as much as possible exact and well informed outside his own discipline. But he is called to serve the truth in a more profound way. He is enjoined to love the Truth above all as absolute and to which he is entirely devoted; if he is a Christian, it is God himself whom he loves." Who speaks this way? It is Maritain, who died yesterday at Toulouse, a great thinker of our time, a master in the art of thinking, living and praying. He died alone and poor, associated with the Little Brothers of Charles de Foucauld. His voice, his person will endure in the tradition of philosophical thought and Catholic meditation. We won't forget his appearance in this place at the closing of the Council, to receive the message to men of culture in the name of Christ our Master.[51]

Not long before Pope Paul VI died on August 6, 1978, he talked about Christian friendship and quoted Cicero's *De Amicitia* to the effect that friendship is "perfect agreement on all things, divine and human, accompanied by benevolence and love."[52] Paul VI mentioned Christ as the perfect friend. Surely this quotation from Cicero also describes the important relationship between Paul VI and Jacques Maritain for the Church in its recognition of religious freedom as one of the universal and fundamental human rights.

50. Barré, *Jacques Raïssa Maritain*, 438.

51. Paul VI, "Morceau inédit extrait de la lettre envoyée à Mgr. Pasquale Macchi," in *40 Cahiers Jacques Maritain* (my translation), 64. Many years before, Maritain had written that genuine fellowship only exists "when a man is firmly and absolutely convinced of a truth, or of what he holds to be a truth, and when he at the same time recognizes the right of those who deny this truth to exist, and to contradict him, and to speak their own mind, not because they are free from truth but because they seek truth in their own way, and because he respects in them human nature and human dignity and those very resources and living springs of the intellect and of conscience which make them potentially capable of attaining the truth he loves": Jacques Maritain, "Truth and Human Fellowship," in *Jacques Maritain, On the Use of Philosophy: Three Essays* (Princeton: Princeton University Press, 1961), 24.

52. Hebblethwaite, *Paul VI*, 707.

JOHN F. MILLARD

Maritain and America

Reflections on a Friendship

On his visit to America in 2008, during the welcoming ceremony at the White House, Pope Benedict XVI said of the United States: "From the dawn of the Republic, America's quest for freedom has been guided by the conviction that the principles governing political and social life are intimately linked to a moral order based on the dominion of God the Creator."[1] His words called to mind those of another great European friend of America, Jacques Maritain, whose 1956 seminars at the University of Chicago were published in 1958 as *Reflections on America.* Maritain writes, "When he who, meeting for the first time either France or America, falls in love at first sight, it is because he is confronted with a moral personality, a moral vocation, something of invaluable dignity, which is spiritual in nature, and which, I think, in the last analysis is quickened, in one way or another, by some spark of the Christian spirit and legacy."[2]

Maritain's friendship with America was deep and genuine. It was a true friendship: Maritain knew America's weaknesses as well her strengths, and he understood that virtue required that a friend be honest about both.

What is friendship? In answering that question I want to call your attention to a wonderful book by Professor John Cuddeback entitled *Friend-*

1. Pope Benedict XVI, address at the White House, April 16, 2008, during his apostolic journey to the United States and visit to the United Nations headquarters

2. Jacques Maritain, *Reflections on America* (New York, Charles Scribner's Sons, 1958), 20. (All references to this work hereafter are placed in the text, in parentheses.)

ship: The Art of Happiness.[3] In discussing friendship, Cuddeback follows Aristotle. He writes: "Full friendship is that relationship of mutual good will that is based upon the virtue, or true goodness, of two persons. It is *based upon* virtue because this kind of relationship can only begin when virtue or goodness is already present. It is also based on virtue inasmuch as virtue or goodness is the main thing that is willed, desired, and sought in the relationship. What does a true friend want most of all? The virtue of his friend: that it be, and increase!"[4]

Of the three kinds of friendships that Aristotle identifies, the third, virtuous friendship, is, in Aristotle's words, "the friendship of men who are good, and alike in virtue."[5] Only to the extent that a person is virtuous, can he share in true friendship. True friendship requires virtue on both sides. People who have become virtuous through effort, Cuddeback points out, can take an unselfish, other-centered position that makes them capable of recognizing true goodness in other persons. Aristotle tells us that, since the good man sees in his friend another self, he feels toward his friend as he feels toward himself. And Cuddeback reminds us that "the most important thing that [two friends] can do for one another is to help each other walk down the path of virtue."[6]

There can be no doubt that Maritain considered himself a friend of America, for he told us so himself. Describing his book as "random reflections on the American scene," Maritain goes on to say, "I am confident that there are true insights at the core of my random reflections.... The truths they contain are most valuable to me, for they are in essence a statement about why I love America" (17). He tells us that he was moved to write *Reflections on America* because he "felt a growing urge to bear witness to this country and to its people—it is a matter of justice and gratitude" (15).

But friendship requires honesty, and so, Maritain writes, "I shall have some opportunity to point out, myself, several of those unfortunate aspects [of America]" (17). Since true friendship, however, can only be between the virtuous, he is quick to add that those aspects "are of small import in comparison with all that I love in this country" (17).

3. The references that follow are from the revised edition of Cuddeback's book, now entitled *True Friendship: Where Virtue Becomes Happiness* (Denver, Colorado: Epic, 2010).

4. Cuddeback, *True Friendship*, 32–33.

5. Aristotle, *Nichomachean Ethics*, trans. W. D. Ross, in *The Basic Works of Aristotle*, ed. Richard McKeon (New York: Random House, 1941), 1156b 7–8.

6. Cuddeback, *True Friendship*, 62.

Reflections on America is fascinating in two ways. First, we see a philosopher thinking about the nature of friendship by reflecting about a country, America, *and* doing so as an act of friendship. Second, we see a friend, Maritain, hard at work fighting for the soul of *his* friend, America.

It is also a book in which we see Maritain at his best—elegant, wry, generous, sometimes a little testy, but most of all insightful and eloquent.

What was Maritain's first impression of America? He tells us that he was confronted with "a sharp contrast between *the people* on the one hand, and, on the other hand, what I would like to call the externally superimposed *structure or ritual of civilization*" (21). Maritain explains that by this structure he means the industrial civilization, born in Europe and carried to America. Maritain writes that "its inner logic, as I knew it—originally grounded as it was on the principle of the fecundity of money and the absolute primacy of individual profit—was, everywhere in the world, inhuman and materialist" (21). He goes on to say that he was forced to wonder "what will be the result of the conflict between the spirit of the people and the logic of the structure" (22) of the industrial civilization.

His answer provides the book's framework for Maritain's "random reflections" on America. We shall return to it shortly to consider his answer. But before we do, it's worth our while to consider which criticisms of America Maritain considers to be just or unjust.

Many who loathe America do so, Maritain shrewdly observes, because "to compensate for their frustration and resentment they need a worldwide scapegoat, a symbolic continent great and powerful enough to arouse mankind's hopes and perverse enough to betray them" (126). Maritain notes that he has never met "any man genuinely aware of the ways of the spirit" (126) who holds this view.

Another canard, in Maritain's view, is that Americans are materialists. In an observation based in part on his own experience, he calls Americans "the least materialist among the modern peoples which have attained the industrial stage" (22). Indeed, Maritain points out that "the ordinary course of activity of American institutions and the innumerable American private groups show[s] us that the ancient Greek and Roman idea of the *civis praelarus*, the dedicated citizen who spends his money in the service of the common good, plays an essential part in American consciousness" (34).

Maritain is deeply aware of America's flaws, the most evident and serious of which, in the 1950's, was overt racism. Maritain's searing condemnation of racism in *Reflections on American* are among the most eloquent passages in the book. Noting that popular prejudice against African Americans was rampant in the North as well as in the South, he describes such racism as "a mixture of fear, a contemptuous superiority complex, and pleasure in humiliating and bullying others" (52). He also notes what he calls the "correct" forms that racial prejudice was taking in some parts of the well-to-do strata of the population. Sparing no words, he calls racism "heart-rending," a "plague" on America and "incompatible with its spirit, the sense of human fellowship" (53). He also points out that "the uncompromising stand [against racism] that Archbishop Rummel has taken in Louisiana on behalf of racial equality has unmistakable significance" (55).

But racism is only part of the story. Maritain notes with approval that the American effort to go "ahead seeking more or less gropingly, but without respite, justice and fairness for all, deserves respect and evinces, within human infirmity, much human grandeur" (57).

Maritain observes in the America of the 1950's a "new-found concern for sex," which finds expression in the assumption that "all that counts is that which can be observed by the senses or by instruments" and, he notes sardonically, in "the preaching of a so-called sex education in which cheap popularized science commingles with soap-opera sentimentality and a most artlessly serious-minded quest for the good" (61–62). With wry wit, he observes that "it is a curious spectacle to see so many people either teaching or learning, through biology and psychology, how to be happy in sexual life, plus a lot of items which, as a rule, and since the beginning of things, nature has its own ready ways of making known to human beings free of Puritan or anti-Puritan complex" (62–63). Spoken as a true Thomist, that.

Let us now return to the question Maritain raised earlier. In answering it, he tells us much about ourselves and a great deal of it is good news. So what *will* be the result of the conflict between the spirit of the people and the logic of the structure of the industrial civilization? Maritain writes that the longer he lived in America, the more he realized that the answer to his question was that "the spirit of the people is gradually breaking the logic of the structure ... [that] the vital, pragmatic, unsystematic pressure exercised by the American people and the American soul on the structures of our modern industrial civilization is transforming from within the inner dynamism and historical trends of the industrial regime" (23).

How was this possible? The answer in its most simple terms is, in Maritain's words, that "there is, in the most existential sense, a strain of Gospel fraternal love deep in the American blood" (86). In Maritain's view, "there is one thing that America knows well, and that she teaches as a great and precious lesson to those who come in contact with her astounding adventure: it is the value and the dignity of the common man, the value and the dignity of the people" (195).

Under the steady, unsystematic pressure of the spirit of the people, stronger than the logic of the structure, Maritain maintains, a crucial change took place in the American economic and social regime. In a strange paradox, the people who lived and toiled under the structure of industrialization kept their souls apart from it. In Maritain's words, "At least as regards the essentials, their souls and vital energy, their dreams, their everyday effort, their idealism and generosity, were running against the grain of the inner logic of the superimposed structure" (22).

Maritain makes it very clear that this response was rooted in the virtues that Americans had learned from the Gospel. The spark of the Gospel was rooted in the American psyche, "deep beneath the hardness and the harshness of the hunt for material interests and advantages" (85). This spark of the Gospel lies deep even in Americans who "more often than not do not think at all of the Gospel" (85). Nothing, Maritain writes, "is more valuable in this poor world than to find a trace of Gospel fraternal love" (85) active in the great mass of a nation.

Maritain sees in America, with its stress on the dignity of work and the dignity of the individual both rooted in the Gospel, fertile soil for the growth of Christian Humanism. "The old merciless struggles between management and labor ... have given way to a new relationship ... of co-operative tension, with enormous social advantages" (109). This is only a beginning for the humanization of the industrial regime. The realization of the American ideal, rooted in the Gospel, will be the work of generations, Maritain acknowledges, but, in his words, "the road is open" (112).

Just to be clear, Maritain writes, "I am far from saying that today's American civilization is a new Christendom, even in outline" (189). But that is not the point for Maritain. "In actual fact, it is in America that I have had a real experience of concrete, existential democracy: not as a set of abstract slogans, or as a lofty ideal, but as an actual, human, working, perpetually tested and perpetually readjusted way of life," (161) a way of life that as a matter of historical fact has always rested not just on the writings of Locke and Jefferson and the Enlightenment, but on the teachings of the Gospel as well.

In writing of the American Founders, Maritain points out that "their philosophy of life, and their political philosophy, their notion of natural law and of human rights, were permeated with concepts worked out by Christian reason and backed by an unshakeable religious feeling." In writing of the Constitution, Maritain speaks of "the spirit and inspirations of this great political Christian document" (182). He is, thus, not surprised to find in America, as he notes, "a certain hidden disposition that is Christian in origin, and appears to me as a kind of humble and remote reminiscence of the Gospel in the inner attitude of people" (83).

Reflecting the Catholic Church's emphasis on the principle of subsidiarity, Maritain notes that "there is in this country a swarming multiplicity of particular communities—self-organized groupings, associations, unions, sodalities, vocational or religious brotherhoods, in which men join forces with one another at the elementary level of their everyday concerns and interests" (162).

Maritain's *Reflections on America* is itself a perfect expression of friendship. In it he fights for the soul of the friend he loves, America. "What the world expects from America," writes Maritain, "is that she keep alive, in human history, a fraternal recognition of the dignity of man, in other words, the terrestrial hope of men in the Gospel" (162). To the extent that America remains rooted in its heritage of the Gospel, there is hope for her future.

II

BEAUTY, ART, AND LOVE

DANIEL B. GALLAGHER

Art, Otherness, and History in Maritain, Gilson, and De Finance

Joseph De Finance's (1904–2000) last and perhaps most original work is an extended philosophical reflection on the significance of otherness.[1] "Every type of human action," he wrote, "is a typology of our attitude towards the other, and more precisely towards the 'otherness' of the other."[2]

One of the most important types of human action considered by De Finance with regard to "otherness" is art. Broadly speaking, art, whether understood mimetically or expressively, initiates with an *apprehension* of the other (*aliud*).[3] Art also aims at the *production* of an "other" (*aliquid*). The artist or craftsman (*aliquis*) seeks to employ a set of acquired skills to generate an object that is either useful, aesthetically pleasing, or some combination thereof. Finally, art is directed to the "other" (*alicui*) as the "recipient" of something akin to a communicative act.

In what follows, I explore the role of otherness in the work of three philosophers who took a particular interest in art against an explicitly Thomistic background: Joseph De Finance, Jacques Maritain, and Étienne Gilson.

Despite the differences between them, De Finance, Maritain, and Gilson all begin with the deceptively elementary Aristotelian-Thomistic distinction between "doing" (*agere*) and "making" (*facere*).[4] According to Aristotle and

1. Joseph de Finance, *De l'Un et de l'Autre: Essai sur l'altérité* (Rome: Editrice Pontificia Università Gregoriana, 1993). English translations from this work are my own.

2. De Finance, *De l'Un et de l'Autre*, vi.

3. The Latin terms given here will be important for my conclusion.

4. Jacques Maritain, *Art and Scholasticism* (New York: Charles Scribner's Sons, 1947), 4–8.

Aquinas, *agere* and *facere* both fall under the domain of the practical intellect. The practical intellect is distinguished from the speculative intellect in that the former is oriented toward something beyond the type of knowledge obtained through the initial cognitive act. Conversely, the speculative intellect terminates in the very cognitive grasp of the object toward which it is directed. The practical intellect comes into play both in the deliberation of moral action (*agere*) and in the deliberation of objects to be produced (*facere*) through the application of artistic skill. According to all three, art is not merely a perfected form of knowledge; it must pass over into the very production of the good to be produced.

For this reason, Maritain vigorously asserts in *Art and Scholasticism* that art is not directed toward the good of the agent but of the object to be made.[5] The virtue corresponding to practical knowledge understood as *facere* is consequently *technê:* that is, the virtue possessed as an intellectual *habitus* that empowers the craftsman or artist to produce precisely the object called for in a given set of circumstances, be they practical or aesthetic. Conversely, the virtue (*aretê*) of prudence (*phronesis*) aims at the good of the agent, although there are certainly external goods that depend on an agent's capacity for making prudent moral choices and acting upon them.

This was the basic distinction that launched Maritain's unique and widely influential *Art and Scholasticsm*. Maritain's goal was to buoy the philosophy of art with what he considered a robust aesthetic philosophy rooted in the metaphysical principles of Aquinas. Considerations of "otherness," however, primarily revolve around the artwork produced and its relationship to the transcendental of beauty rather than the psychological and historical considerations which will come to the fore in his later work and which are highlighted in the work of De Finance.

Like Maritain, Étienne Gilson nurtured a keen interest in beauty and its imbeddedness in artistic activity. Although Gilson shared the basic Aristotelian-Thomistic principles that inspired Maritain, he devoted his early energies to engaging in a polemic with those who held art to be a form of knowledge. He particularly had in mind the idealist philosophy pervading the field of aesthetics as seen in the Hegelian tendencies of Benedetto Croce, R. G. Collingood, Roger Fry, and others.[6] Art, Gilson argued, was

5. Maritain, *Art and Scholasticism*, 6–8, 10–16, 44–45, 68.

6. Étienne Gilson, *The Arts of the Beautiful* (New York: Charles Scribner's Sons, 1965), 13–23, 26, 30–31, 104–19.

not primarily a form of pure knowledge but a type of know-how. The difficulty lies in delineating a meaningful distinction between these two types of knowledge and articulating the repercussions of that distinction upon the "other" produced by the artist. In short, works of art are the product of intelligent action, but an action that lies somewhere between pure speculative and practical knowledge. Gilson adopts a line of reasoning similar to Maritain's in that he establishes beauty as the ultimate end of the fine arts, specifying that beauty is neither purely intellectual (for it is related to appetite) nor exclusively sensible (for it is related to intellect). Gilson differs from Maritain in that he downplays the link between the epistemological stage of artistic production and the stage of execution in which the other is actually produced.

We can gain further insight into this difference between Maritain and Gilson by comparing and contrasting their approaches to art, knowledge, and otherness with De Finance's approach. De Finance's primary conviction is that "the full meaning of art emerges only at the level of interpersonal relations."[7] At the same time, he insists that this relational and social character of art does not seem to bear upon its essence. As is evident from his placement of *ars* within a conceptual framework constituted by the *agere/facere* distinction that stands at the basis of both Maritain and Gilson, De Finance regards the essence of art to consist neither in pure intellection nor in intersubjective communication, but rather in a unique form of human action directed toward another object (*aliquid aliud*) that displays the features of appropriateness, suitability, and goodness.

De Finance's key example in *De l'Un et de l'Autre* is a shepherd boy who finds himself whittling a stick merely for the sake of pleasure.[8] De Finance explains that even though this budding artist may enjoy his pastime in the blissful solitude of a remote pasture, his work reveals something of his character, including both his "unconscious" and "conscious" tendencies. De Finance thus bears an uncanny resemblance to the later Maritain in his immediate perception of the psychological traits of artistic activity. For De Finance, the spontaneity of art is undeniable. It is not a deductive conclusion drawn from syllogistic reasoning. And yet, as we shall see, Maritain is reluctant to leave behind the rigor of such reasoning when it comes to a

7. De Finance, *De l'Un et de l'Autre*, 125–26.

8. See Paul S. Wingert, *Primitive Art: Its Traditions and Styles* (New York: Oxford University Press, 1962).

philosophical reflection upon art and beauty. De Finance himself offers a word of caution. The unconscious at work in artistic production is spiritual and therefore quite different from that espoused by Freudian psychology. It results not merely from the firing of uncontrollable impulses and internal "pressures," but from one's personal ideals and fundamental moral dispositions. De Finance draws attention to the fact that the shepherd boy's choice to carve a human head rather than an eagle might indeed be more significant than we would first think.[9]

De Finance then proceeds to make a provocative observation: "Art is therefore before all else an expression, a *non-conceptual* objectification in an external work—not in a mental word or oral discourse—of that which is active or latent in the consciousness and subconsciousness of the subject and which, very often, is incapable of being said."[10] This is quite different from the position assumed by De Finance's former mentor Étienne Gilson. Gilson maintained that there is a certain terminal point between the knowledge of the object to be produced and the physical execution of that object in paint, clay, stone, or wood. The artist's main task is to remove the physical obstacles standing in the way of realizing the artwork in the external world. Consequently, De Finance stands remarkably closer to Maritain who, even at the time of *Art and Scholasticism*, viewed the movement from creative intuition to creative production in a more dynamic and seamless way.

At the same time, we find that De Finance does not align himself with a strictly expressive theory of art, insofar as he holds that the "signs" detected in the shepherd boy's sculpted staff by an astute psychologist do not necessarily suggest that the child intended them to be communicated. Hence De Finance maintains that although it is practically impossible to imagine that children who are utterly alone would find any interest in inventing a language, it is entirely conceivable that they would make artworks simply for the sake of their own enjoyment. This is the springboard from which art moves in the direction of a communal phenomenon, acquiring the variety of nuances typical of communication and social interaction and thus opening channels for a correlated philosophy of history.

De Finance's pivotal conclusion is the following: "Eventually, step by step as art progressed, the social element became more important, not

9. De Finance, *De l'Un et de l'Autre*, 118.
10. Ibid., 127.

only for the reason that the artwork, in what it expresses and in the way it expresses it, goes on to influence society, but also insofar as the intention to communicate, to express oneself to others, to attract their attention, assumes greater importance and perhaps even the place of *greatest* importance" (emphasis mine).[11]

The salience of De Finance's conclusion lies not only in the fact that "otherness" now takes center stage in his theory of the social and communicative dimensions of art, but that this "otherness" emerges through the progression of history—both of the individual and of mankind. De Finance's suggestion lends itself to a more detailed exploration of how he compares with the later Maritain, who was much more progressive in the way he related the philosophy of art to philosophical psychology and the philosophy of history.

Throughout his life, Jacques Maritain remained ambivalent about the nature and scope of modern psychology and the philosophy of history. He attributed his distaste of the former to Freud, and his ambivalence over the latter to Hegel. "Because of my distrust of Hegel," he wrote, "I was, in my youth, somewhat prejudiced against the very notion of the philosophy of history."[12] Maritain was most critical of the Hegelian sublimation of history into metaphysics. In *On the Philosophy of History*, Maritain reconsidered the intrinsic value of a linear conception of history to be embodied in the Judeo-Christian tradition. He offered a series of "axiomatic" and "typological" formulas to support such a linear conception philosophically. These formulas revolve around Maritain's conviction that to engage in a study of the philosophy of history is not to do metaphysics, but moral philosophy.

Maritain has been criticized for adhering to a brand of Thomism that fails to take sufficient account of the historical dimensions of human existence. Francesca Aran Murphy, for one, has criticized Maritain for a certain short-sightedness of historical vision.[13] Murphy thus places Maritain in what Bernard Lonergan has called the "classicist" perspective as distinguished from the "empirical" perspective.[14] The classicist perspective ex-

11. Ibid., 116.

12. Jacques Maritian, *On the Philosophy of History*, ed. Joseph W. Evans (New York: Charles Scribner's Sons, 1957), ix–x.

13. Francesca Aran Murphy, *Christ the Form of Beauty* (Edinburgh: TT Clark, 1995), 60.

14. Bernard Lonergan, *A Second Collection: Papers by Bernard Lonergan*, ed. W. F. J. Ryan and Bernard J. Tyrell (London, Darton, Longman Todd, 1974), 5–6.

tracts the artwork from its historical and cultural particularity in order to hone in on its significance as a trans-historical and trans-cultural object of perception. While not going to a Hegelian extreme, the classicist perspective tends to view art as a privileged moment in the process of the spiritual maturation of mankind. Umberto Eco, advocating a "historiographical" approach to aesthetics, similarly criticized Maritain for a lack of empirical perspective.[15] Art, Eco insists, cannot be detached from the historical-cultural milieu from which it arises, which in turn entails that we explicitly acknowledge the "otherness" of the object under study. By collecting a seemingly disparate set of artifacts and relating them to one other through an exacting process of interpretation, the "other" comes alive "for me" once again in the present moment, but only because I have respected the object as "other."

De Finance's approach to the historicity of art both complements Maritain's but also expands upon it considerably. His primary focus on "otherness" and his subsequent placement of art within the broader historical horizon that ultimately qualifies otherness opens space for the type of psychology that Maritain found attractive in his later years. The conscious and unconscious "pulsions" discussed in *Creative Intuition in Art and Poetry*[16] would not be possible apart from the category of time that allows the spiritual subject to reflect upon the data of perception and penetrate the core of that which makes a thing to be what it is and to be beautiful.

Murphy is correct in noting that Maritain tended to emphasize the objectivity of being, truth, and beauty throughout most of his career. However, his turn to historical considerations in philosophy did not wait until the publication of *On the Philosophy of History* in 1957. In 1952, Maritain presented his famous series of lectures on art and poetry which would eventually be collected into *Creative Intuition in Art and Poetry* in 1954. The material presented therein builds on the Thomistic foundations he had begun to lay in *Art and Scholasticism* between 1918 and 1919. *Creative Intuition in Art and Poetry* already begins to reveal the dynamic conception of history suggested by De Finance but scarcely evident in the work of Gilson.

15. See Umberto Eco, *La definizione dell'arte*, 2nd ed. (Milano: Garzanti, 1984), 100–10. See also his *Art and Beauty in the Middle Ages*, trans. Hugh Bredin (New Haven: Yale University Press, 1986), 4–16; and his *The Aesthetics of Thomas Aquinas*, trans. Hugh Breden (Cambridge: Harvard University Press, 1988), 22, 39–46.

16. Jacques Maritain, *Creative Intution in Art and Poetry* (New York: Published by Pantheon Books, Inc., for the Bollingen Foundation, 1953), 65–76, 79–80.

I would suggest that, in the end, Maritain viewed art and history as coupled, though not, of course, in an absolutist or deterministic sense.[17] He suggests, rather, that there has been a gradual disclosure of human subjectivity through art over time. Like De Finance, Maritain considered this disclosure as a contingent, though nonetheless historical event. It is spontaneous, but ordered—not towards anything beyond itself (as in Hegel's Absolute), nor with respect only to itself (as with Heidegger's *archē*), but rather as a way of contemplating things in the world both as objects-in-themselves and as objects-of-consciousness. Though Maritain rejects the Kantian epistemological separation between *noumena* and *phenomena*, his theory of creative intuition might help to explain to someone who does accept such a separation how a deeper understanding of the former is possible through the latter.[18] In his later philosophy, and in a vein remarkably similar to De Finance, Maritain began to take seriously the respective roles of history and psychology in facilitating this deeper understanding.

Art, as Maritain understands it, is coupled to history by way of induction. De Finance likewise stresses the "gradual" and "step-by-step" development of the social and cultural dimensions of art through time. Maritain writes that the objective content of the philosophy of history "consists of universal objects of thought, which are either the typical features of a given historical age or some essential aspect of human history in general, and which are inductively abstracted from historical data."[19] The data provided by history is "non-scientific." By this Maritain means that it is "not universal, not necessary, and not raised to the level of abstract intelligibility."[20] Art objects are not of history, nor from history, but in history. We recognize artworks as produced in time but also, argues Maritain, as conveyances of a trans-historical human spirit; that is, a free spirit that can recollect the past and project itself into the future.

At the same time, Maritain continued to maintain that philosophy itself is primarily deductive. This highlights a significant divergence from De Finance, whose approach to the philosophy of otherness, including art, is con-

17. Cf. Stephen Rocker's interesting proposal in "Hegel and Maritain on Philosophy of Art: Incompatibility or Complimentarity?" *Études maritainiennes* 25 (2001): 70–78.

18. See Manuel M. Davenport, "Kant and Maritain on the Nature of Art," *British Journal of Aesthetics* 12 (1972): 359–68.

19. Maritain, *Philosophy of History*, 10–11.

20. Ibid., 12.

siderably more open to the phenomenology of human experience and—so to speak—less tethered to Baroque-Thomistic conceptions of metaphysics and ontology. According to Maritain, philosophy cannot find adequate rest in what is merely particular and contingent. It rather seeks what is universal and necessary. Despite his gradual turn to the subjective and historical dimensions of creative intuition and artistic action, Maritain generally adheres to Thomistic metaphysical principles more ostensibly than does De Finance. Maritain asserts that "induction and philosophical truths are and must be joined together in order to have the objective content of the philosophy of history."[21] Yet it is always tempting to push this "joining together" in the direction of an all-out synthesis. Induction may lead us to recognize and penetrate philosophical truths, but we cannot deduce historical conclusions from philosophical truths. "Neither induction alone nor philosophical deduction alone are sufficient. They must complement one another."[22]

As previously mentioned, we can see Maritain working out some of the practical consequences of his reflections on the philosophy of art, psychology, and history in *Creative Intuition in Art and Poetry.* The study of art as an historical phenomenon must proceed inductively. A philosophical reflection on the nature of art, however, can draw upon the results of deductive reasoning. The philosophy of history—and similarly the philosophy of art—must always draw from the power of deductive reasoning which aims at universality and necessity. According to Maritain, the philosophy of history is "not merely conjectural, because it is never a mere induction—there is always some rational necessity involved."[23]

Maritain carries the dynamic interplay of induction and deduction a bit further in *Creative Intuition in Art and Poetry.* Whereas thirty years earlier he had begun his study of the philosophy of art more deductively, here he begins with an inductive study of Eastern artistic traditions.[24] He explains how Eastern art tends to focus solely on things rather than on the self. Conversely, Western art, especially since the Renaissance, turns progressively toward the subject. "The Things and the artist's Self—," Maritain asks, "what can we learn on this subject from the typical forms in which the creative effort of man's eyes and hands has manifested itself in the course of the centuries?" As we read *Creative Intuition in Art and Poetry,* it turns

21. Ibid., 31.

22. Ibid., 35.

23. Ibid., 38.

24. Maritain, *Creative Intuition,* 112–24.

out that what we can learn on this subject can be learned only by employing both induction and deduction. Man perceives things in time, but his very perception of things leads to a trans-historical cognition of himself as "other." Both these dimensions are present in the original creation of an artwork. The artist neither prescinds from the historicity of the objects with which he works and creates, nor does he prescind from his own trans-historical consciousness and subjectivity. Similarly, philosophical reflection on art can never prescind from art's historicity, nor can philosophical reflection on history prescind from art's subjectivity and the appropriation of the "other" (*aliud*) within oneself (*in se*). They are coupled, but not confused.

As I have suggested, we might also contrast Maritain and De Finance at the level of sympathy each has for the Kantian distinction between the thing-as-known from the thing-in-itself. De Finance at least takes seriously the implications of the Kantian distinction and the need to confront it seriously.[25] Maritain is notably less sympathetic to the Kantian project to the point that he views Eastern art as the outstanding example of how focused attention to the object actually leads to a more complete discovery of one's self as "other." "The more the personality of the Oriental artists succeeds in forgetting itself and immolating itself in Things, the more, in point of fact, it is present and revives in the work."[26] By stretching ever more intently toward the historical concreteness of the object, the artist more fully imbues the artwork with his own subjectivity without sacrificing the ontological richness of the "other" as existing apart from him. However, insofar as the subject retains his unique subjectivity and the artwork its unique objectivity, there is no fusion or absorption involved that would abrogate the respective identity of subject or object or mitigate the distinctive aspect of "otherness" present in both.

I would suggest that, for Maritain, art ultimately relates to history in the following way: through history, art moves from a consideration of the human person as object towards a consideration of the human person as subject. Moreover, this historical movement in the West is not fully perceived until it is contrasted with the history of art in the East. Eastern art discloses the subjectivity of the self through the concentrated and meditative focus on the object as object, all the while respecting its otherness and recogniz-

25. See De Finance, *De l'Un et de l'Autre,* 99–108.
26. Maritain, *Creative Intuition,* 115.

ing one's own otherness through it. Western art discloses the subjectivity of the self through a more deliberate and gradual turning away from the person as object to the person as quasi self-enclosed subject.

So how does the Maritain of *Creative Intuition in Art and Poetry* and *On the Philosophy of History* relate to De Finance's suggestion that in the "progression of art" the "the social element became more important" and "the intention to communicate, to express oneself to others, to attract their attention, assumes greater importance and perhaps even the place of *greatest* importance?" He and De Finance seem to share the conviction that the philosophy of art must include a more penetrating analysis of otherness, its appropriation by the spiritual subject, and its expression in art and poetry. The "other" produced by the artist is indelibly stamped with the subjective and psychic characteristics of the spirit, such that the artwork is naturally disposed to be communicated to another spiritual being. Risking a gross generalization, I would dare say that in this regard Maritain shows himself a more "progressive" Thomist than Gilson, though considerably less so than De Finance.

Gilson emerges as the most "mimetic" and, for lack of a better term, "conservative" of the three, in that he tends to emphasize the ontological boundaries between artist, artwork, and the reality according to which the art object is produced. In short, a work of art (*aliud*) is produced by an artist (*ab alio*) according to the pattern that results from an encounter of artistic skill and aesthetic vision based on some existing object in the natural world (*secundum aliquid*). I would thus summarize Gilson's view of artistic production as: *aliud ab alio secundum aliquid fit* (something comes about from someone according to some pattern).

Maritain's position is complex insofar as it underwent considerable development between *Art and Scholasticism* and *Creative Intuition in Art and Poetry*. On the basis of both the distinction—and analogy—of technical skill in the case of art and of prudence in the case of the moral life, Maritain distinguishes himself from Gilson in that he places the accent on the artist (*aliquis*) and the use of the practical intellect throughout the entire process of producing an artwork (*alterius*) that is a good in itself (*bonum*). I would thus summarize the early-Maritain as: *aliquis ad bonum alterius facit* (someone makes for the good of some other thing).[27]

27. Note that the use of the verb *facere* rather than *fieri* underscores the creative action of the agent which, Maritain suggests, is of greater interest within a humanistic philosophy.

The later-Maritain shifts his attention to the subjective appropriation of the external world through "intuition" and the poetic "pulsions" involved in the production of a beautiful work. The other produced through the process of creative intuition ineluctably bears the imprint of the subject responsible for its existence. The artist (*aliquis*) thus produces an artwork (*aliquid*) which reflects the object as known and is intuited by the soul of the artist (*quoad aliud in se*).[28] Hence the caveat of the later Maritain: *aliquis aliud quoad aliud in se facit* (someone makes something insofar as that thing exists within himself).

De Finance, given his primary interest in "otherness" rather than in art *per se*, thickens the interconnections between artist, artwork, and audience by delineating both the objective and subjective dimensions of artist and audience. Nevertheless, De Finance never relinquished the Aristotelian-Thomistic principles which he shared with Maritain and Gilson. Furthermore, like Maritain, De Finance is sympathetic to a more anthropocentric approach to the phenomenon of art. On the other hand, like Gilson, he finds great value in the fundamentally mimetic aspects of artistic epistemology. For De Finance, the artist (*aliquis*), who exists and acts in the world as "other" in the sense of *alius* and in the sense of *aliud*, makes an artwork (*aliud*) precisely within the horizon of another receiving subject (*alicui*). Thus, I would summarize De Finance in the following way: *aliquis, quoad alius et aliud, aliud alicui facit* (someone, insofar as he is a "someone else" and a "something else," makes something for someone else).

So to summarize our three philosophers on the "otherness" of art: (1) for Gilson, *aliud ab alio secundum aliquid fit* (something is made by someone according to some pattern); (2) for the early Maritain, *aliquis ad bonum alterius facit* (someone makes for the good of something else); (3) for the late Maritain, *aliquis aliud quoad aliud in se facit* (someone makes something as it exists within himself); (4) and for De Finance, *aliquis, quoad alius et aliud, aliud alicui facit* (someone, as someone else and something else, makes something for someone else).

If nothing else, a comparison of De Finance, Maritain, and Gilson demonstrates that interfacing Thomistic philosophy with contemporary philosophies—especially when it comes to identity, otherness, and intelligibility—is far from easy or straightforward. This becomes paradigmatic in

28. Note that the antecedent of *se* here is *aliquis* rather than *aliquid*.

the case of the philosophy of art. De Finance is unique due to the breadth of his philosophical influences and his approach to "otherness" as a meaningful and urgent philosophical question. Whether or not one is convinced of the overall success of De Finance's project of constructing a systematic philosophy of otherness, and whether or not one agrees that such a primary emphasis on otherness can be sustained with traditional Thomistic metaphysics, such an emphasis sheds new light, I believe, on the distinctiveness of artistic activity and the privileged role it plays in our understanding of the metaphysics of identity and otherness.

JAMES G. HANINK

On Love's Object

Maritain, Pascal, and Spaemann

I. An Epitaph as Prelude

Rainer Maria Rilke led friends to believe that he was dying, not of his leukemia, but of the blood poisoning caused by the thorn of a rose. He asked that his gravestone carry only these few words.

> Rose, Oh pure contradiction, Desire
> To be no one's sleep under so many
> Eyelids.

Like much of his poetry, this epitaph is at once lyrical and enigmatic. Perhaps the rose symbolizes a love whose thorns prick. It is a plausible interpretation, since Rilke repeatedly sought love and then rejected it.[1]

Robert Spaemann, however, cites Rilke's epitaph to mark the contrast between a person's successive states and a person's core self. He writes,

> If I am not someone who can be 'meant' as who I am, I am not 'someone' at all, but only 'something'; I possess no necessary principle of inner unity. Not being someone else's 'Thou', I cannot be my own 'I', but only a succession of unowned states—'a longing to be no man's sleep under so many eyelids'. (Rilke)[2]

1. See Hans J. Zweig, "Postscript," www.rilke-unraveled.com/ (Retrieved July 22, 2008). The translation of the original German is Zweig's. Romano Guardini sees Rilke as "one of the most thoroughgoing individualists of modern times." See Guardini's *Rilke's Duino Elegies: An Interpretation*, trans. K. G. Knight (London: Darwen Finlayson, 1961), 304.

2. Robert Spaemann, *Persons*, trans. Oliver O'Donovan. (Oxford University Press, 2006), 78.

An intriguing appropriation, it seems. But why should we listen to what a philosopher says about a poet? And how is it that a philosopher is reading a poet? Didn't Plato seal the enmity between the two?[3]

Jacques and Raïssa Maritain, of course, reject this enmity.[4] For them, poetry can incite philosophy, and philosophy can illuminate poetry.[5] They wept for a world too quick to dismiss poetic intuition and philosophical intelligence. Such a world ignores those who could be its tutors in love.

II. Love's Lesson

Jacques Maritain served as a draftsman for what Paul VI and John Paul II called a "civilization of love."[6] In his *The Person and the Common Good*, Maritain offers an early sketch of this civilization. When we turn to this classic, we first think of it as a Thomist charter for a new social order. Therein, we recall, Maritain distinguishes between the person and the individual. But, in doing so, he affirms the unity of the human being. "Our whole being," he writes, "is an individual by reason of that which is in us that derives from matter, and a person by reason of that which derives from spirit."[7] A person, an embodied spirit, is a unified whole and so transcends the social order; an individual is but a part of the social totality.

A further thesis comes into play in Maritain's prospectus for a new social order. It is his identification of *love* as the way we know the other as person. Looking to the nexus between love and the person and personality, he asks us to consider that "perhaps the most apposite approach to the philosophical discovery of personality is the study of the relation between personality and love."[8]

3. Plato, *Republic* 608 a6–b2.

4. Here Martin Heidegger is an ally. See his "What are Poets For?" in *Poetry, Language, Thought*, trans. Albert Hofstadter (New York: Harper Row, 1971), 96. He notes that Rilke's poetry teaches that "love has not been learned." Haim Gordon speculates whether Rilke's *Duino Elegies*, published in 1923, helped Heidegger work out his account of *Dasein* in *Being and Time*, published in 1927. See Haim Gordon, "Heidegger on Poetry and Thinking: Some Educational Implications," The Paideia Project: Proceedings of the 20th World Congress of Philosophy, bu.edu/wcp/Papers/Cont/ContGord.htm. (retrieved July 22, 2008).

5. Both must reverence the real. Guardini insists that "Real poetry is an affirmation, not simply of what the poet feels or thinks, but also of what *is*" (Guardini, *Rilke's Duino Elegies*, 303).

6. Paul VI, "Sensitive Love in the Defense of Life," closing address of the 1975 Holy Year; John Paul II, *Sollicitudo Rei Socialis*, 33.

7. Jacques Maritain, *The Person and the Common Good*, trans. John J. Fitzgerald (Notre Dame, Indiana: University of Notre Dame Press, 1966), 43.

8. Maritain, *Person and the Common Good*, 13.

III. Pascal's Problem

Maritain readily acknowledges that this "apposite approach" faces a serious problem, one that Blaise Pascal has set for us. In his *Pensées* he poses a hard question: "Would we love the substance of a person's soul, in the abstract, whatever qualities might be in it?" Immediately he answers, "That is not possible, and it would be wrong. Therefore we never love anyone, but only qualities."[9] If this be so, love never reaches to the person; it must satisfy itself with observable qualities.

Pascal, moreover, can readily enlist commonsense considerations to support his argument, however brusquely he states it. First, we only become aware of a person through his or her qualities. Second, it is a person's qualities that either do or do not attract us. Third, any major change in a person's qualities ordinarily leads us to change our view of that person and so, it seems, can affect our love for that person. And, fourth, we rightly resolve any forensic question about a person's identity over time by reviewing a person's observable qualities. There are, then, pressing reasons to take seriously what we might call Pascal's "empirical quality thesis" with regard to the object of love. If it stands, Maritain's avenue to love proves to be impassible.

IV. Maritain's Response

Yet Maritain has a response to Pascal, and it is robustly metaphysical. "Love is not concerned with qualities. They are not the object of our love. We love the deepest, most substantial and hidden, the most *existing* reality of the beloved being."[10] To be sure, this reality is not empirically observable. But it is critical to our understanding the person in four ways. First, it is the metaphysical center of the person that gives rise to, and sustains, his or her empirical qualities. Second, in our experience, this metaphysical center integrates the qualities of a person rather than separating itself from them. Third, this center is the *sine qua non* of personal action, since no quality or group of qualities can act alone. Fourth, love engages the person in a giving of self, not just the presenting of qualities. It is the personal

9. Blaise Pascal, *Pensées* #688 (Krailsheimer translation). One might, though, read Pascal as rejecting the view thus expressed. Whether this is in fact the case I leave for Pascal scholars.

10. Maritain, *Person and the Common Good*, 38–39.

center, as well, that receives the other. Thus Raïssa Maritain finds that the "essence of love is in the communication of oneself, with fullness of joy and delight in the possession of the beloved."[11] There are, then, also pressing reasons to take seriously what we might call Maritain's "metaphysical center thesis." And yet, despite this marshalling of reasons for their respective positions, Maritain and Pascal remain sharply at odds with one another.

V. Toward Resolution: Spaemann's Test Case

Have we come then to an irresolvable impasse? Or might we find a way to adjudicate between Maritain and Pascal's contending views of love's object? A dialectical resolution recommends itself, and Robert Spaemann offers a thought experiment to initiate adjudication. "Suppose," he suggests, "super-scientists simulated a double of someone whom we loved." Well, what then? "Suppose," he continues, "they succeed in deceiving us. Now, if they later tell us that they had substituted the double for our beloved, would we not feel violated? Would it not be impossible to love the substitute in the same way?"[12] My sense is that we would surely feel violated and that we could not love the substitute in the same way. But there is more at issue than my possibly idiosyncratic "sense." We would be violated because the scientists had deceived us; we would be especially violated because they supplanted the "who" that we love with a "what." And because the substitute is only a *virtual* person, we could not love the substitute as we love the beloved. The substitute is just a collection of qualities, and strictly speaking, only a simulation of such a collection. In contrast, the beloved is a real person.

Of all the ways we personally interact with one another, love is the richest and most intimate. As such, it is that which is most foundational. If love were to prove counterfeit, all else would be put in jeopardy. Spaemann, for his part, grounds his realism in the relation of reciprocity between persons. He writes,

> The centre of being (*Selbstein*) that evokes our transcendence, the other person, stands to us in a relation of reciprocity. I am a part of her world, as she is a part of mine. I exist for her as she exists for me. It is a reality for me that I exist for her and

11. Raïssa Maritain, *Journal*, ed. Jacques Maritain (Albany, New York: Magi Books, 1974), 219.

12. Spaemann, *Persons*, 76.

that she knows she exists for me. On this reciprocal relation is founded the metaphysical realism that is decisive for persons.[13]

Note: he does not speak of the special allure of selected qualities but rather of the mutual understanding of persons who recognize each other as distinct but united centers of being.[14]

There are further key considerations that Spaemann's thought experiment helps bring to mind. It invites us to explore three instructive distinctions. The first is the distinction between indexical and qualitative identification. The second is that between naming and describing. The last is that between a person and a specimen. Let's look at each of these differences in turn.

First, the beloved is *someone,* and so I can identify her with a singular and particularizing referent, for example, "my first love" or four decades later "the love of my life." Then I might speak about the qualities of my spouse. In contrast, the super-scientists who would deceive me cannot so identify their projected substitute. They must, instead, fashion it according to a list of specifications and hope that they have the right list. They must, as it were, follow a recipe—and a very long one. As Spaemann points out, "Objects of intention are defined by their attributes, qualitatively. The object of love, on the other hand, is identified indexically; there is no indeterminacy in love's reference."[15] No team of super-scientists can reduce my beloved, who has a numerical identity, to any set of descriptive qualities—nor can I.

Second, I know my beloved by name. While I might write a poem in praise of her finest qualities, or lamenting those less so, it would be absurd to give any of them a proper name. To do so would be to misuse a name in that it confuses a person with a non-indexical descriptive quality and thus trivializes the person and misconstrues the property. Spaemann rightly observes that "No description can replace *naming.*"[16] We pay great attention

13. Ibid., 78.

14. W. Norris Clarke, S.J., makes a like point: "The whole key to a realist epistemology like that of St. Thomas is that action is the 'self-revelation of being,' that it reveals a being as *this kind of actor* on me, which is equivalent to saying it really exists and has this kind of *nature* = an abiding center of acting and being acted on." See his *The One and the Many: A Contemporary Thomistic Metaphysics* (Notre Dame, Indiana: University of Notre Dame Press, 2001), 12. John W. Carlson, too, argues that the person is the critical context for metaphysical realism. See his *Understanding Our Being: Introduction to Speculative Philosophy in the Perennial Tradition* (Washington, D.C.: Catholic University of America Press, 2008).

15. Spaemann, *Persons,* 76.

16. Ibid., 29.

to names, especially the names we give our children. Because we see them as unique, we want to capture something of this uniqueness in the names we choose for them.

Third, my beloved is a person and, as such, she cannot give rise to specimens of the person that she is. A specimen is an instance of a type, and it is a pathology to love a type rather than a person. The cloning of human beings is, for related reasons, pathological. The beloved is unique and irreplaceable, as is every person. In contrast, specimens are fungible; they invite "trading-up," as is the fashion, for example, in looking for a younger "trophy wife" or a wealthier "sugar daddy."

To be sure, each of us is a human being. And each human being is a member of the class *Homo sapiens*; but as a person each human being transcends his or her biological class. Because no human person is a typical human being, no one is "just another human being." Spaemann, alert to such considerations, advances an insightful thesis: "We call human beings 'persons', because they are unlike all other living beings in the *way* they are *what* they are."[17] To be sure, not all persons are human. Thus he perceptively observes that "'Person' … is an analogical concept, like 'being.'"[18] The biology of the individual leads to the physiology of attraction; the metaphysics of the person leads to the language of analogy and to the object of love.[19]

Where, then, has the adjudication of the pivotal debate between Maritain and Pascal led us? Spaemann's thought experiment initiates an unfolding reflection on what it is to be a person. *Contra* Pascal, it helps us identify the distortions that arise from reducing the uniqueness of the person to the qualities of the individual and thus preventing love from reaching to the

17. Ibid., 165.

18. Ibid., 68.

19. Both come into play in these lines from W.B. Yeats's "When You are Old":

How many loved your moments of glad grace,
And loved your beauty with love false or true,
But one man loved the pilgrim soul in you,
And loved the sorrows of your changing face;

And bending down beside the glowing bars,
Murmured, a little sadly, how Love fled
And paced upon the mountains overhead
And hid his face amid a crowd of stars.

I thank Anne Barbeau Gardiner for drawing attention to the poetic and personalist significance of William Shakespeare's Sonnet 116 and W.B. Yeats's "When You are Old."

beloved. This adjudication, in sum, encourages us to follow Maritain's way of love as the "most apposite" way to understand the human person. With this understanding, we can best build-up the civilization of love for which he served as a draftsman.

VI. A First Test: the Taking of Vows

The civilization of love, to be sure, serves us as an ideal which we often betray. A first test, I submit, of this civilization of love is how we see and honor the love between husband and wife. Can we vow this love? Can we promise fidelity to it?

What if love is but a feeling, albeit the strongest of our feelings?[20] If we have no guarantee that we can control our feelings and especially not this strongest of feelings, how can spouses responsibly promise to love one another until death separates them? And if we can only love a selection of changing personal qualities, as Pascal claims, then should we not expect our feelings to change? How can we promise fidelity to our spousal love? But there is more: if we deny metaphysics, must we not see *ourselves* as merely a changing collection of personal qualities, as David Hume (intermittently) believed?[21]

But spousal love is a self-donation; it is not a feeling, however strong. Feelings characteristically attend this giving of self. Passion is often a catalyst for love; but spousal love can both embrace and transform passion. We can, moreover, give ourselves in love only if we ourselves are more than simply a selection of qualities. And, following Jacques Maritain and Robert Spaemann, a pivotal claim of this essay remains: we love a person rather than simply a selection of personal qualities. Metaphysics brings us beyond empirical qualities to the core self. This metaphysical center cannot be the object of empirical observation. Since personhood itself is not intrinsically restricted to material conditions, personhood is a pure perfection.[22] In any case, it is this person, this "someone," who alone makes intelligible our shared human form of life.

20. Bertrand Russell, *Autobiography* (London: George Allen and Unwin, 1967), 197–99.

21. David Hume, *A Treatise on Human Nature*, "Appendix." For an extension of Hume, see Derek Parfit, "Later Selves and Moral Principles," in *Philosophy and Personal Relations*, ed. A. Montefiore (London: Routledge and Kegan Paul, 1973), 144.

22. For this point, see John W. Carlson, *Understanding Our Being*, 81.

Yet marriage vows do not stand alone; they are a distinctive sort of promise. Promising itself is a mark of being a person. In promising, a person reaches beyond the here-and-now; only a free and intelligent center of action could hope to do this. G. K. Chesterton gets to the heart of the question and the challenge it issues: "The man who makes a vow makes an appointment with himself at some distant time or place," but adds that "[t]he danger of it is that he himself should not keep the appointment."[23] Indeed; even if my friends "get me to the church on time," can I—or they—count on what I promise while there?

Spaemann elucidates what is at stake. "When we make an actual promise in history ... we rise above our normal immersion in the stream of time."[24] Marriage is a communion of persons. But can it be irrevocable? Mustn't we every day negotiate a maze of contingencies? Yet a person can rise above "the givens" of nature, both without and within. Spaemann develops the point: "The nature of every living being is subject to change, and persons, who 'have' a nature are not exempt [although] their growth is not merely a function of spontaneous natural energy, but subject to a higher law of personal identity."[25] And what of sexual relations? They draw us into "the sub-personal stream of life," yet the personal communion of marriage can fashion them into a "source of living order."[26] It can fashion the ties that bind. Chesterton throws down the gauntlet; in marriage vows a man writes "his oath upon the heavens, as the record of his highest moment."[27] If this be so, we can appreciate why Jacques Maritain was keen, near the end of his life, to write a commentary on Scripture's *The Song of Songs*.[28]

VII. A Second Test: the "Least Little Ones"

A second test in building a civilization of love is how we care for the least little ones. In our context, these are the ones whose identity as persons some deny: the very young, the very old, and the most severely damaged. Those who deny the personhood of these least little ones deny, as

23. G. K. Chesterton, "A Defense of Rash Vows," from his *The Defendant* (Rockford, Maryland: Wildside Press, 2005), 24.

24. Spaemann, *Persons*, 223–24.

25. Ibid., 227.

26. Ibid., 229.

27. Chesterton, *The Defendant*, 27.

28. See Jacques Maritain, *Untrammeled Approaches*, trans. Bernard Doering, preface by Ernst R. Korn (Heinz R. Schmitz) (Notre Dame, Indiana: University of Notre Dame Press, 1997), Ch. XIX, 443–94.

well, that they can be the objects of intelligent personal love. We cannot so love them, because they lack the qualities that distinguish *us* as persons; we cannot love them as persons, because they are not persons. Peter Singer, among others, advocates this restrictivist view.[29]

Jacques Maritain, of course, rejected any attack on the unborn, the very old, or the severely damaged. He rejected, too, any attempt to drive a wedge between being a human being and being a person. What is perhaps less known is that despite his familiarity with the role of DNA in human development, he insisted that the human embryo, indeed, even the human fetus in its earlier stages, could not be a human being. The moral standing of the unborn, rather, supposedly depends on a virtual humanity that comes with a kind of "evolutive" life trajectory. Maritain based his position on St. Thomas's ill-informed embryology, together with the surprising view that this embryology is critical to a Thomist metaphysics of evolution.[30]

Happily, Robert Spaemann's anthropology helps him correct the *de facto* dualisms of both Singer and Maritain. To separate the biological and the personal, he argues, is to ignore "that personhood is situated in the *life* of human beings."[31] Our animality, "the medium of personal realization," puts us in a network of personal kinship relations of ethical import.[32] And what is this import? Not only, he writes, is there "no graduated transition from a 'something' to 'someone'" but "[i]t is only because we treat human beings from the start as someone, not as something," that they develop the properties typical of the species.[33] We intuitively grasp that our lives are unified at their core. Thus we do not say "'on such and such a date there was born some thing from which I later developed.'"[34] And why not? Because, he tells us, "the person is the mode in which a human being exists."[35] The point is a metaphysical one, and Maritain's delayed hominization thesis undercuts the unity of the human person.[36]

29. Peter Singer, *Practical Ethics*, second edition (Cambridge: Cambridge University Press, 1993).

30. For Maritain's position, see James G. Hanink, "Jacques Maritain and the Embryo: a Master's Muddles," presented at the University Faculty for Life Conference, Marquette University, 2008.

31. Spaemann, *Persons*, 239.

32. Ibid., 240.

33. Ibid., 244.

34. Ibid., 245.

35. Ibid., 245.

36. For an important, but not persuasive, account of how our approach to the status of the embryo ought to put metaphysics aside in favor of ethics, see Brian V. Johnstone, CSSR, "The Human Embryo: The Person and the Gift," *Life and Learning: Proceedings of the University Faculty for Life*, Vol. XVII, 489–505.

The plight of the severely damaged invites further reflection. No such damage displaces the humanity of the one who suffers it. And the damaged one is always a 'someone' rather than a something. The severely disabled can, if we let them, be our teachers. For Spaemann, they are "the paradigm for a human community of recognizing *selves*, rather than simply valuing useful or attractive *properties*."[37]

There persists a consequentialist urge to put the lives of the very young, the very old, and the severely damaged at a lesser value than our own lives. Species membership isn't enough to end the easy talk of cost-benefit analysis. Here Spaemann looks to the incommensurable dignity of the person, indicating that he prefers "to speak of human 'dignity' (*Würde*) rather than human 'value' (*Wert*)." He contends that "The *value* of ten people may be more than that of one, but ten are no more than one in point of dignity. [E]ach [person] is uniquely situated in relation to every other."[38] Because of this dignity, each one has a name, whatever his or her qualities; because of it we should call each one by name, as befits a person.[39]

VIII. Envoi: Roses, once more

These reflections on love's object began with a poet's epitaph about a rose and a thorn. Of a rose and its name, Shakespeare's Juliet has famously raised a question.[40] (The Bard, we recall, also insists the "Love is not love / Which alters when it alteration finds....[41]) Rainer Maria Rilke's rose is darkly enigmatic. Romano Guardini finds Rilke unable to reach to "the integrating centre" of the person.[42] So be it. Jacques Maritain thought that sometimes great poetry just is enigmatic, but illuminatingly so; and he put forward *The Song of Songs* in support of his claim. He was keenly interested in the disputed identity of that poem's rose (II, vs. 1–2):

37. Spaemann, *Persons*, 244.

38. Ibid., 185.

39. Simone Weil charges Jacques Maritain with himself placing too much weight on the qualities of a person. Eric O. Springsted contends that Weil's emphasis on the impersonal advances the thesis that "if we are to be wholly and infinitely committed to making space for human souls in the world, the commitment cannot depend on their interesting—or our interested—features." See his "Beyond the Personal: Weil's Critique of Maritain," in *Harvard Theological Review*, 98/2 (2005): 218.

40. William Shakespeare, *Romeo and Juliet*, Act II. Scene II.

41. William Shakespeare, Sonnet 116.

42. Guardini, *Rilke's Duino Elegies*, 304.

She
1. I am the lily of Sharon
The rose of the low places.

He
2. Like a rose amid the brambles
Is my love among all other women.

For him, this rose speaks for the beloved, the Church, rooted as She is in the Chosen of Israel.[43] Raïssa Maritain, a daughter of Israel, wrote of another—and heraldic—rose:

A cloud in the sky,
Ezekiel's chariot
Flashing by.
... Roses glow,
Then you appear
And the tears flow
In the thin air
Upon your face
O messenger.[44]

For both Maritains, the rose retains the enigmatic and yet announces the mystery of the person.

And for both the Maritains, the object of love is the person, whole and entire. Blaise Pascal notwithstanding, and *pace* the many despisers of metaphysics, they teach us well. Robert Spaemann greatly enriches their lesson. It is a preamble to a civilization of love.

43. Jacques Maritain, "The Song of Songs," *Untrammeled Approaches*, Chapter XIX, 443–94.

44. See "Raïssa Maritain: Philosopher, Poet, Mystic," by Michael Sherwin, OP. Her poem "The Cloud," is translated by a Benedictine of Stanbrook Abbey. See Catholic Education Center, www.catholiceducation.org (retrieved July 29, 2008).

JOHN MARSON DUNAWAY

Un seul amour en nous

Human and Divine Love in Maritain and Literature

In *Le Désert de l'amour,* François Mauriac has given us a richly ambivalent trope in the character of Maria Cross.[1] The object of desire of both Dr. Paul Courrèges and his son Raymond, she is a kept woman with a reputation to match. But Mauriac once said that his vocation as a novelist was to highlight both the human weaknesses of saints and the hidden nobility of sinners, and there is a redemptive transformation taking place in this apparently lost soul called Maria Cross, so she becomes an instrument of the workings of divine grace in the story. By the end of the novel, her mysterious influence has moved Raymond Courrèges and his father from being potential rivals to the point of exploring the possibilities of reconciliation in their formerly strained relationship. The most profound statement in the novel is spoken by Maria on her sick bed to Dr. Courrèges:

> I see everything so clearly now. I understand what I never understood before ... the people we think we love ... the passions that end so miserably ... now, at last, I know the truth.... No, not passions, but one single passion [*Non pas des amours, mais un seul amour en nous*].[2]

Jacques Maritain, whose *modus operandi* in philosophizing was to distinguish in order to unite, would not have stated it the way Mauriac does.

1. François Mauriac, *Le Désert de l'amour* (Paris: Grasset, 1925).

2. François Mauriac, *A Mauriac Reader,* trans. Gerard Hopkins (New York: Farrar, Straus, and Giroux, 1968), 242.

Indeed, there are a whole variety of forms of love in humankind that Maritain examines in his philosophy. In his essay on "Love and Friendship," Maritain shows that both Love and Friendship are forms of *l'amour de dilection*, which Joseph Evans has translated as *disinterested love*. Quoting Raïssa, Jacques observes that "the essence of friendship is in desire for the good of one's friend, strong enough to sacrifice oneself for him."[3] This is the form of *amitié*, whose perfection Christ was describing when he said "Greater love hath no man than this, that a man lay down his life for his friends."[4]

"A genius for friendship" is a phrase that recurs repeatedly in descriptions of Jacques Maritain. The celebrated "*grandes amitiés*" of Meudon were eventually expanded to include many significant relationships with artists and intellectuals on both sides of the Atlantic, in cities like Versailles, Rome, New York, Princeton, and Chicago. Such diverse figures as Jean Cocteau, Julien Green, Allen Tate and Caroline Gordon, Maurice Sachs, Georges Rouault, Giovanni Montini, Thomas Merton, and Arthur Lourié were drawn—by Maritain's personal warmth and kindness as well as his intellect—into the "*centre de rayonnement*" that he, Raïssa, and Véra always sought to make of their home. Godfather to many a convert, faithful companion to pilgrims of the absolute on several continents, Jacques knew existentially whereof he spoke when he addressed the topic of friendship.

At the same time, it would be difficult to find a man more passionately devoted to his spouse. Raïssa was the love of his life. When she died, he felt himself inconsolably diminished. The woman who had entered with him into a suicide pact during their Sorbonne days, the companion who had shared fifty-six years of marriage with him, his collaborator in writing and in reaching out to the intelligentsia of France and North America, she was a true soul-mate. So Jacques was also well acquainted with the topic when he spoke of marital love.

From his reflections on "Love and Friendship," it is clear that Maritain saw both human and divine love involved in *l'amour de dilection* or disinterested love. And it is just precisely this interaction between human and divine love that for a long time has particularly interested me in the literature of the Western tradition. Courtly love, that seductively charming invention

3. Jacques Maritain, *Notebooks*, trans. Joseph Evans (Albany, N.Y.: Magi Books, 1984), 220. (All page references to this essay are hereafter placed in the text, in parentheses.)

4. John 15:13 (all biblical citations are from the King James Version).

of the twelfth century, has always had a powerful appeal to the Western psyche. Even today, with the deconstruction of relationships between the sexes and the assault on traditional notions of love, marriage, and the family, the male who worships the object of his affections from afar and seeks through serving her in total submissiveness to win her attentions is a recurring theme in popular culture. Theorists suggest that one influence on the birth of the courtly vision of romantic love was the rise of the Cult of the Virgin Mary. The exalted place attributed to Mary must certainly have caused men to regard women as more than heirs of the sin of Eve.

Another strong paradigm that must have exerted at least a modicum of influence on the courtly love movement is found in the most sexually explicit and perhaps the most spiritually profound book of the biblical canon, Solomon's *Song of Songs*. It is certainly not surprising that near the end of his life Maritain wrote one of his most brilliant essays on the *Song of Songs* and even provided a new "translation" of the text. After all, Saint Thomas is said to have pronounced a sublime oral commentary on Solomon's *Song* on his deathbed. The multiple levels of meaning in *Song of Songs*—from explicit sexuality to soaring mystical desire—provide an admirable example of the richness of analogous forms of love and friendship explored philosophically by Maritain. Though he had no desire to diminish the poetic beauty of the *Song* on its literal level of meaning, he saw three principle allegorical interpretations. It is a dialogue between: 1) Yahweh and the chosen people; 2) Christ and his Bride, the Church; and 3) "God and the soul wholly devoted to him in the secret of mystical contemplation."[5] And one of the key concepts he introduced in his commentary was the notion of *l'amour fou* (or mad love), a favorite expression of André Breton and the Surrealists, and one that returns to do significant duty in the essay on "Love and Friendship" as well.

In the essay I wrote for Douglas Ollivant's *Jacques Maritain and the Many Ways of Knowing*, I observed that

> Breton's doctrine of the poetic consciousness is in some ways not terribly far from that of Maritain. Breton was fond of the phrase *l'amour fou* ... to describe poetic inspiration. It is the contradiction of material determinism and logical discursive reasoning. This perfect, free spontaneity is what happens when beauty, in its supreme innocence, becomes "the perfect mirror in which all that has been and all

5. Jacques Maritain, *Approches sans entraves* (Paris: Fayard, 1973), 534 (my translation).

that is called to be is admirably bathed in what is going to be this time" [*Les Vases communicants*, 167]. For both Maritain and Breton, then, there is a magic moment of creative intuition in the poet in which something novel and unique is born through mad love.[6]

As the King and his bride in *Song of Songs* are consumed with *l'amour fou*, so are Yahweh and his chosen people, Christ and the Church, and God and the individual contemplative soul.

Dante Alighieri at first perceived the goal of his poetic quest to be the lovely Beatrice Portinari, whom he had seen only three times before her untimely death in 1290 in Florence. Most contemporary readers of the *Commedia* read only the first canticle, often forgetting that both the purpose and the motivation for this descent into infernal suffering and sin are his eventual reunion with Beatrice. Dante's involvement in the *Dolce Stil Nuovo* movement, in which he, Guido Cavalcanti, and others sought to refine courtly poetry, inherited from the Provençal school a doctrine of romantic love that was supposed to ennoble the lover. The sublimation of desire was reflected in the conventionalized description of the process of falling in love. The lover always was attracted not so much by the bodily form or facial features as by something in the beloved's eyes. In the *Vita nuova*, Dante describes the process as follows:

> The power of Love borne in my lady's eyes
> Imparts its grace to all she looks upon.
> All turn to gaze at her when she walks by,
> And when she greets a man his heart beats fast,
> The color leaves his face, he bows his head
> And sighs to think of all his imperfections.
> Anger and pride are forced to flee from her.
> Help me to honor her, most gracious ladies.[7]

Even before the great vision of the *Commedia*, Dante thus portrayed Beatrice allegorically, in the *Vita Nuova*, as a figure with a religious aura. But in the *Divine Comedy*, as the pilgrim undergoes the transformation of the journey, he realizes that the ultimate goal of his quest will be the beatific vision. The first depiction of love we see in the *Commedia* is the story

6. Douglas Ollivant, *Jacques Maritain and the Many Ways of Knowing* (Washington, DC: Catholic University Press, 2002), 315.

7. Dante Alighieri, *The Portable Dante*, trans. and ed. Mark Musa (New York: Penguin Books, 1995), 616.

of Paolo and Francesca, a typical tale of romantic love between handsome young Italian nobles. The problem is that Francesca is married to Paolo's brother, who discovers them *en flagrant délit* and summarily executes them on the spot. Dante the pilgrim so deeply identifies with them that when he hears Francesca's tearful narrative, he faints. His own form of love has not been purified by experience, by suffering and by prayer. He will have to contemplate the consequences of sin in *Inferno* and the purification by fire in *Purgatorio* before his will reaches the point of being merged with God's at the entrance to *Paradiso*.

Even then, however, he is not able to gaze directly upon the Godhead, but when he looks into the eyes of Beatrice, who has replaced Virgil as his guide into Paradise, in her eyes he sees the reflection of the divine glory. A youthful romantic infatuation has been transformed by grace into the instrument of the pilgrim's purification, so that he is prepared to behold God.

In Julien Green's finest novel, the protagonist, Joseph Day, is a fanatically pious redheaded student at a southern university (modeled after Green's alma mater, the University of Virginia in Charlottesville). Joseph's childhood in a remote, primitive mountain region has ill prepared him for the libertine ways of the college town where he comes for his studies. The eponymous character in the story, Moïra, is a brazen mulatto temptress. Moïra represents for Joseph the epitome of sexuality, which he fears as the way to certain damnation. Joseph's rigid puritanical morality and condemnatory attitude toward all who fail to live by it are ultimately tamed at the end of the story when he succumbs to Moïra's seductive charms and then murders her in a rage at having fallen from his imaginary pedestal. But he refuses to flee and turns himself in to the authorities, showing signs of having gained a new compassion toward the sinners he once condemned. In "Love and Friendship," Maritain says of authentic human love: "Man ordinarily attains to it only after a certain maturation in the experience of life and in suffering" (223). The story of Joseph Day, as well as that of Dante the pilgrim, seems an apt illustration of such a principle.

Jacques Maritain was a longtime friend of Julien Green. If André Gide represented the darker side of Green (encouraging him to write more explicitly about his temptations), it was Maritain who exerted the most salutary influence on his life. Still, Maritain never made Green feel judged. Rather, he encouraged him to see the powerful spirituality of his inner vision. He once said of Green: "I find it marvelous that an American should be the greatest writer of our time."[8] Green, for his part, wrote in his *Journal* that "One of the greatest favors ever granted to me by God was to place Jacques on my path in 1924."[9]

It would not be difficult to make a case for the proposition that the Maritains' godfather, Léon Bloy, was an early case study for the multiple levels of love and friendship that are eventually catalogued in Maritain's essay. Both in his fiction and in his life, Bloy exemplified the mysterious workings of divine grace through the medium of human love and desire. In Bloy's autobiographical novel, *Le Désespéré* (*The Desperate One*, 1886), the protagonist, Marchenoir, is smitten with a prostitute named Véronique whose life is radically transformed into that of a saintly, selfless woman. Véronique heroically sacrifices her physical beauty (both her hair and all her teeth) in order not to be a source of temptation for Marchenoir. Not only beauty, but poverty and suffering are the tools that God uses to prepare Marchenoir for his prophetic vocation, lived out in rage at the world's smug indifference to God. Maritain once wrote of Bloy, "Instead of being a whited sepulchre like the Pharisees of all times, he was a charred, blackened cathedral. The *white part* was inside, deep in the tabernacle."[10]

The *Song of Songs* is not the only part of the Bible that uses human love to help us understand God's love. In several of the prophets, Israel's unfaithfulness to the covenant is depicted in terms of a marital relationship. Israel has "gone a whoring," forsaking Yahweh for the pagan gods and goddesses of the Canaanites. The fact that these religions practiced fertility rites and deployed temple prostitutes makes the imagery even more vivid. Yahweh is a jealous God who expects faithfulness from his chosen people. In Hosea, he is depicted as the patient, forgiving husband, loving his wife in spite of her whoredom and reinstating her in the covenant relationship. In Isaiah 62:4, God speaks to unfaithful Israel: "Thou shalt no more be termed Forsaken; neither shall thy land any more be termed Desolate: but thou shalt be called Hephzibah, and thy land Beulah: for the Lord delighteth in thee, and thy land shall be married."

8. Jacques Maritain, "Fidélité à l'esprit," *Renaissance de Fleury*, no. 75 (October 1970), my translation.

9. Julien Green, *Diary 1928–1957*, trans. Anne Green (New York: Harcourt, Brace and World, 1964), 278.

10. Jacques Maritain, "Introduction" to Léon Bloy, *Pilgrim of the Absolute*, trans. John Coleman and Harry Lorin Binsse, ed. Raïssa Maritain (New York: Pantheon, 1947), 23.

In Matthew 22:1–14, Christ compares the Kingdom of Heaven to a marriage feast, and, in Revelation, John's eschatological depiction of the believer's union with God in glory is that of the marriage feast of the Lamb with his Bride, the church. And perhaps most revelatory of all is Paul's extended comparison of the marriage relationship to that of Christ and the church in the fifth chapter of Ephesians. After giving instructions to both spouses and quoting that marvelous phrase in Genesis 2:24 about the husband and wife becoming "one flesh," he concludes in verse 32 with this comment: "This is a great mystery, but I speak concerning Christ and the church." Indeed, it *is* a deep mystery, this miracle of two humans becoming one, and even more so the miracle of a human becoming one with the Creator. This double mystery, as Raïssa and Jacques Maritain have shown, can be fruitfully explored for a richer understanding of love and friendship.

One of the points that gave me serious pause in Maritain's essay is his insistence that "if a soul has entered into mad, boundless love for God, then it is necessary for it to renounce human mad, boundless love" (228). I understand that my love for Trish should not supercede my love for God, and on occasion I've wondered whether it had not approached the place of idolatry. It has indeed been what I personally would call *amour fou* for nearly a half-century now. Maritain goes on in this same paragraph to suggest that if the soul enters into *amour fou* for God and is married, it does not necessarily have to take a vow of chastity such as he and Raïssa did (aren't we married believers all relieved to hear that?), but he or she does have to sacrifice *amour fou* for his or her spouse. "Because," he continues, "disinterested love of such a kind that the Beloved is truly and really given *the Whole* of the Lover, has to be unique in the soul, and if such a love (*amour fou*) is given to God, it has to be given only to Him" (228).

Later he observes that "carnal intercourse between spouses is not at all an obstacle to the mystical life or to contemplation, even very high" (248), and he cites numerous examples of married contemplatives and mystics among Jews, Muslims, and Christians. But he maintains that at some point in their progress toward union with God, these souls will inevitably not be able to move any higher without renouncing the exclusive claims of *amour fou* for any human. "In mad, boundless love does not the lover give himself to the beloved as to his Whole, of which he makes himself a part? My Whole is my Unique. Already in the natural order, in human mad, boundless love, the total gift that the lover makes of himself entails and requires an absolute exclusiveness" (248–49). He points out, with good reason, that Abraham's paternal love for his only promised son Isaac was not *amour fou*. And neither was Mary's maternal love for Jesus. We are helped to understand that this is true when Maritain offers the following footnote: "What I mean is that Mary very clearly had mad, boundless love for Jesus, *God* and man, but that her *maternal* love for Jesus, *man* and God, being *perfectly* ruled by charity, was not a mad, boundless love" (251).

At this juncture in his argument, Maritain describes a hypothetical scenario that admirers of Clive Staples Lewis will find ironically true-to-life. "If a man loves a woman with mad, boundless love, he will not consent to give her so far as immolation, even to God. (He will struggle against God, he will be broken)" (251). Readers will certainly recognize the desperate, inconsolable Lewis of *A Grief Observed* in this description. William Sloane Coffin, in his famous sermon after the auto accident that claimed the life of his 24-year-old son, says that God does not take our loved ones from us in this kind of sudden, tragic event. He is just as shocked and deeply wounded as we are in those circumstances.

A Joseph Day or a Maria Cross, or even a Marchenoir has doubtless not yet "entered into mad, boundless love for God." These, rather, are fictional examples of humans who begin to explore the limits of human love and are thereby prepared to experience in some measure the motivation for selfless giving that is genuine love for God. It is in literary heroes like the Lover in *Song of Songs* or Dante's pilgrim or Georges Bernanos's protagonists that we see the more elevated forms of *amour fou* that Maritain is exploring in his essay. As Maritain puts it, "Romantic love ... should be present as much as possible in marriage as an initial stimulant and starting point" (243). However, the purpose of the marriage relationship is not to bring romantic love to perfection but to transmute it into a nobler, more elevated or disinterested form of love. This process Maritain refers to as "an infinitely deeper and more mysterious, alchemical operation" (243).

Such a discussion of the relationship between human and divine love will naturally lead us to speak of things we would normally describe as mystical. However, mysticism is a word that has perhaps always been fraught with misunderstandings, and how much more so nowadays, when the bookshelves at Barnes and Noble that carry the label of mysticism are filled with witchcraft, astrology, telepathy, magic, and New Age philosophy. So it is eminently instructive to read in Maritain's essay that the expression "mystical" should not be construed as automatically synonymous with contemplative life. I suppose Maritain might say that all true contemplatives are mystics but all mystics aren't necessarily contemplatives. Those who commit themselves to the *vita activa* of discipleship, he maintains, are also endowed with the gifts of the Holy Spirit that open the way to union with God. They are given the grace of what he calls a "masked or unapparent contemplation" which, rather than consisting in their way of praying, may lie instead "in their way of walking, or in their way of looking at a poor man or at suffering" (234). This, too, I believe, is what Maritain would call a form of *amour fou* for God.

Love for God and love for our neighbor are simply like the two sides of the coin of charity, but Maritain takes care to trace "a distinction between the predominant regime of friendship (in which the active life has not crossed the threshold of the mystical state) and the predominant regime of mad, boundless love (in which contemplation is *open* in the 'contemplatives'—and *masked* in the 'actives')" (238, n.). He finds an analogous distinction in two very similar attitudes toward our neighbor. "Under the predominant regime of friendship with God it is in trying *to love our neighbor as Jesus loved him* that we love our brothers; and ... under the predominant regime of mad, boundless love for God it is ALSO (and first) *in seeing Jesus in our neighbor* that we love the latter" (238, n.); and he quotes Matthew 25, where Jesus tells the elect that he was hungry and they gave him food under the guise of "the least of these."

I'm sure Maritain would have placed Mother Teresa in this latter category. In her letters and talks to her nuns, she constantly invoked her mantra of the five fingers, which represented the five incomparable words of Jesus: "You did it unto me." It was her way of motivating them to be faithful to the vocation of the Missionaries of Charity. Indeed, Mother Teresa's own personal vocation seemed to be motivated by that vision. Now I have always been a great admirer of Mother Teresa, regardless of what Christopher Hitchens has to say about her. Still, I must confess a degree of discomfort with some of the terms in which she expresses her spirituality in *Come By My Light*. The problem for me is one that Simone Weil put her brilliant finger on, namely, the questionable nature of an expression like "loving one's neighbor in the Lord." A crucial element of the story in Matthew is that the elect actually fed the hungry without realizing it was Jesus they were feeding. "God is not present," Weil insists, "even if we invoke him, where the afflicted are merely regarded as an occasion for doing good."[11] Was Mother Teresa guilty of regarding the poor and dying as an occasion for doing good? If she was, she needed to read what Weil wrote about precisely that passage in Matthew: "He who gives bread to the famished sufferer for the love of God will not be thanked by Christ. He has already had his reward in this thought itself. Christ thanks those who do not know to whom they are giving food."[12]

The recently deceased French novelist Vladimir Volkoff, who was also a devout Orthodox Christian, is quoted in a book of interviews as saying this about the spiritual significance of human love:

> The act of love has an immense symbolic importance.... The more seriousness, the more religiosity, the more sense of the sacred, the more of what the liturgy called 'the fear of God' we put in the act of love, the more spiritual nourishment we will receive, it seems to me.[13]

Of course, it is not without significance that in the Orthodox Church priests are allowed to take a wife. Still, there is also the requirement of celibacy for those Orthodox priests who are to be bishops. God founded the institution of the family long before he established the temple or the church. The blood of Jesus that was shed to redeem the human race from the curse of sin was the blood passed down from Adam to Abraham, through Ruth and Rahab, through David and the rest of his lineage. We are direct descendants of the first Adam and inherit his guilt through our physical heredity, but we're also grafted into the root of Jesse and co-heirs with the Son of Man through our spiritual adoption. The family of God is the Body of Christ, which is being prepared to become his Bride.

In Milton's *Paradise Lost*, after Adam and Eve have fallen victim to Satan's guile, they begin to contemplate in great anguish the scope and con-

11. Simone Weil, *Waiting for God*, trans. Emma Craufurd (New York: G. P. Putnam's Sons, 1951), 93.

12. Weil, *Waiting for God*, 94. Mary Poplin, author of *Finding Calcutta: What Mother Teresa Taught Me About Meaningful Work and Service* (Downers Grove, Illinois: InterVarsity Press, 2008), says "Mother used to say they should be grateful to the poor because they helped them love God more because God wasn't there to directly tend him, but he was in the distressing guise of the poor. I don't think she would have thought about it as an occasion for doing good, but an occasion to love God.... My own belief is that God so worked through her, she could no longer distinguish His presence." Quoted from email to the author dated 29 March 2008.

13. Jacqueline Bruller, *Vladimir Volkoff: L'Exil est ma patrie: Entretiens* (Paris: Le Centurion, 1982), 177.

sequences of their sin. Realizing that their guilt will be passed inexorably on to their entire progeny for ages to come, they are tempted to end Eve's recently-revealed pregnancy. This is the darkest moment of despair in the poem, and Milton makes it clear just how close to the grand design of Lucifer is the taking of unborn life. We need to be reminded in this day of on-demand abortion that the first divine command recorded in Scripture is for humanity to be fruitful and multiply. The "great and primordial blessing" (245), as Maritain calls it, as far as the earthly destiny of married couples is concerned, is the privilege of participating with God in the ongoing, continuous act of creation.

Percy Shelley, as Maritain observes, said that Dante understood the secrets of love better than any other poet. Maritain, for his part, insists that the author of *Song of Songs* "was a man profoundly versed, much more than Dante himself, in the things of profane love, the experience of human mad, boundless love, and of the carnal love which is normally linked to it" (252). Still, Maritain suggests that it is entirely conceivable that the biblical poet may have already renounced the flesh before he wrote *Song of Songs* and most certainly had renounced human *amour fou*.

So how does the vow of chastity or celibacy fit into Maritain's exploration of friendship and love? Well, even though he states clearly that normal conjugal relations between husband and wife are not incompatible with a lifestyle of contemplation, we also know that he and Raïssa themselves willingly embraced a vow of chastity as a part of their commitment as oblates, so it is no surprise to see him end his essay with a description of how well chastity fits with the more elevated forms of *amour fou* for God. "He who loves a human person with mad, boundless love gives himself to this person in his body and in his soul. He who enters into a state of life dedicated to mad, boundless love for God must give to God his body as well as his soul. His soul gives itself to Him by love, his body by chastity" (255).

Finally, Maritain points out quite cogently that the humanity of Jesus, since it is such an integral part of the object of contemplation in the life of the Christian contemplative, provides us with a powerfully persuasive example. "That to which the Christian contemplative has his eyes constantly attached is, at the same time as the one and triune God, a man perfectly chaste, born of the most chaste of Virgins, and who Himself is God. How would the Christian who aspires to contemplation not feel himself drawn also to a life of continence or of chastity—not, once more, as to a necessary condition (except, for some, because of the religious state), but as to something which better accords with his desires?" (255).

Jacques's and Raïssa's union produced no earthly offspring. The family that they built was an unusually close-knit trio, Raïssa and her sister Vera forming the Mary and Martha pattern and Jacques the wise and kindly patriarch. Their commitment to chastity channeled their parental desires into the apostolate of producing spiritual offspring, and the number of converts and godchildren who revered them like parents was impressive. With such a great cloud of witnesses surrounding us, then, is it not incumbent upon us not to let "Love and Friendship" remain just a theme for a conference? Those of us who teach Catholic philosophy and literature are called to join the Maritains in making our classrooms and our homes *centres de rayonnement* too. By causing an atmosphere of disinterested *amitié* to reign in the classroom, and by cultivating our own infectious *amour fou* of God, we in our turn can be pilgrims of the absolute, applying and embodying today the lessons of a living perennial philosophy.

GLENN STATILE

Forgiveness and Its Discontents

I. The Many Facets of Forgiveness

Saint Augustine informs us that the full measure of love is to love without measure. This being the case, it therefore follows that forgiveness is a perfectly suitable topic to dwell upon in a book dedicated to the kindred themes of love and friendship, for forgiveness is a gift bestowed upon us by the immeasurable love of God. In theological terms, one might go so far as to say that forgiveness is the gift which continually rescues salvation history and keeps our hopes for eternal life alive. No less a scribe than William Shakespeare once called upon the attitude of forgiveness in his literary epitaph when bidding farewell to his loyal public in the epilogue to his final play, *The Tempest*. It is at this point that Prospero, the Duke of Milan, issues the following plea to the audience: "As you from crimes would pardon'd be,/Let your indulgence set me free."

While forgiveness is a mandatory condition for living a proper Christian life, it is not completely clear as to what is meant by it. Yet it is nevertheless always pleasing to extol its virtues. Waxing poetical, we might say that forgiveness is a gem which has many facets, or a gift which allows the many splendors of love and friendship to shine forth in the fullness of their heavenly raiment. Yet, while admittedly rhapsodic, the application of such a poetic coating to the unvarnished concept of forgiveness only sidesteps the underlying persistent problem of its definition which, like Wordsworth's world, is always with us.

Peering at forgiveness through the looking glass of faith, reason, and science yields a kaleidoscopic array of conceptual hues that can make it seem utterly equivocal. One particularly knotty problem bearing on the meaning of forgiveness has to do with the various semantic intersections one encounters when forgiveness bumps up against such kindred terms as: pardon, absolution, clemency, remission, reconciliation, excuse, exculpate, and amnesty. Both etymologically and semantically the concept of forgiveness is tied to the concept of gift: *perdonare* in Italian; *pardoner* in French; and *vergeben* in German, for example, all inscribe the word for gift within a word that suggests a gift of great moral significance—forgiveness. And of course there is that old but overly familiar proverb: forgive and forget. While not identical, the act of forgiving is often linked to a loss of recollection, even in the case of God—"It is I, I, who wipe out, for my own sake, your offenses; your sins I remember no more."[1]

Thinkers such as Jacques Derrida even go so far as to employ the logical *aporias* and inconsistencies which they derive from an analysis of forgiveness as a basis for maintaining that forgiveness is impossible for anyone to dispense.[2] Derrida maintained, for example, with an hyperbole that borders upon philosophical affectation, that only what is unforgivable meets the criteria for actually being forgiven. He further held that acts of purported forgiveness function as weapons by which we impose our sovereignty or ulterior motives upon others. Thus, according to Derrida, when we forgive, our purpose is not to give but, ultimately, to take by gaining some type of long range psychological advantage over another person. This might be true to the extent that what passes for human forgiveness might sometimes be a subterfuge—and hence not an authentic act of forgiveness. Human forgiveness is always imperfect given our fallen condition. Additionally, one need not be a post-modern deconstructionist from Algiers with a predilection for philosophical scandal in order to throw believers a curve ball. One of my favorite mystical writers, Julian of Norwich in her *Revelations of Divine Love*, openly avers that God does not forgive since he is incapable of being offended. What he does, according to Julian, is to continue to give us the gift of His infinite love despite our ongoing rejection. My aim in this essay is twofold: 1) To shed some light upon what is meant by human forgiveness from the Catholic perspective; and 2) To consider whether the

1. Isaiah 43:25, *Saint Joseph New Catholic Edition* (New York: Catholic Book Publishing Company, 1963).

2. See for example what Derrida says about forgiveness in John D. Caputo, Mark Dooley, and Michael J. Scanlon, eds., *Questioning God* (Bloomington/Indianapolis, Indiana: Indiana University Press, 2001), 21–72.

evolutionary or scientific approach to the problem of forgiveness has anything to offer the Christian conception of forgiveness.

II. To Err is Human, to Forgive Humane

For people of faith, divine forgiveness provides the ontological starting point for any possible extension of the concept of forgiveness. Divine forgiveness is the subject matter of Psalm 50 (the *Miserere*). In verse six of this prayer of repentance, King David quite strikingly says that sin is a grievance only against God (*tibi soli peccavi*). While we offend other human beings with our acts of selfishness and injustice, we do not, in any theologically technical sense of the term, sin against them. And, if we do not sin against them, then they cannot forgive us unless forgiveness can be extended to offenses other than sin. For Alexander Pope, forgiveness, one might argue, is the prerogative of God alone: "To err is human, to forgive divine."[3] On the other hand, such a poetic exclamation could also be interpreted as meaning that we, in some perhaps analogous way, imitate God when we forgive.

My focus here concerns the status of human forgiveness in the sense of one person forgiving another. There are, however, opposing ways by which the concept of human forgiveness might be contracted or expanded. By a contraction of human forgiveness, I refer to the ultra-fuzzy concept of self-forgiveness, in which not two but only one person is allegedly involved in the forgiving process. Pop psychology and new age religion instruct us to forgive ourselves, but never come close to telling us anything significant about the epistemology of such a daunting philosophical task. Neither will I attempt to do so. One interesting danger when dealing with the issue of self-forgiveness, however, is the possibility that one's so-called act of self-exoneration might be premature. If we forgive ourselves too quickly, in the absence of remorse and proper penance, then we only increase the risk of behaving in the same way that initially prompted our need for self-forgiveness. Christian self-forgiveness, assuming it is possible, requires that we esteem ourselves highly enough to be worthy of forgiveness, but never to the narcissistic extent that we sidestep the gauntlet of self-examination and repentance. A proper relationship to God, in relation to whom we are both beloved children and subordinate creatures, offers perhaps the only

3. Alexander Pope, *The Works of Alexander Pope*, ed. William Warburton, vol. 1: *Essay on Criticism* (New York: William Durell, 1807), Part I, line 325.

legitimate basis for achieving the proper psychological balance necessary for real self-forgiveness.

On the other hand, forgiveness involving groups, institutions, nations and the like represents an expansion upon the basic model of one-to-one interpersonal forgiveness. Desmond Tutu's book entitled *No Future Without Forgiveness* is symbolic of the late 20th century elevation of forgiveness into a principle of social justice within the political arena. The author of *The Prince* would no doubt declare the notion of political forgiveness to be oxymoronic. Of the many complexities involved in attempting to make philosophical sense out of any extension of forgiveness into the political arena, I find the following to be of great interest. In the case of the Truth and Reconciliation Committee in post-apartheid South Africa, truth served as both a necessary and sufficient condition for amnesty. Those guilty of apartheid era crimes were granted amnesty by the newly elected Mandela government simply by coming clean and confessing to everything they had done. No remorse was requested or required. Thus, in a quite literal sense, it was the truth which in this instance set these moral scoundrels free.

In the case of divine forgiveness, we are absolved of our sins by God. Note that this does not necessarily imply that some stain or blot has been purged or erased from the soul, although such a view does enjoy scriptural support. In verse nine of the *Miserere*, for example, King David petitions God to purify him of his sin with hyssop so that he might be cleansed and made whiter than snow. In *Works of Love*, Søren Kierkegaard even describes divine forgiveness as a counterpart to creation, for in an act of divine forgiveness God might be said to *decreate* or cast something which exists back into nothingness. But if evil is a privation of being, as St. Augustine contends, then the forgiveness of our sins by God actually restores us to an elevated spiritual state. It augments rather than depletes us, in a way which is analogous to the anomaly that once attached itself to the old phlogiston theory during the early days of modern chemistry when phlogiston-depleted substances would, surprisingly, end up weighing more after the removal of this hypothetical element than they did when it was supposedly still present. Although God is undoubtedly pleased when one of his creatures returns to the fold of grace, we nevertheless do not theologically ascribe any change whatsoever to God's unchanging nature. Yet we the sinners are changed dramatically in the *remissio peccatorum* of the confessional. As Aquinas pointed out in his innovative treatment of the sacrament of penance in Part III of the *Summa Theologica*, such a change occurs when sinners are forgiven their sins by the conjunction of the formal sacramental causality of God's grace, which is mediated *in persona Christi* by the priestly confessor, and the materially penitent acts of contrition, confession, and satisfaction.[4]

We use the language of forgiveness all the time in connection with our interpersonal relationships with other human beings. Moreover, even though the prayer was given to us by Christ himself, it is we the people, God's people, who in the Lord's Prayer continually invoke that divine forgiveness be granted to us only contingently upon our extension of forgiveness to others: *et dimitte nobis debita nostra, sicut et nos dimittimus debitoribus nostris.* While our being is analogous to that of God, according to Aquinas, it is not equally as clear, at least to me, as to what would constitute the basis for arguing that human forgiveness is analogous to that of divine forgiveness. God forgives us our sins, whereas we forgive only offenses or crimes, and not sins, committed against our persons. Perhaps there is too much of an asymmetry between the cases of divine and human forgiveness ever to contemplate such an analogous link. When God forgives, we are spiritually healed with no effect upon Himself. But when we forgive others, while no corresponding ontological change occurs in the forgiven, both forgiver and forgiven derive whatever emotional benefits ensue from the healing power of human forgiveness. As is sometimes said, when we forgive, the prisoner we set free is none other than ourselves. But despite these differences between the cases of human and divine forgiveness, one important similarity is that in both cases there is, if not in the ontological sense, an emotional or spiritual benefit which accrues to the forgiven that stems from the affirmation of love which has been extended in the process. Such a benefit, albeit unquantifiable and immeasurable, and thus perhaps unsatisfactory for those who would demand scientific precision, is nevertheless phenomenologically real and authentically holy. Whereas divine forgiveness might be characterized as a divine action in which God's healing grace and love is communicated to us, human forgiveness, on the other hand, is actualized by the adoption of a loving attitude, or state of being, on the part of the human forgiver which in turn impacts the state of being of the forgiven. As all good marriage counselors know, or ought to know: a happy marriage is the union of two good forgivers.

4. Thomas Aquinas, *Summa theologiae* III, qq. 84–90; *Supplementum*, qq. 1–15.

While the Lord's Prayer stipulates that forgiveness constitutes a real component of our human repertoire of actions and attitudes, it is nevertheless the case that the concept of human forgiveness remains for the most part neglected by mainstream Catholic theology, although books galore have been written upon the subject and are easily found upon the pop psychology shelf in your neighborhood bookstore. Saint Thomas Aquinas barely scratches the surface of what human forgiveness entails. When he does refer to human forgiveness, he does so almost exclusively in the context of the divine. Such neglect is due to the fact that human forgiveness is linked by Thomas to the divine grace that is a *sine qua non* of its conferral. The restoration of a fractured human relationship in the case of human forgiveness cannot take place except in the presence of God's grace. Even when Thomas deals directly with the text which petitions God to withhold divine forgiveness in the absence of prior human forgiveness in his commentaries upon the gospel of Matthew and the Lord's Prayer, he does not probe too deeply into any independent mystery associated with human forgiveness. He does, however, exemplify the meaning of this contingent petition via his analysis of the parable of the unmerciful servant in *Matthew* 18:23–35 in the former work.[5] Just as in the case of this ungrateful servant, people who are unwilling to forgive those who have offended them simultaneously demonstrate a sense of *ingratitude* to God and thus are not properly disposed to receive divine forgiveness.

It is important to remind ourselves that the Christian call to forgiveness does not derive from the Decalogue but from the Beatitudes: "Blessed are the merciful, for they shall obtain mercy." We imitate God more perfectly when we fulfill the full spirit of the Law which Jesus shares with us in the Sermon on the Mount than when we merely comply with the prescriptive and proscriptive rules set forth in the commandments. From the minimalist baseline for holiness represented by the commandments, human forgiveness is rightly perceived as a kind of supererogatory attitude by which we rise to the Everest of our human condition. And as Dante informs us in Canto XXXIII of his *Purgatorio*, after himself ascending to the earthly paradise which sits atop Mount Purgatory, only after scaling such a summit are we then *puro e disposto a salire a le stelle* (pure and prepared to climb unto the stars).

5. See Thomas Aquinas, *Lectura Super Matthaeum, Reportatio*, 18.1.3.

III. Nice Guys Finish Last

While the Christian or theological understanding of forgiveness provides many of us with our working model of what forgiveness actually means, the literature on forgiveness abounds with other, what one might call secular, models of forgiveness. These secular models can interact, overlap, or compete with each other as well as with the Christian model. When we are ensured by faith that our Christian understanding of a particular issue is correct, then we must resist the temptation to allow secular novelties to lead us astray. But when well recognized gaps exist in what we believe on the basis of faith, then it is only fitting that we consider what the sciences or philosophical reflection have to offer. *Fides quaerens intellectum* is just as valid a motto today as it ever was. One example of a secular model of forgiveness is the *health* model. Many experiments have been conducted, for example, as in the case of prayer, to try to demonstrate the physiological advantages of forgiveness. Another such secular model is what one might dub the *game-theoretic* model in which strategies of forgiveness are compared with other competitive strategies in order to determine which yields the greatest quantifiable measure for cooperative success in the pursuit of goals which maximize self-interest.[6] However, the focus of this section will be to examine and assess the philosophical credentials of the *evolutionary* model of forgiveness.

The massive literature in sociobiology and evolutionary psychology purports to provide us with a not-so-kind evolutionary interpretation of altruism. The sociobiological verdict against the Christian interpretation of altruism or *caritas* can be best summed up in the words of that great Darwinian scholar, Leo Durocher, who in the title of his autobiographical memoir about his life in baseball reminded us of a well-known competitive and survivalist truism: nice guys finish last. Thinkers who attempt to extend evolutionary theory to both animal and human behavior have spilled much ink in an effort to convince us that truly selfless and charitable instincts and attitudes are not suitable for survival on that great playing and slaying field of Natural Selection. The same kind and caliber of evolution-

6. See Colm O'Riordan, "A Forgiving Strategy for the Iterated Prisoner's Dilemma," in *Journal of Artificial Societies and Social Simulation*, Volume 3, No. 4. (This is available at http://www.soc.surrey.ac.uk.Jasss/3/4/3/.html.) See, also, Robert Axelrod, *The Evolution of Cooperation* (New York: Basic Books, 1984) and Robert Axelrod, *The Complexity of Cooperation: Agent-Based Models of Competition and Collaboration* (Princeton, New Jersey: Princeton University Press, 1997).

ary reasoning is also applied to the concept of forgiveness. According to evolutionary theory, the rise and persistence of forgiveness in human civilization is due to its fitness as a means for survival, and not to any transcendent claim upon our commitments and behavior.

Materialist exponents of evolutionary theory can concoct an explanation to cover almost every facet of human behavior, but glibness is no substitute for knowledge. After all, both Marxist theory and Freudian psychoanalysis boasted a kind of explanatory omniscience in their heyday, and just look at how far it got them. Sociobiologist David Buss gives an evolutionary explanation as to why men and women forgive differently in cases of infidelity. He says that men are less likely to forgive a partner who is impregnated by another man, whereas a woman is more likely to forgive the father of her children. The man presumably has no genetic investment in the progeny of another male, while the woman, as we all know so well, easily forgives her husband's cheating heart as long as he keeps his checkbook close to hearth and home. I don't know about you, but I would rate the psychological sagacity of such an evolutionary interpretation as unworthy even of the wisdom promulgated by the most trite of predictions to be found within a Chinese fortune cookie.

But of course I am being a bit unfair to both evolutionary theory and Chinese fortune cookies. The old adage which says that men forget but never forgive, while women forgive but never forget has, for all of its hyperbole, both the ring and sting of social truth. Research into the existence of a forgiveness instinct within human nature is a legitimate and currently ongoing scientific enterprise, funded by no less than the deep pockets of the Templeton Foundation. Such an instinct, like the infamous God gene of recent memory, has not been discovered in our genetic constitution or our neural wiring. But like Chesterton's quip in regard to the most outstanding fact about the missing link in evolutionary theory, the forgiveness instinct is still missing. Belief in the existence of such a biological instinct is not necessarily damaging to the spiritual pedigree of forgiveness. Christianity, after all, is a religion based upon the principle of incarnation. Just because a forgiveness instinct might be rooted in our physical nature does not mean that it has no spiritual significance. Research into animal behavior, for example, strongly indicates the existence of mechanisms that are thought to be analogous, to use the language of primatologist Frans De Waal, to those that prompt the so-called human instinct to forgive.

According to the evolutionary interpretation, the persistence of forgiveness as a virtue in our civilization must be due to the fact that success in healing broken relationships and in overcoming the compulsion to exact revenge must have been advantageous for the survival of the human species in the distant past. Evolutionary interpretations of this type coupled with the postulation of some sort of forgiveness instinct accomplish little more, however, than a public acknowledgement or confession of one's allegiance to the wide explanatory horizons of natural selection. Logicians call this begging the question. But it would be wrong to conclude that the psychological dynamics and neural foundations of forgiveness as understood from an evolutionary perspective have nothing to offer the Christian conception of forgiveness, although a significant portion of what passes for forgiveness research from an evolutionary perspective deals not with authentic Christian forgiveness, but with a kind of mockery of forgiveness that treats it as a subtle tool of self-promotion within a utilitarian framework.

One example of how an evolutionary or at least scientific approach to forgiveness can enhance our understanding about how Christian forgiveness functions in our lives comes from research done on the feeling known as empathy. According to recent work in both standard psychology and neuropsychology, one of the conditions that can trigger the alleged evolutionary based forgiveness instinct is called *careworthiness*, which is defined by psychologist Michael McCullough as the condition of a transgressor which makes him or her an appropriate target for kindness and compassion.[7] As might be expected, there is a high correlation between those we are willing to forgive and the percentage of our genes that they share. Yet this is not the end of the story. According to neuroscientific studies, forgiveness is most likely to be triggered when we care for someone, whether there is a close genetic relationship between us and the people we care for or not. Additionally, we are more likely to care for others, say these studies, if we empathize with their situation and mindset. When people feel empathy toward those who have wronged them, they do not experience any increase, on the average, in the activity of the prefrontal cortex that usually

7. Michael McCullough, *Beyond Revenge: The Evolution of the Forgiveness Instinct* (Hoboken, New Jersey: Jossey-Bass, 2008), 147–49. See also, A. B. Newberg, E. G. d'Aquili, S. K. Newberg, V. deMarici, "The Neuropsychological Correlates of Forgiveness," in *Forgiveness: Theory, Research, and Practice*, ed. M. E. McCullough, K. I. Pargament, C. E. Thoresen (New York: Guilford, 2000), 91–110.

accompanies the desire for revenge.[8] If we can manipulate the conditions that induce empathy, either clinically or medically, then we might be able to create (whether we should or not is another story) the kind of psychological climate that will facilitate our loving others as we love ourselves. For while to know all is certainly not to forgive all as is sometimes said, being able to share the same psychological perspective as someone else who has harmed you is to make of them, in the word's of Aristotle's remarks on friendship, a kind of second self.

IV. Concluding Remarks

Those who are discontent with the Christian concept of forgiveness try to get around it in various ways. One way is by arguing that forgiveness is both humanly and philosophically impossible; another is by trying to demonstrate that on a deeper level forgiveness is just as motivated by self-interest as any other kind of behavior or attitude; and yet another is that the so-called spirituality of forgiveness is a sham that should be completely reinterpreted by the biological imperatives that form our personalities. As a person of faith, I prefer to engage in philosophical argument and not to quarrel with those who do not share my views. In saying so, I adopt both a Chestertonian, as well as a fraternal, attitude toward those with whom I disagree. About his relationship with his brother Cecil, the great Chesterton once said that, while they always argued, they never quarreled. As believers in an incarnational religion, we should not necessarily expect the full mystery of human forgiveness to be unraveled without any help from our embodied condition. Neither should we expect forgiveness to be completely understood in strictly biological terms without any spiritual remainder. What is required is the kind of multi-layered approach to explanation that Aristotle pioneered over two millennia ago. As I began an essay on forgiveness upon a literary note with quotes from St. Augustine and Shakespeare, in the interests of symmetry I will conclude in a similar literary vein, but this time with a quote from Mark Twain, who tells us that: "forgiveness is the fragrance that the violet sheds on the heal that has crushed it."

8. McCullough, *Beyond Revenge*, 148–49.

III

FRIENDSHIP, VIRTUE, AND DUTY

HERBERT E. HARTMANN

The Role of Love in Practical Reasoning

I. Introduction

For the premoderns, the philosophical study of moral matters originally begins with the study of men as engaged in *praxis*, proper human action. But with Aristotle it does not begin with the study of just any human action, but with the study of the virtuous action of a publicly recognized virtuous man. In such actions, and in such men, we find the measure of correct conduct and being, and the realization of human being in its nature and *telos*. Significantly, in such actions, and in such men, we find no conflict between human appetitive inclinations and human reason. In fact, here we find only the harmonious and congruent functioning of appetite and reason. Right reason and right love are found together, united as one principle of being and action.

It seems reasonable that, if a human being is to function properly, the principle of his action should be one as well as being proper to his being. The one principle of human action is the intellect and the appetite, working in union to codetermine in their respective manners the act of choice. Thus, the principle of human action requires the uniting, and the harmonious functioning, of two powers, intellectual and appetitive, *as if* they were one, right reason and right love.

For a variety of reasons, among them the influence of Kant, modern moral philosophy most often begins its study of morals with the situation of those individuals that Aristotle would label 'the morally strong' or 'the morally weak,' that is, not those exhibiting the perfected mode of human being. In short, modern ethical thought begins with the condition that we find most commonly in persons, their present natural state, and not with the more perfected natural state of the human person. In this common condition, the moral agent finds himself divided: his appetitive inclinations oppose the commands of his reason. The moral agent is out of sorts, and in conflict, with himself, unable coherently and harmoniously to act according to one correct unified principle in his being. The state of nature for man is a state of war between his concrete reason and his appetite. Modern moral philosophy discovers its *principal task* is thus to offer the means to resolve this radical conflict in the moral agent's being. Its concentration on this separation and the ensuing war for self-control within the moral agent leads modern moral philosophy to look outside the conflicting parties in the agent's soul and to look exclusively to an abstract or pure reason alone to clarify and thus resolve this conflict from the reason's superior being and its superior and impartial dictates. Philosophy from its own autonomous and sovereign resource, philosophic reason, alone determines what is right for us to do. The role of the appetite is to follow the command of the universal reason. As Robert Sokolowski remarks, in such a situation: "We are tempted to look for criteria or methods of reasoning that will generate our obligations for us. We think it might be possible for us abstractly to recognize what is right."[1] Thus, for many modern moral philosophers, the measure of rectitude is to be sought *in* universal reason and *by* reason alone, that is, in separation from the inclinations and appetites of our whole natural being. The appetites and their inclinations are seen more as the source of the moral problem and not as a contributing source or principle of its resolution. For the human appetitive structure in its natural, animal givenness is no longer seen as a proper principle of free and moral human action. Love finds little or no role in modern moral thought.

In his Tanner Lectures[2] and in the book, *Reasons of Love*,[3] Harry Frankfurt declares himself deeply unsatisfied with the accounts of reason, appetite, and love found in contemporary moral philosophy. In his attempt

1. Robert Sokolowski, *The God of Faith and Reason* (Washington, D.C.: Catholic University Press, 1982, 1995), 63.

2. Harry Frankfurt, *Taking Ourselves Seriously and Getting It Right* (Stanford: Stanford University Press, 2006). (All page references to this work are hereafter placed in the text, in parentheses.)

3. Harry Frankfurt, *The Reasons of Love* (Princeton: Princeton University Press, 2004).

to expound the true foundations of practical or normative philosophy, he begins, not with the separation of inclination and reason; rather, he returns philosophical attention, as did Aristotle, to the good unified agents, those who love and know the human good. To be precise, unlike Aristotle, Frankfurt does not return to the perfected or virtuous man and the virtuous action as such, but he does return to the reasonable man, as one would find him in our common law tradition before administrative law minimized this tradition. For Frankfurt, the good human action originates in love, and that means for him, in practical reason working in harmony with the whole of man, including his appetites and not in abstract reasoning alone.

Frankfurt establishes the proper foundation of human action upon two major teachings. First, he rejects the understanding of reason that is employed in contemporary normative philosophy, and proposes to replace that notion of reason with a true and proper account of practical reasoning. Labeling this account "volitional reasoning," he finds that practical reasoning is rooted in our first caring or loving, in our first *taking something as* important. Our norms are not first based upon a theoretical, formal and abstract "normative or value realism." Without first loving, there is no practical reasoning. Thus, the reasons for our actions are all reasons of love. Values merely known, even very evident values, if they are not loved, cannot function as the foundation of our practical thinking. What we, in fact, care about and love, what we take as truly important to us, grounds our *praxis* by "creating" and ordering the effective final ends of our *praxis*.

Secondly, in order to complete this foundation of practical reasoning, Frankfurt believes that we must be able to provide answers to the following questions as well. What are we to care about? How are we to measure the relative importance to us of the various things about which we care? How are we to get it right? "Our understanding of what to care about, then, that is the ultimate touchstone and basis of our practical reasoning" (28).

In examining what we do love in order to find the grounds of normativity, Frankfurt finds that our loves have two forms. "The ground of normativity is relative in part to the common nature of human beings and in part to individual experience and character" (48). Some of our loves reflect "fundamental necessities of the will" that "are solidly entrenched in our human nature from the start." These are "the elementary constituents of volitional reason itself" (38). Thus, he teaches that the natural necessities of our will and of our human nature are the basis for, and become experienced as, the volitional necessities grounding our loves, and thus they ground our normative and practical reasoning. The fact that grounds our norms is that some of our loves reflect experienced natural volitional necessities. "We cannot bring ourselves to be wholly indifferent to these things, much less categorically opposed to them" (38).

All of our actions and their reasons are rooted in our fundamental loves, and our loves follow from the teachings of our nature. These first volitional necessities, those entrenched in our nature, provide the basic measure or standard of our good loves and of our norms. They found our understanding of moral or practical rationality. If the final ends that structure and order our lives and loves are those arising from these fundamental necessities of our nature, then we will have "gotten our life right" in a significant and fundamental manner. Thus, Frankfurt teaches that the decisive rational warrant for our moral laws is in a primary and significant sense, rooted in human nature itself.

Frankfurt finds these volitional necessities to be universal, necessary, absolute, unchangeable, irreducible and objective.

II. The Rational Value of Love in Human Life

Before our conscious and rational life develops, we necessarily care about particular things. "If there were nothing that we cared about—if our response to the world were utterly and uniformly flat—there would be no reason for us to care about anything" (20). In fact, "the world is everywhere infused for us with importance" (20). We begin to reason practically because we first love. We are beings in the world because the objects in the world are known to be fitting or unfitting for our well-being. Our personal identity is originally defined for us, and later by us, by our caring for certain things and by our caring about them in an ordered hierarchical manner. If we are asked the Socratic question "how are we to live?" we find that we have already begun to answer this question in our mode of being before our reason has considered it. The question of the examined life concerns the question of whether we have explicitly ordered our loves on a foundation which has an objective basis or whether we have merely accepted an order of loves without an examined and rationally considered foundation. Before such questions are asked or considered, we are always already on our way to an answer in our affective, caring mode of living.

> It is by caring about things that we infuse the world with importance. This provides us with stable ambitions and concerns; it marks our interests and our goals. The importance that our caring creates for us defines the framework of standards and aims in terms of which we endeavor to conduct our lives.... Insofar as he does care about certain things, this determines how he thinks it important for him to conduct his life. The totality of the various things that a person cares about—together with his ordering of how important to him they are—effectively specifies his answer to the question of how to live.[4]

The question concerning how one is to live is not a question of abstract reason. Socrates died precisely because his inquiry, which was driven by this question, questioned and undermined the loves, and thus the lives, of his fellow citizens.

> Love commits us to significant requirements and limitations. These are boundaries that delineate the substance and the structure of our wills. That is, they define what—as active beings—we most intimately and essentially are.... It (love) profoundly shapes our personal identities and the ways in which we experience our lives (3).

Long before we study moral philosophy, we have an ethical mode of being. Long before we have any sciences, we, in our lives, are already committed in our *ethos* to certain goods and modes of conduct. Before, and even without science, this loving is essential to human life. To live a human life, "we need goals."[5] Thus the first formation of our character is dependent upon the customs which form our moral education in our home and community. Our lives are meaningful insofar as we have final purposes that we value, that provide us with aims and ambitions. Frankfurt here cites Aristotle: without final purposes or ends for our desire, our desires are "empty and vain."[6] Thus, like Aristotle, Frankfurt wants to ground practical reasoning in our first having final goods in our mode of being. "But how is it that things may come to have for us a terminal value that is independent of their usefulness for pursuing other goals? In what acceptable way can our need for final ends be met? It is love, I believe, that meets this need.... Love is the originating source of terminal value."[7] Practical reason sets our final ends "by identifying what it is that we love."[8] Practical reason within our act of practical reasoning is not an autonomous self-creative reason;

4. Frankfurt, *The Reasons of Love*, 23.
5. Ibid., 52.
6. Ibid., 52.
7. Ibid., 55.
8. Ibid., 55, n. 9.

rather, it is a notion founded upon our loves and is not an unconditioned principle.

> By its very nature, loving entails both that we regard its objects as valuable in themselves and that we have no choice but to adopt those objects as our final ends. Insofar as love is the creator both of inherent or terminal value and importance, then, it is the ultimate ground of practical rationality.[9]

Man's nature is to love. Love founds his practical reasoning. Human existence for an agent has no meaning, no direction, no order and no *raison d'etre* without his first loving. Thus, it is not surprising to find Frankfurt reject with several arguments what he takes to be the reigning understanding of reason's use in ethics: that abstract rational necessities are of themselves, as intelligible, the source and foundation of our practical reasoning.

> We need to understand, however, that the ambition to provide an exhaustively rational warrant for the way in which we are to conduct our lives is misconceived. The pan-rationalistic fantasy of demonstrating—from the ground up—how we must reason to live is incoherent and must be abandoned.[10]

Frankfurt looks around himself and finds men acting seriously and correctly in defending their lives, in seeking to avoid illness and suffering, in disinterestedly loving their spouses and their children. He finds that in these human lives, these commitments are not primarily grounded in any consideration of universal moral principles. They do not depend upon even the assumption that good reasons could be found. Does a man need a reason, especially one grounded in a universal moral principle, to save his drowning wife in preference to another? Rather, "these commitments are innate in us. They are not based upon deliberation. They are not responses to any commands of rationality. The commands to which they do in fact respond are grounded in a source that is constituted not by judgments and reasons, but by a particular mode of caring about things. They are commands of love."[11]

What modern moral philosophy needs to understand is that the authority of the moral law is not merely the authority of reason itself, of pure rationality. "The normative authority of reason ... cannot be what accounts for the normative authority of morality" (21). The mere understanding of moral value does not by itself make it important to the knower to be mor-

9. Ibid., 56.

10. Ibid., 28.

11. Ibid., 29.

al or to do the act commanded. He needs first to care about the act and morality. He needs first to identify it as his good. Some argue that we are morally obliged to care about certain things, and that these obligations do not depend upon any subjective considerations. But for Frankfurt what matters is whether the agent identifies these "obligations" as binding upon him, whether he finds them to be important for him. Reason alone cannot motivate us to be moral. Given our nature, when one is reasoning practically, the issue of importance is more fundamental than the issue of abstract morality.[12]

Moral values and their importance are rooted in the particular loves present in the individual. "Unless a person knows what he already cares about, therefore, he cannot determine what he has reason to care about" (23). In order to answer the normative question "What should he care about?" he must first answer the non-normative question "What does he actually care about?"[13] Thus, for Frankfurt: "There can be no well-ordered inquiry into the question of how one has reason to live" because this purely rational inquiry is dependent upon volitional necessities that provide the basis for any practically rational inquiry. As Aristotle would say, ethics cannot be taught to one merely because he is rational, like mathematics can be. Without starting with what people actually take as their good, their ethical *doxa* based upon their loves, one does not have the method proper to conduct a practical inquiry.[14]

What Frankfurt has proven is that any inherent value as recognized by pure reason is not effective as such in the practical order. He rejects as "not truly viable" those philosophers who claim that "certain things have an inherent value that is altogether independent of any subjective states or condition."[15]

If we love some values or goods naturally, then those goods are primarily known as important, as desirable. These goods are not merely known, but rather they are known practically, that is, as valuable, as desirable, as good for the agent. As loved, such values are known as dependent "on our subjective states or condition."[16] Thus, practical knowledge is a knowledge essentially 'conditioned by subjective conditions' in the knower. He knows these values as good for him, as fitting for him.

12. Ibid., 57, n. 10.

13. Ibid., 26.

14. Aristotle, *Metaphysics*, VII, 3, 1029b 4–8.

15. Frankfurt, *The Reasons of Love*, 56.

16. Ibid., 56.

III. Human Nature as the Foundation of the Foundation

Having shown that our loves ground our practical reasoning, our second task is to explicate the rational warrant that Frankfurt finds for the fundamental volitional necessities of our love. He finds that there exist "fundamental necessities of the will" which are "solidly entrenched in our human nature." They "are not transient creatures of social prescription or of cultural habit." Indeed, they are elementary constituents of volitional reason itself. "Our moral norms are grounded in the loves we cannot but have as undeformed human beings" (43).

As human beings we have volitional necessities that are "universal" (37), "irreducible" (37), "necessary" (45), "unconditional" (45), "absolute" (46), "unchangeable" (46), and "objective" (47). There are normative truths that are 'inescapable' because "they are determined by volitional necessities that we cannot alter or elude" (34). The foundations for our moral norms for Frankfurt are stated clearly: "for normative guidance in understanding what we should want or what we should do, there can be no authority superior to the welcome necessities of our own nature" (51).

Our reason can come to know these natural necessities because, through a philosophical clarification of our actual fundamental loves, we can come to identify the essential and natural requirements and boundaries of our will. Our loves provide "the only legitimate authority" (51) upon which our norms can properly and finally rely. Our norms reflect our wholehearted loves, and our wholehearted loves reflect the volitional necessities of our nature. Our wholehearted love "expresses what we, as active individuals, cannot help being. We have no recourse other than to accept its dictates" (51). The potencies of our nature cannot be understood or truly known until they are actualized and exercised in our *praxis*.

For Frankfurt, what a human person is is known through what a person loves, and some of those loves are so fundamental to our nature that we cannot but come to know what a human being is in our clarifying what we fundamentally must love.

How does Frankfurt reason to this vision of our moral laws as grounded in our nature? He begins questioning David Hume's thought, which "appears to rule out the possibility of providing any rational basis for deciding what we are to care about" (29). For Hume asserts that "'tis not contrary to reason to prefer the destruction of the whole world to the scratching of my finger (29)." As Frankfurt clarifies, "In this purely formal sense of rationality, his choice (to choose to destroy the world rather than to choose not to scratch his finger) is not at all irrational" (29).

Although logically and formally rational, Frankfurt asserts that such a choice is commonly and more properly described as "crazy," as "wildly irrational," as "lunatic," and as "inhuman." Later, he describes this choice as "defective" (30) and as the product of a "deformed will" (39). These legitimate epithets are "literal denials that the person is a rational creature" (30). To Frankfurt, this means that there is a familiar and natural human mode of rationality in addition to abstract, formal rationality. He asserts *that we all*, unless defective, *recognize* a rationality based upon, and limited in its rational considerations by, volitional structures and necessities. "They limit what it is in fact possible for us to care about, what we can accept as reasons for action, and what we can actually bring ourselves to do" (31). There exist moral norms that we recognize, that we understand to be intelligible constraints upon what "one" can choose and do. These rules and measures are "necessary," "irreducible," "unchanging," and "objective." But their rational character is of a different rationality than the formal reasoning predominantly found in modern philosophy since Descartes. The succinct response to Hume is: Violations of volitional rationality are not inconceivable. Rather, what stands in their way is that they are unthinkable (31).

This rationality is not value-free. This rationality "does not permit us to be open-minded and judicious about everything. It requires that certain choices be utterly out of the question" (31). Some choices are "unthinkable" because the volitional rationality is grounded "in ourselves," in our person. It is grounded "only in what we cannot help caring about and cannot help considering important" (33).

Although we can err, Frankfurt claims that this rationality is nevertheless objective, not in the sense of its being external to our minds as an object; rather, "its objectivity consists just in the fact that it is outside the scope of voluntary control" (34). It is grounded in the volitional necessities blossoming forth from the nature of the human will, "a reality that is within ourselves" (34). For our will is "a thing as real as any reality outside us. The truth about it does not depend upon what we think it is, or upon what we wish it were" (50).

As a clear paradigm manifesting evidence of this objective volitional reality, Frankfurt offers our desire for self-preservation. "Its importance is recognized by everyone, and it radiates everywhere" (38). In other texts, he offers parental love and "similarly primitive and protean concerns" (38), which provide *self-evident reasons for our acting.* We cannot bring ourselves to be wholly indifferent to avoiding serious injury or illness, to maintaining minimal contact with other human beings, to be free of chronic suffering and endlessly stupefying boredom. One does not need to provide a reason for the choices. They stand as reasonable before and without one's offering any reasons.

Those who deny these goods are "flatly incomprehensible" to us. They make no sense to us. It is not merely that they are in error or mistaken; they are "deformed." Reasoning from purposes we, as reasonable moral agents, cannot identify with, we are unable to reason practically with such men. Thus, Frankfurt rejects those thinkers who hold that an act is right only if it can be justified to other rational beings. Such thinkers do not grasp the unique character of practical reasoning. A serious ethical choice requires that the rational understanding be both true and the desire correct. There is no practical truth without a correct appetite also guiding the reason. As Frankfurt comments, "those whom we seek to convince must be volitionally rational as well" (39–40).

These objective constraints of volitional rationality are grounded primarily in our will, and in that sense only are they subjective. Since these constraints or determinations arise from the natural constitution of the will, they are not coercive, even though they are necessary and irresistible. They are *natural necessities,* and thus they are neither violent nor coercive (45). Nor is the agent merely a passive recipient of these limits. Rather, given his practical experience and moral education, he identifies these goods as his goods and takes upon himself responsibility for them. By identifying himself with the desire, "he acknowledges that satisfying it is to be assigned some position in the order of his preferences and priorities. If he externalizes the desire, he determines to give it no position in that order at all" (11). "The necessities of love are imposed upon him, then, by himself. It is by his own will that he does what they require" (45). We have here a grounded and cogent notion of human freedom.

For Frankfurt, then, the principles of morality, the moral laws, elaborate and elucidate universal and categorical necessities that constrain the human will. Because there are natural volitional necessities limiting and guiding our loves and our choices, our reason, *after having experienced* these loved goods and our judgment concerning them, can then clarify and articulate the moral laws. Because a philosopher has studied how humans have shaped their lives in accordance with a number of fundamental human goods—fundamental loves—he can then elaborate the rule and measure of human action in his moral philosophy. These laws are based upon the objective necessities of our nature as they have been displayed in their actual developed operations. Having experienced the loves and the goods as loved by men, the philosopher can formulate a notion of a serious and perfected human being, a reasonable human being. From an analysis of his life, one can promulgate moral principles that can clarify the true human loves and inspire others to live correctly.

The truths of morality are a reflection of the volitional necessities that ground them. These volitional necessities have to be experienced, identified, clarified, and elucidated before the philosopher can formulate any moral law. Frankfurt's point is that they are effective and functioning in human lives without a prior 'scientific' formulation, and that they are the basis of all ensuing formulations of moral norms. Thus, the moral laws, as based in our volitional necessities or natural inclinations, are objective, even though they are not evident to our theoretical reason before our nature enacts itself in loving and living. Rather, they only become evident to our reason after they have functioned as actually structuring our loves, and thus our practical reasoning and judgment. The reasons of love are the reasons of our volitional nature enacted.

JONATHAN J. SANFORD

Aristotle, Aquinas, and the Christian Elevation of Pagan Friendship

A theoretically adequate understanding of the Christian conception of friendship requires both a significant adoption and adaptation of the pagan Aristotle's reflections on friendship. To argue for this thesis, I explore in this paper how Aquinas uses his own understanding of the uniquely Christian conception of love to resolve four difficulties in Aristotle's theory that arise from a comparison between our three greatest objects of love: God, our friends, and our selves.[1] These difficulties, which I call Love's Dilemmas, result from the cross purposes that self-love and love of other as another self put us in. I explore the steps in Aristotle's treatment of love and friendship that force him into these quandaries, then Aristotle's solutions to the first three of them, and then look to how Aquinas resolves all four of them. Aristotle's difficulties prove enduring for some Aristotelians, but not for Christian Aristotelians following Aquinas's lead.

I. Aristotle on the Formation of Fulfilling Friendships

One finds in Aristotle's reflections two prerequisite conditions for friendship to obtain. These are more or less well met in perfect and imperfect friendships respectively, and can be characterized as self-love and commu-

1. See also, L. Gregory Jones, in "The Theological Transformation of Aristotelian Friendship in the Thought of St. Thomas Aquinas," in *The New Scholasticism* 61 (1987): 373–99.

nity.[2] About either of these two conditions a legitimate claim to ultimate priority can be made. Self-love is prior with respect to the sorts of voluntary relationships we undertake. The community is prior with respect to the involuntary relationships and the obligations born from them that undergird the voluntary ones, such as those we owe our parents.[3] From one's parents, one receives goods of an elemental sort—that is, goods without which other goods are impossible, such as life, and so the recipient is eternally in debt. These, and others like them (Aristotle mentions particularly the relation between teacher and student), are at their best unequal friendships, not because they cannot be grounded on the pursuit of virtues as supreme goods, but because the mutual love and affection one finds in them is disproportional between the two parties. However, in a fulfilling friendship between equals which has been voluntarily pursued, the reception and distribution of benefits is mutual, the goods shared are profoundly important (though not as elemental as life), and the reciprocated love and affection, which is a certain perfection of community, is proportional between the parties.

Aristotle's ethics, taken as a whole, is predicated on what I am calling self-love. The task of the mature moral agent is to pursue well his happiness, which is the activity of his soul in accordance with complete excellence (I, 13, 1102a 5–6). It is because, amongst other things, friendship (*φιλία*) is, "indeed some excellence, or is with excellence" (VIII, 1, 1155a 3–4), that Aristotle undertakes its examination in Books VIII and IX of the *Nicomachean Ethics*. Aristotle leaves open the question whether friendship really is an excellence (*ἀρετή*), or merely an activity involving excellence. Even if we count friendship to be an excellence, it is still left open whether it is an excellence surpassing justice, or the greatest type of justice (VIII, 1, 1155a 26–28).[4] In any event, Aristotle tends to analyze friendship in the

2. For more extensive treatments, see chapters 14–16 of John M. Cooper's, *Reason and Emotion* (Princeton, New Jersey: Princeton University Press, 1999); Lorrain Smith Pangle, *Aristotle and the Philosophy of Friendship* (Cambridge: Cambridge University Press, 2003); and Suzanne Stern-Gillet, *Aristotle's Philosophy of Friendship* (Albany: State University of New York Press, 1994).

3. Aristotle, *Ethica Nicomachea*, ed. I. Bywater (Oxford: Clarendon Press, 1954 [1894]), VIII 14, 1163 b 13–27. Translations to follow are my own. (All references to the *Nicomachean Ethics* are hereafter placed in the text, in parentheses.) I have consulted those of W.D. Ross in *The Complete Works of Aristotle*, Vol. 2, ed. Jonathan Barnes (Princeton, New Jersey: Princeton University Press, 1995 [1984]).

4. See Robert Sokolowski's "Phenomenology of Friendship," *Review of Metaphysics* 55 (2002): 451–70.

same way he analyzes excellences. Like the excellences, friendship is not simply expedient, but καλόν (beautiful and noble), and choice-worthy for that reason alone (VIII, 1, 1155a 28–29). In seeking friendships we seek some good for ourselves, but Aristotle's claim regarding the structure of fulfilling friendships indicates that friends are goods of a special sort: "The marks of friendship towards one's neighbors, and those things by which friendships are defined, seem to have emanated from one's relation to himself" (IX, 4, 1166a 1–2). The degree of intimacy in friendships implied here could not be greater, and it is this intimacy that make of our friends goods of a unique sort. Nevertheless, the grounds for this claim of intimacy with our friends ought to strike us as odd, given Aristotle's own rejection, at the end of Book V (V, 11, 1138b 5–8), of the Platonic notion of justice as a virtue of the self in anything more than a metaphorical sense. Aristotle registers a similar unease about whether a man can, in the literal sense, be a friend with himself in Book IX (IX, 4, 1166a 33–1166b 2), but he does not let this prevent him from using the metaphor of friendship with, or love for, oneself as a model for friendship in its literal sense.

What is it about love for oneself that provides the paradigm for friendships with others? In loving himself, a man wishes first to live, then to live well, and to continue to live well as the self he is, a self that Aristotle designates as being particularly identifiable with that part of himself by which he thinks—his *νοῦς* (IX, 4, 1166a 17–19). It is these same things that a man wishes for his friend, "for he is related to his friend just as he related to himself (for indeed, his friend is another self)" (IX, 4, 1166a 30–32). Friendships are then not merely great goods that humans choose to pursue; they are rather extensions and permutations of our very selves. They are, to borrow Plato's expression, ourselves writ large, written, that is, in such a way that we can read ourselves in them. This transference of self-love to love of another as oneself indicates the point of perfection of that other prerequisite of friendship, namely community.

One way to see the necessary role of community in fulfilling friendships is to note again friendship's similarity to justice. Aristotle marks out one of the distinctive features of justice vis-à-vis the other excellences, as the good of another (V, 1, 1130a 3–5). Friendship holds this distinction, too. Every type of friendship implies some type of community (VIII, 12, 1161b 11), but in the maximally fulfilling friendships, it is not enough merely to wish well for our friends and to have that wishing well reciprocated. We must be mutual goods to each other, and goods of the greatest sort. That is why Aristotle writes that, "To a friend we say one ought to wish him good for his own sake" (VIII, 2, 1155b 31); and, "Indeed, the good person in becoming a friend becomes a good to his friend" (VIII, 5, 1157b 33–34). The good that the good friend becomes to his friend is, in fact, the very same good that his own friend has become to him: a shared path to, and sharer in, what Aristotle eventually argues to be the greatest activity, contemplation.

Aristotle argues that friendship is necessary to our happiness, and gives three reasons for why a person, if he or she is to be happy, needs friends. The first two of these reasons would seem to reduce friendships to instrumental, rather than constituent, goods.[5] The first does this by claiming we need friends because they are goods to us (IX, 9, 1169b 8–10), the second, by claiming we need friends so as to have others to whom to do good things (IX, 9, 1169b 10–14). If these were, in fact, the main reasons for why we, to be happy, need friends, then our motivation for pursuing friendships would be no better than a consistent utilitarian would have for doing anything: that is, opting for the result of a calculation concerning maximization of benefits. But Aristotle is no Benthamite, and, as we would expect, these are not the only, or by any stretch the most important, reasons. There is a third reason which points to what Mansini has aptly termed, "the intrinsic goodness of friendship."[6] It is with this third reason that we can see our friends truly to be constituent goods of our happiness.

This third, more natural (φυσικώτερον), and most important reason why the flourishing person needs friends is predicated on the observation that life essentially is perceiving and thinking (IX, 9, 1170a 18–19), a claim that Aristotle makes not just in this chapter but at the height of his description of God in the *Metaphysics*, where he claims that the actuality of thought is life, and that God himself is that actuality.[7] The highlights of Aristotle's third argument, that which reveals the deepest reason for why friendship is naturally desirable for a virtuous person (IX, 9, 1170a 13–14), stress the fundamental desirability of life and the social nature of the hu-

5. Martha Nussbaum, *The Fragility of Goodness* (Cambridge: Cambridge University Press, 1986), 365.

6. Guy Mansini, "Aristotle on Needing Friends," *American Catholic Philosophical Quarterly* 72 (1998): 405–17, 407.

7. Aristotle, *Metaphysics* XII, 7, 1072b 26–27.

man being (IX, 9, 1170b 3–12, 19). Our friends complete our social nature. They are, for us, mirrors for ourselves, since "we are able to contemplate better those living near us than ourselves and their actions better than our own" (IX, 9, 1169b 33–35).

The irreplaceable goods of sharing insights and perceptions, of discussing matters of the greatest moment as well as those more trivial, represent some of the most satisfying activities of beings who are from the very beginning of their lives communal. But it is precisely the activities of perception and thought that are most godlike. It is not merely our social natures that are fulfilled in this activity, but our social nature as emblematic of that best thing in us—our mark of divinity (X, 7, 1177b 26–1178a 8). It is our friends who are our best helpmates in bringing to actuality our best potentiality, and it is we in turn who do this for our friends. Through such relationships, friends enable each other to do the most beautiful of deeds, securing for themselves as well as for the common good all the greatest goods (IX, 8, 1169a 7–11). At their apex, these friendships encourage and enable those activities which lead to divinization.

II. Frustration at the Heart of Fulfilling Friendships: Aristotle and Love's Dilemmas

To be sure, becoming divinized is a great good for any man, but its achievement, when measured from Aristotle's perspective, would seem to come at considerable cost, most importantly including: (Cost 1) the loss of one's human nature; (Cost 2) the loss of one's friends; and, (Cost 3) the loss of oneself as a friend to one's friends. It is clear that these losses will indeed result from divinization because to be a god implies, amongst other things, the following: first (Implication of Divination 1),[8] to be so far beyond the limits of human association as to be incapable of being in any sort of community open to friendship with mere mortals (VIII, 7, 1158b 33–36); and second (Implication of Divinization 2) to enjoy the perfection of self-sufficiency, which for Aristotle implies the continuous activity of thinking thought itself for those who aspire to be God (or thinking oneself if one is God),[9] and entails an absolute lack of concern for any others, even

8. See Aristotle, *Magna Moralia* II, 11, 1208b 27–30.

9. Aristotle, *Metaphysics* XII, 9, 1074b 15–30.

to the point of making no provisions for the development of moral virtue (X, 8, 1178b 3–23).[10]

It is self-love that motivates us to pursue complete friendships, and so, too, is it self-love that sets us on the path to divinization as the most complete realization of our potential flourishing, the primary mark of which is the activity of contemplative wisdom (X, 7, 1177a 12–18). Aristotle leaves unresolved the question of whether this best thing in us is divine or just divine-like, and the extent of his conviction that it is possible to complete the process of divinization is hard to gauge. Nevertheless, the exhortation to model ourselves as much as possible on God's contemplative activity is clear enough (X, 7, 1177b 30–31, 33–34; 1178a 2–3, 5–7), even if how exactly that is possible for beings who are wed to knowing through abstraction from sense-perceptions is not. The happiness that flows from our human life, a life of just and brave acts, and of friendly relations, is merely secondary in comparison to the exalted life of a self-sufficient god (X, 8, 1178a 9–21), and Aristotle implies an obligation to live according to the best thing in us, which is derived from that view of flourishing upon which the whole of Aristotle's ethics is predicated (I, 7, 1097b 20–1098a 7). If we are to be all we can be, then we must strive with all our might to be a god, even if that means leaving our friends behind.

Aristotle does not shrink from facing the difficulty his exhortation to become divine raises for what we are to wish for our friends, suggesting that in fact one *should hold back* from wishing for his friend to become divinized (VIII, 7, 1159a 3–8). One of the friends becoming a god means the end of the friendship, for there is no friendship between god and man once measurable equality has been stretched beyond its breaking point (VIII, 7, 1158b 29–34). Is it possible, then, for an Aristotelian thoroughly to love his friend as himself? It is in Aristotle's proposed solution, or as Aquinas saw it, dual solution,[11] to this riddle that we see love of self, and love of other as self, break down; for we must conclude that, for a strict Aristotelian, the answer to the question is "no" (VIII, 7, 1159a 8–12). Aristotle stresses that we are to wish the greatest goods *to the human being* in friendship; that is to say, to the human being *qua* human being, not to the human being *qua* potential divinity. We want to keep our friend, not lose him, even if he should

10. See Jerome G. Hanus, OSB., in "Friendship in Aristotle's Ethics," *The Modern Schoolman* 50 (1973): 351–63.

11. Thomas Aquinas, *Sententia libri Ethicorum*, 1637–38.

be lost because he has received the greatest of all goods for himself. It is insofar as our friend is a human being that we wish for him the greatest goods, and we are, Aristotle suggests, wise to fall short of wishing him fully to actualize his potential divinity.

What breaks apart the harmonious composition of perfected self-love and community on display in Aristotle's solution to this riddle is the fact that we must still want *ourselves* to become divinized, and presumably so, too, must our friend want himself to become divinized, since he too is a good man. This is to say, the self-love that points ourselves and our friends ultimately in the direction of achieving self-sufficiency as gods entails that we want to move beyond our human friendships, but, at the same time, our desire to remain with our friends while still restricted to our human social lives (social lives that can and indeed optimally do include philosophizing together) makes us wish that our good friends not become gods. It is the case, then, that Aristotle's analyses of friendship and contemplation put our best wishes—the wish to become divinized and the wish to love our friends as other selves—at cross-purposes, for we want more for ourselves than we should want for our friends. It is precisely the unbridgeable inequality between gods and men, on the one hand, and the real possibility of our becoming gods, on the other, that forces Aristotle into a solution fraught with two inconsistencies: *we do want to become gods, but we also do not want our friendships to cease; and we do wish the best goods for our friends, but we do not wish for them their greatest good.* There are three dilemmas that can be derived from these two inconsistencies. Aristotle's wisdom is to be found in recognizing them as problems, but his attempted solutions to them leave much to be desired.

(Dilemma 1) Should we really wish for ourselves the greatest good of divinization, which entails complete self-sufficiency, at the cost of our distinctively social human nature; or ought we to prefer our human estate over actualizing our potential for divinization? Aristotle answers that "yes," we should strive our upmost for divinization, given the fact that the intellect most of all is our essence and that its most perfect activity is what constitutes our greatest happiness.

(Dilemma 2) Should we wish our friends the greatest goods, including their divinization, at the cost of depriving us of their friendship and love; or should we wish them to remain our friends at the cost to them of actualizing their potential for divinization? Aristotle's answer is "no," we should not wish our friends to become divinized, for to do so is contrary to our desire to hold on to all true goods, and surely friendship is one of the greatest of those. So, even though we want ourselves to become gods, we do not want our friends to escape our human community, which is a necessary condition to our enjoying their friendship.

(Dilemma 3) Should we wish ourselves the greatest goods, including our divinization, at the cost of depriving our friends of the good of our own friendship and love; or, should we, out of love for our friends, be willing to forgo actualizing our potential for divinization? This I take to be a related, but different, question to that posed in the first dilemma. The first asks whether we should really want to abandon all that belongs to us *qua* our human estate. This third question asks whether our love for our friends should extend to a special concern that our friend have all the goods he wants. The most fulfilling friendships are based on mutual goodwill and affection, and to want to escape the bonds of our friendship for the sake of becoming divinized seems to entail, even if not fully realized, a willingness to deprive our friends of a great good, namely ourselves. If we are honest about this, we would realize that this is, in fact, to wish for our friends an evil. Aristotle seems not to appreciate the full force of this third dilemma, but it is clear that his answer to this question would be "yes," we ought to wish our own divinization even though it entails an evil for our friends.

Aristotle's answers to these dilemmas give rise to a fourth difficulty. Aristotle insists, not just upon the compatibility, but also upon the unity of all the virtues (V, 1, 1130a 5–13; VI, 13, 1144b 30–1145a 11). But if one becomes a god, then, on Aristotle's understanding, the moral virtues which guide our passions are abandoned (X, 8, 1178b–23), which undermines the claim regarding the unity of the virtues. Hence: (Dilemma 4) An Aristotelian must give up on the unity of the virtues, or give up on his treatment of love and friendship.

III. Overcoming Love's Dilemmas: Aquinas on Friendship with God and Neighbor

My claim is that Aquinas overcomes Love's Dilemmas in his treatment of *caritas* in the *Summa theologiae*. What I mean by this is not that Aquinas provides the contrary answer to each of these dilemmas, but that his own unique absorption of the Aristotelian treatment of love and friendship into a Christian model eliminates Love's Dilemmas altogether. Yet, it must be said, Aquinas makes no mention of these problems in the *Summa theologiae*,[12] or that he is solving them.[13] I am then claiming for Aquinas's treatment of love and friendship more success than he himself acknowledges.[14]

I turn here only to those parts of Aquinas's treatment of love and friendship that are needed to show that he provides the denouement for the point of crisis in Aristotle's story.[15] I draw, moreover, from a portion of Aquinas's work that is explicitly theological, and this for two main reasons. First, although Aquinas treats of friendship in several places,[16] it is his treatment of charity in *ST* II-II, qq. 23–27 that represents the full flowering of his theory. Second, it is Aristotle himself who has introduced the theological perspective on friendship with his speculations about divinization and its effect on human friendship, and thus it is fitting to respond to the difficulties he raises in kind.

There are, so to speak, three directions Aquinas's treatment of love and friendship takes in addressing Love's Dilemmas. First, he moves *below* the depth that Aristotle's treatment reaches, insofar as God's love for us is prior to all our loves, and so undergirds every friendship, including friendship with God. Second, he moves *above* what Aristotle considers the ceiling of human associations, stretching the human community to the heavens. Third, he penetrates far deeper *into* the intrinsic goodness of human friendship, by showing how it is not just modeled on the good that is God's own, but is brought to even greater perfection by joining in God's own activity. The first two directions are locatable in the initial questions on *caritas* in the *ST* II-II, qq. 23–27, but the third stretches us beyond those questions and is to be found in a consideration of God's inter-personal relationship within his Trinitarian nature.

We find the two necessary prerequisites in the Aristotelian model of

12. See David H. Calhoun's "Can Human Beings Be Friends of God?" *The Modern Schoolman*, 66 (1989): 209–19.

13. Aquinas, *Sententia libri Ethicorum*, 1637–38.

14. Thomas Aquinas, *Summa theologiae* (hereafter ST) II-II, q. 26, a. 7 and qq. 184–186 need to be discussed for a fuller defense of my claim.

15. For more comprehensive accounts, see Don Adams, "Love of God *And* One's Neighbor: Thomistic Charity," *Faith and Philosophy* 11 (1994): 207–23; Joseph Bobik, "Aquinas on Friendship with God," *American Catholic Philosophical Quarterly* 60 (1986): 257–71; David M. Gallagher, "Desire for Beatitude and Love of Friendship in Thomas Aquinas," *Medieval Studies* 58 (1996): 1–47; and Daniel Schwartz, *Aquinas on Friendship* (Oxford: Clarendon Press, 2007).

16. Aquinas, *ST* I-II q. 4, a. 8 denies that we need human friends to complete our happiness,

friendship to be still operable in Aquinas's self-love and community. Aquinas adds a new dimension to these prerequisites, however, one that undergirds them both when, by identifying *caritas* with *amicitia*,[17] he grounds these two prerequisites on a deeper community, namely that between God and man.[18] God first loves us, and calls us his friends.[19] This love expresses itself to us as God's own happiness, which is our end and object.[20] God's happiness, like all of God's perfections, is one with himself, and so in communicating to us his happiness as our end, God has presented to man, as the very foundation of charity, his own self. It is by means of the Incarnation of the second person of the Trinity that this fellowship with God is made possible. It is through the Son's *kenosis* that the radical inequality between God and man, which renders friendship between God and man impossible for Aristotle, is overcome and the human community is stretched into the heavenly.

God, then, serves as the principal object of charity. Aquinas argues in *ST* II-II, q. 27 that God is to be loved not just first, but directly (a. 4), wholly (a. 5), and without measure (a. 6). Aquinas is careful to show in qq. 26–27, however, that this love does not stop with God, but extends to three other objects: our selves, our neighbors, and our bodies, and in that order. The reasons that love for oneself is prior to love for one's neighbors are both scriptural and philosophical. Both Leviticus 19:18 and Matthew 22:39 command us to love our neighbors as ourselves. The biblical mandate clearly holds up the love we have for ourselves as a model for the love we ought to have for our friends.

By way of extra-biblical reasons, Aquinas argues that man is a unity with himself, which is a state more powerful than being unified in fellowship with his friends;[21] and this love (*amor*), which is not strictly speaking friendship (*amicitia*), because it is the expression of self-unity and not merely the union of community, provides the foundation upon which we

---

but does not deny that we need friendship to be happy. Progress on a description of friendship in earlier sections is assumed in the treatment of supernatural friendship in *ST* II-II, qq. 23–27.

17. See Paul J. Wadell, C.P. *Friendship and the Moral Life* (Notre Dame, Indiana: University of Notre Dame Press, 1989).

18. Aquinas, *ST*, II-II, q. 23, a. 1.

19. Aquinas, *ST*, II-II, q. 23, *sed contra*, citing John 15:15.

20. Aquinas, *ST* II-II, q. 23, a. 4.

21. Aquinas, *ST* II-II, q. 25, a. 4.

incorporate our friends into our friendship for God. We see, then, that Aquinas affirms those same Aristotelian points of community and self-love as origins for friendship.

God's befriending us is absolutely prior, and it perfects the natural love we have for ourselves, which is our will for perfection; and out of the combination of these two loves, our love for our neighbor grows.[22] For Aquinas, the richest community is a community of love whose source is God himself. We are indeed unified with our neighbors, but the foundation of that unity is our association with God himself. Aquinas argues that one sign that we ought to love ourselves more than our friends is that we ought not to follow our friends when they would lead us into sin. We are to brook no fellowship that jeopardizes the one God has founded with us, and it is precisely this fellowship with God that we share with our true friends.

What, then, we are to love in our friends (if we are to love them rightly) is *their own* participation in God's happiness.[23] We find in this notion echoes of Aristotle's claim that in regarding our friends we are in fact contemplating the perfection we ourselves are participating in. For Aquinas, it is clear that what human friends are contemplating in perfected friendship is both their individual *and* their mutual participation in God's happiness, which is God himself.

Finally, it seems that we can find one other way in which Aquinas's identification of *amicitia* with *caritas* oversteps the dilemmas we found in Aristotle. This consideration takes us beyond the explicit comments Aquinas makes in *ST* II-II, qq. 23–27, but certainly not beyond what is implied in those questions.[24] For Aristotle, part of God's perfection is his self-sufficiency. This entails the lack of all need, including, as Aristotle sees it, the need for any community. For Aquinas, on the other hand, God is the perfected community itself—a community of superabundant activity, rather than one of need-based co-dependency. God is a Trinity of persons who models in his own nature the community we can, through Christ, hope to be adopted into. The happiness that God communicates to us, and that serves as the foundation both for our perfected self-love and our perfected love of neighbor as ourselves, is the shared beatitude of the community of Divine Persons.

22. Aquinas, *ST* II-II, q. 26, a. 4.

23. Aquinas, *ST* II-II, q. 25, a. 12.

24. See, again, Jones's article, cited above (note #1).

Aquinas's understanding of God's self-revelation as a God of redeeming love in the Incarnation enables him to overcome the weaknesses of Aristotle's treatments of love and friendship *without* abandoning the principles of Aristotle's theory. What makes this possible is the expansion of the human community to make room for the divine. God becomes like us, and having thus entered the human family makes possible our reception into the divine. Aristotle's fundamental limit on friendship, that friendship always presupposes community, remains intact. What changes is a radical expansion of our community. With this expansion, there is no longer a conflict between wishing what is best for ourselves and what is best for our friends: we both wish and work towards our mutual divinization, and in doing so we strive to bring to still greater perfection our incorporation into the community which is the Trinitarian God. The apparent conflict between the virtues of contemplative wisdom and friendship is overcome, for our one true goal of perfected good—our happiness in contemplative union (*visio*) with God—is that which we share with our friends, and so remains motivationally consistent as that goal towards which right reason directs us throughout all our choices, including those that involve our friends.

Not only is friendship with God the goal of a well lived Christian life, and our love for our friends perfected rather than defeated through our incorporation into God's activity, but this charity provides the very form, or essence, of all the virtues by serving as their efficient cause.[25] Since each of the virtues has its efficient cause in charity, we find in charity the ultimate point of unity between all of the virtues. Thus, we discover, as well, a way for an Aristotelian not to have to face a choice between giving up on the unity of the virtues or on an Aristotelian treatment of love and friendship. This difficulty, like the others, no longer exists for the Christian Aristotelian who follows Aquinas in grounding all goods in God's charity.[26]

25. Aquinas, *ST* II-II, q. 23, a. 8 ad 1.

26. Thanks to members of the American Maritain Association and the Philosophy Department of Niagara University for their comments, and to Pamela Osborn.

JOSÉ MARIA J. YULO

Love's Imperative

A Study of Kant and Kolbe

> *Let us follow for a moment the clue of the martyr and the suicide; and take the case of courage.... He must not merely cling to life, for then he will be a coward, and will not escape. He must not merely wait for death, for then he will be a suicide, and will not escape. He must seek his life in a spirit of furious indifference to it; he must desire life like water and yet drink death like wine.*
>
> —G. K. Chesterton[1]

When commenting on the residual, though potent, effects that Thomas Hobbes' *Leviathan* has had on the Western mind since its inception, former Franciscan University Professor Benjamin Wiker struck a lamentable note. Wiker cited the coupling of humanity's most sundry or sordid desires legitimized as "rights," and the construction of governments to guarantee in effect such liberties.[2] This, Wiker saw as becoming more and more commonplace as modern society struggled to discover, or perhaps rediscover, a non-transcendent morality. The rationality of Hobbes's own ensuing Age of Enlightenment seemingly held little sway in the public ethos, as Wiker correctly pointed to the Englishman's paradigm being a product of willful declaration, rather than reasoned argument.[3]

1. G. K. Chesterton, *Orthodoxy* (New York: Image Books, 2001), 94.
2. Benjamin Wiker, *10 Books that Screwed Up the World* (Washington, DC: Regnery Publishing, 2008), 31.
3. Wiker, *10 Books*, 37.

When faced with this accordingly short, nasty, and brutish perspective on human nature, today's students normally pursue one of two alternatives. First, there is the begrudging, yet inevitable, embrace of dismal turgidity—a rationalization at some points born of reflex, at others of premature cynicism. Second, there appears a partial acceptance of the premise, but a rejection of the declaration-spawned conclusion.

In the pursuit of the latter avenue, the non-transcendent sourcing of morality is maintained. However, instead of resignedly coping with central-planning-generated virtues, a reborn, humanly-derived system of ethics is offered. Integral to this, however, is the establishment of reason as the chief agency through which one acts ethically. Unlike ancient pagan philosophy, the realm of the *eide* is ventured upon, this time without any Socratic *daimon* as travel guide. There are few thinkers who so closely approach these hinterlands as Immanuel Kant. Kant's categorical imperative is possibly the most refined of the non-transcendent ethical systems, though the contemporary secular culture at times seems blithely unaware of its tenure.

This being said, there are two points of intrigue with regard to the German's thought. From what, exactly, does the imperative come? Since Kant is dealing with a purely human source of his moral philosophy, this would of necessity emanate from nowhere else. Next, what are the extents of its commands, or put in another way, can Kant's moral vision lead to theistic philosophy's cardinal virtue, love? The categorical imperative may possibly arrive at human goods, even those shared by a majority of persons. However, can these goods equate with the call to community and sanctity found in Christian thought?

For the purpose of providing a paradigm for these latter queries, this paper will set Kant's philosophy against the life of Fr. Maximilian Kolbe. Fr. Kolbe, the martyr of Auschwitz, led a life of love for God and his fellow man so whole in its calling that one, at times, is unsurprised by his final and most famous act of sacrifice. In allowing his life to be exchanged for a prisoner designated to die from isolation at the baleful camp, the Pole bore testament to his faith's highest ideals. What prompted his final, fateful choice? And how close does his faith's own imperative approach love? The priest will be compared to Kant in that the former, through his faith, presented an adherence to something beyond human imperatives. Ultimately, this essay will seek to answer whether the differences between imperatives and attainments truly separate Kant from Kolbe.

In Kant's *Fundamental Principles of the Metaphysics of Morals,* the German arrived at the conclusion that nature intended what was best for the human will. Nature, a seemingly benevolent, albeit intentionally deliberate entity in itself, granted reason as the means through which a good will was achieved. Contrasted to the siren song of the inclinations, reason sought "the establishment of a good will as its highest practical destination."[4] Kant claimed this end of the good will to be likewise determined by reason, the faculty hastening the will's arrival to said destination. This arrival effectively served as reason's only source of satisfaction.

Building from this spare infrastructure, Kant next intended to elaborate on the concept of a likewise minimalist will which was "highly esteemed for itself, and is good without a view to anything further."[5] The concept of duty was, therefore, necessary in this task although it hinted at various non-objective limitations. Leaving aside actions undertaken with duty in mind, since these may be duly affected by inclinations, Kant stressed the importance of acting "from duty."[6]

Here, several beneficial avenues to action are opened. It is a duty, for example, to maintain one's life. Kant emphasized, however, that this call to action ought not to be done "as duty requires"[7] because there are human inclinations which direct this course. Rather, the preservation of life should be performed without regard to self-love, and without trepidation. Hence, the only remaining command would stem *from* duty, which gave the act "moral worth."[8]

Kant added the capacity to be "beneficent when we can"[9] to the possible motivations for acting as from duty requires. For this, he hypothesized the sorrowful philanthropist, an individual so immersed in his own misgivings that he did and could not feel the plight of those who potentially might benefit from his generosity. This melancholy effectively divorced the philanthropist from his fellow man, thus severing any inclination to do good for the purposes of bettering his community. In this case, should the donor somehow manage to wrest himself away from his troubles to act benevolently toward his objects, simply moving from the direct commands of duty, he might possess "genuine moral worth."[10]

4. Immanuel Kant, *Fundamental Principles of the Metaphysics of Morals,* trans. Thomas K. Abbott (Indianapolis: Bobbs-Merrill, 1949), 14.

5. Kant, *Fundamental Principles,* 14.

6. Ibid., 15.

7. Ibid.

8. Ibid.

9. Ibid.

10. Ibid., 16.

Apart from these two alternatives to acting *from* duty, Kant reinforced fundamental principles of the singular linearity of such actions. The objects of benefit from dutiful acts are not to be the main focus, since the moral worth of "an action done from duty derives ... not from the purpose which is to be attained, but from the maxim by which it is determined...."[11] Hence, what is of import is strictly the will, or "principle of volition,"[12] bolstering said acts.

Lastly, Kant elevated acting from duty to being akin to following legal statutes. Here, "Duty is the necessity of acting from respect for the law...."[13] Proceeding from a mere inclination for a preferred effect on the object of an action is insufficient for Kant, insufficient because he "cannot have respect for it just for this reason that it is an effect and not an energy of the will."[14] Inclinations are to be overcome, not simply by neglecting them, but rather by allowing them to be overwhelmed by something more objectively powerful. The victor in this sense is a will-spawned law. It is not difficult to see a Mosaic Golden Calf caveat with this final fundamental of duty. Following acting from duty, and stressing the will and not the object of benefit, what seems to command Kant is a humanly-derived metaphysical principle: obeying a law because the will has stripped away all tangential inclination, revealing at last an imperative which the subject wills to be there.

Returning home to nature's initial effort to employ reason to bring about a good will, Kant asked "what sort of law that can be the conception of which must determine the will, even without paying any regard to the effect expected from it, in order that this will may be called good absolutely and without qualification?"[15] Kant offered what would come to be the calling card for his moral thought, the categorical imperative: the law an individual establishes as worthy of respect, owing to its being a product of duty as previously discussed, that wherein "I am never to act otherwise than so that I could also will that my maxim should become a universal law."[16]

It is worthwhile noting some peculiar instances that occur within Kant's chain of reasoning leading to the categorical imperative. Somehow, nature endows human beings with rationality, enabling them to reach good wills, as charted by reason. The command to act in accordance with such a

11. Ibid., 17.
12. Ibid.
13. Ibid., 18.
14. Ibid.
15. Ibid., 19.
16. Ibid.

will manifests itself in the form of duty, perhaps to emphasize the distance between such a motivation and acts born from inclination. These acts from duty are to be conceived in the most spare linearity, their worth being assessed via the will choosing them. Such a choosing will ought to adhere to a law it itself establishes, again to thwart any pull from desired-inclined effects. Up to this point, the linearity mentioned, which almost makes it seem that Kant's agent is acting in a vacuum, is an abundantly solitary endeavor. Individuals are to act with little regard to anything other than themselves. Suddenly, however, when the objective, culminating law that finally indicates a good will is formed, it is broadcast to humanity writ large, perhaps paralleling the theoretical expansion *ex nihilo* of the universe. We know what is best for each other by coming up with moral goods while completely being divorced from each other.

Similar observations have been found throughout historical analysis of Kantian ethics. The Oxford Jesuit Fr. Frederick Copleston, when commenting on the German as part of his *A History of Philosophy*, pointed out that the set of acts done "in accordance with duty is much wider than the class of actions performed for the sake of duty."[17] The larger set of actions done in accordance with duty, which may possess variable shades of inclination, Copleston stated may not necessarily be "morally wrong."[18] However, these acts, according to Kant, lack moral worth since they are not performed from duty. In this case, Copleston posited the contrasting cases of a person who saved his own life because he had an inclination to do so, and of a suicide. In the former example, this may not be a moral act. However, it is not "an immoral action in the sense in which suicide is immoral."[19]

In addition, Copleston wrote of the odd proportionality represented by acting for duty's sake. Since Kant implies that greater moral value arises in proportion to the disinclination of performing such acts, it follows that, as Copleston put it, "the more we have to overcome ourselves to do our duty, the more moral we are."[20] Thus, provided an individual overcome his tendencies, "it seems to follow that the baser a man's inclinations are, the higher is his moral value. . . ."[21] To this, the Jesuit struck at the implicit Manichean, or Heraclitean paradigm of warring inclinations and duties. This view

17. Frederick Copleston, *A History of Philosophy* (New York: Image Books, 1994), vol. 6, 316.

18. Copleston, *History*, vol. 6, 316.

19. Ibid.

20. Ibid., 317.

21. Ibid.

would be contrary to the "integrated personality, in whom the inclination and duty coincide."[22] Likewise, Copleston realized the potential, if not deliberate, challenge this Kantian line of reasoning would present to natural law. This is most odd, in a sense, considering that the German endeavored to author, with reason as ghostwriter, a transcendent-free version of this *logos*.

Joining Copleston in this examination of Kant's ethical thought many years later was the contemporary British philosopher Roger Scruton. In his *A Short History of Modern Philosophy*, Scruton focused on the categorical imperative's vaunted objectivity. The categorical imperative's commands, written in terms of ought and should, may or may not reach validity, but as Scruton stated, "they certainly claim it."[23] Though the imperative may have been argued by Kant to possess *a priori* validity, this command presupposed a postulated ideal world. In this realm, "the agent sees himself as one among many, of equal importance with them, deserving and giving respect on the basis of reason alone, and not on the basis of those empirical conditions which create distinctions between people."[24] The agent, solely bound by his nature as a rational being, follows a moral law not merely universal, but necessary as well.

Scruton asked if the original Kantian claim to objectivity could be maintained. Noting the difficulties which begin arising from this point, particularly the adjudging of *a priori* validity of the categorical imperative, Scruton wrote that Kant "recognizes that it is no more sufficient in the case of practical reasoning than it is in the case of scientific understanding to make such a claim."[25] Ultimately, Kant "left the gap between his metaphysics and his morals unclosed."[26]

Notwithstanding these critiques on the possible limitations of Kantian ethical thought, it now follows to see whether these arguments help or hinder this most developed of non-transcendent moral systems in arriving at actions and states typically the province of theistic truths. In order to advance in this direction, an examination of the life and death of Fr. Maximilian Kolbe is required.

22. Ibid.

23. Roger Scruton. *A Short History of Modern Philosophy* (London: Routledge Classics, 1995), 154.

24. Scruton. *Short History*, 155.

25. Ibid., 156.

26. Ibid.

As a young man in his twenties, Maximilian Kolbe once asked his mother Maria, "Pray that I will love without limits."[27] The entreaty was most appropriate for the man later considered the martyr of Auschwitz. Before examining the act for which he is most famous—his decision to volunteer to suffer another man's death sentence—it would be worthwhile to delve into accounts of Fr. Kolbe's earlier life and career. From these, it is possible to construct a model offering unique perspectives regarding the ethical framework constructed by Kant.

In the spring of 1930, Fr. Kolbe and four accompanying Franciscan Brothers traveled via mail steamer to the Orient. Their destination was Japan where, in the city of Nagasaki, Fr. Kolbe would teach philosophy at the local seminary and publish a Japanese language religious magazine. The latter involved learning the language as quickly as possible while living in the most trying of conditions. The priest would often find himself sick from eating cuisine he was not accustomed to, coupled with his already complicating tuberculosis. However, as one of the Brothers put it: "We're sleeping on straw ... we eat from benches and sit on the ground. The poverty is extreme but we are very happy...."[28]

In addition to the well-suffered hardships, Fr. Kolbe had to return at intervals to Poland to give an accounting of his efforts to his superiors during Provincial Chapter meetings. Successfully convincing his audiences to allow him to found a friary and train Japanese who wished to join, Kolbe noted, "a good religious is good not because he does much, but because he obeys."[29]

Poverty alone could not drain the Franciscan's mission that aspired "to be one in will with Mary of the great fiat ... to be perfectly united to the will of God."[30] Through this unity of faith and will, Fr. Kolbe stressed to his flock the importance of allowing God to "transform you into a knight of love who, with others, will conquer the whole world, not in the sense of capturing it, but of freeing it."[31]

When war finally came to Poland, Kolbe and members of his friary were initially held at the internment camp of Amtitz. There the priest, facing starvation, caused his fellow inmates bewilderment by distributing his meager day's rations to the most needy prisoners. Soon, rumors began

27. Patricia Treece, *A Man for Others* (San Francisco: Harper and Row, 1982), viii.

28. Treece, *A Man for Others*, 46.

29. Ibid., 48.

30. Ibid., 73.

31. Ibid.

spreading of the prisoners' release. Younger Brothers implored Kolbe to hide himself at local convents for fear of what the Germans might do to him on the way home. As Plato once responded to Crito's plea, the priest refused the call and remained. God, said he, "wanted otherwise."[32] This steadfastness was later attributed by a fellow Franciscan to Kolbe's "supernatural obedience."[33]

A few points are most clear and distinct in these accounts illuminating the priest's character. Unlike Kant's good will, Kolbe's own volition does not itself spawn a course of duty it must follow. The trait of obedience appeared many more times in the various reminiscences on Kolbe's life. For those who knew him, this quality was perhaps only matched by Kolbe's piety. The priest's will was good because he surrendered it to an ultimately better one. This divine will assigned duties that, when followed, led not to a hypothesized ideal world, but to the real-world emancipation of all. It may be debated as to the presence or absence of any Kantian inclinations which possibly affected Fr. Kolbe's decisions and actions. However, since the priest humbly surrendered his will instead of allowing it the godlike abilities to author its own duties, it is reasonable to hold that Kolbe's will is freer from inclination than Kant's ideal good will. Kant divorces desired effects from his good will through duty. Ultimately, the adherence to self-duty is itself a desired effect. On the other hand, Kolbe allows another will, regarded as infinitely more benevolent than his own, to work through him.

In the end, this will which works through Kolbe can be best seen in the priest's actions during the summer of 1941 at the dreaded block 14 at Auschwitz. In response to the attempted escape of a fellow prisoner, Kolbe and five hundred and ninety-nine others were assembled and meticulously lined up in accordance to height by their German captors. The commanding officer at the time informed the prisoners that, though the lone escapee had been caught, ten of those assembled were condemned to die from starvation. Remarkably, Fr. Kolbe himself was passed over in the selection. Yet, when the condemned were being made ready for their dark fate, a forty-year-old Polish sergeant, Francis Gajowniczek, implored: "My wife and my children."[34]

Almost immediately, there appeared someone assertively, though peace-

32. Ibid., 85.

33. Ibid.

34. Ibid., 170.

ably, making his way through the ranks of those spared. It was Kolbe. In polite, flawless German, the priest announced, "I wish to make a request please.... I want to die in place of this prisoner."[35] The guards were dumbfounded, and Kolbe persisted, "I have no wife or children. Besides, I'm old and not good for anything. He's in better condition."[36] When commanded by the commandant to say who he was, he replied, "A Catholic priest."[37]

Even in the cramped, filthy, penal block chosen for the captives' slow execution from starvation, Kolbe led others in prayer and heard as many confessions as he could. So placid was the priest's suffering, a fate he bore for another, that the SS guards on call remarked: "*So einen wie diesen Pfarrer haben wir hier noch nicht gehabt. Das muss ein ganz aussergewohnlicher Mensch sein*; We've never had a priest here like this one. He must be a wholly exceptional man."[38] Finally, after two weeks, Fr. Kolbe was one of four surviving prisoners who were given fatal injections of carbolic acid. Upon death, an eyewitness account stated: "Father Kolbe was sitting upright.... His body was not dirty like the others, but clean and bright.... His eyes were open. Serene and pure, his face was radiant."[39]

Fr. Maximilian Kolbe's faithful obedience has been earlier noted. Yet aside from this separation from Kant's own humanly-derived imperative, there are more telling points of divergence made clearer by the priest's final act.

Previously, Kant's ethical framework was shown to be able to ascertain meticulously what was right for fellow human beings from the very distant and peculiar perch of being in conceptual isolation from them. This was not the case with Kolbe. Since the priest did not, through reason, manufacture routes to the good will via self-generated legal ordinances, he would seem to have been in constant contact with the transcendent source of his imperatives. It is this constant companionship with God, reminding the priest of his relationship to his fellow human beings, that solidifies Kolbe's final resolve. Love is more manifestly clear and possible when viewing oneself as part of a community of distinct fellows—a perspective Kant, for all his elegance in construction, does not maintain.

Next, the issue raised by Fr. Copleston deserves revisiting. The Jesuit argued that Kant favored actions born out of the rifts carved between in-

35. Ibid., 170–71.
36. Ibid., 171.
37. Ibid.
38. Ibid., 175.
39. Ibid., 176.

clinations and duties. As discussed, the more one has to overcome one's baser inclinations, the greater the moral value of the dutiful act. However, it is very possible that Maximilian Kolbe represented Copleston's integrated personality, one whose duties and inclinations in fact coincided. Simply from the historical accounts, Kolbe's actions in 1941 and before did not speak of the suppression of the priest's undisclosed desires, in order to provide for his flock. Rather, Kolbe almost joyously took to his assigned fate, alleviating the suffering of all save himself every step of the way. It raises the question whether Kant would have considered these examples of lesser moral worth by dint of Kolbe's being inclined to perform them.

Lastly, there is a fundamental difference in the way both Immanuel Kant and Fr. Maximilian Kolbe chose to deal with human inclinations. It is, up to this point, obvious that both men valued selflessness as central to their moral worldviews. That Kant was even able to arrive at this juncture *sans* a transcendent source for his categorical imperative was and is most noteworthy. A survey of the older and more modern secular moralities shows many who fall far short of the German's skill and adherence to reason. In fact, so telling is his work that modern secular ethicists' shortcomings in this field reflexively imbue Kant's theory with a touch of near-transcendence. However, to construct a moral duty and view it as a law is not, as Kant said, to overwhelm the inclinations; it is to choose not to deal with them.

Kolbe, like the savior he followed, wished and loved selflessly for the betterment of all, even his enemies. Though he may, as mentioned, have possessed inclinations which coincided with his duties, the priest knew all too well the limits of his mortal shell. To suffer the most dire torture, isolation, and death required Kolbe truly and fully to surrender his will to God's. Once done, he was able not merely to ignore the inclinations for survival, or to despair, but actually to confront these inclinations and reject them.

Whether or not Kant's categorical imperative would encompass the actions of Fr. Kolbe is subject to further debate. It remains to be seen whether the potentially universal command to alleviate human suffering clashes with a similar command to preserve one's own life in light of injustice. What is not arguable is the fundamental distinction between the natures of humanly and divinely derived ethical commands—the uniqueness, beyond human reason, of love's imperative.

IV

LOVE, FRIENDSHIP, AND THE POLITICAL COMMUNITY

JOHN J. CONLEY, SJ

Friendship and Political Virtue

Rereading Aristotle

Whereas contemporary ethics tends to confine the phenomenon of friendship to the sphere of the private, Aristotle conceived friendship as central to the public life of the *polis*. The virtues engendered by friendship were central for the execution of a citizen's duties toward fellow citizens and paramount for the successful functioning of the constitution of a particular state. The purpose of this paper is to examine the relationship between friendship and political order proposed by Aristotle in Book VIII of the *Nicomachean Ethics*[1] and to indicate its relevance for contemporary politics.

I. Aristotelian Friendship

For Aristotle, all political associations inevitably require the virtues of friendship because any commitment to justice requires affection for the others with whom one is pursuing a common goal. "Between friends there is no need for justice, but people who are just still need the quality of friendship; and indeed friendliness is considered to be justice in its fullest sense. It is not only a necessary thing but a splendid one" (VIII, 1, 1155a 25). As examples of political associations requiring interpersonal affection to pursue their collective aims, Aristotle cites religious guilds, artisan cooperatives, naval trusts, even military combines in which fellow soldiers agree on an

1. The citations from Aristotle are based on the Thomson-Tredennick translation. See Aristotle, *The Nicomachean Ethics*, trans. J. A. K. Thomson and Hugh Tredennick, 3rd ed. (London: Penguin Books, 2004). References to this work are hereafter placed within the text.

equitable division of plunder (VIII, 9, 1160a 9–30). Self-interest is not sufficient to ground such enterprises. Affection and fidelity for other members of the group, sealed through religious rituals and sacrifices, are essential for the durability and success of the association. In the broader *polis*, the pursuit of the common good by citizens under the tutelage of legitimate authority requires self-sacrificial esteem for fellow citizens if the *polis* is to have a reasonable chance of fulfilling its collective goals. Unaccompanied by its citizens' mutual sense of a common origin and a common destiny, the state cannot defend an order of justice shaped by the *telos* of the common good.

In the Aristotelian typology, human friendship operates along three dominant models. In the first type of friendship, that of utility, an affectionate relationship develops between several persons out of mutual interest in certain future benefits. The relationship is often hierarchical in nature: teacher/student; master/apprentice; expert/novice. In the second type of friendship, the erotic, the affection between the partners is focused on the acquisition of pleasure. Romantic relationships express both the intensity and the fragility of this particular form of affection. In the third type of friendship, the mature or the authentic, the partners love each other for their own sake, not because of the economic or romantic benefits the other partner might bring. In this atmosphere of disinterested but mutually sacrificial love, stable growth in virtue is the most assured.

Although the interpersonal esteem central to the execution of justice in the state bears characteristics of all three types of friendship, it bears principally the traits of the first, more utilitarian type: an affection built on mutual benefits through services rendered. "Friendships between fellow citizens and fellow tribesmen or fellow voyagers and such are more evidently friendships of association, because they seem to be based as it were on a sort of compact" (VIII, 12, 1161b 13–15). It is not the highest form of friendship, in which one is devoted to another simply for the other's sake. But the cardinal virtue of justice can neither be cultivated nor expressed independently of the virtues of social affection, such as benevolence, fostered by such mutually interested friendship.

For Aristotle, friendship is not simply a generic quality essential to political interaction; the virtues typical of particular kinds of friendship are necessary for the flourishing of specific types of political regimes. The father-child relationship perfects the type of directive benevolence essential for monarchy. The relationship between husband and wife, conceived as a type of mild subordination, develops the virtues of consultation and deference essential for aristocracy. The relationship among siblings encourages the virtues of egalitarian concertation necessary for a vibrant democracy.

The virtues of protectiveness and filial piety in the parent-child relationship parallel the benevolent virtues necessary for the proper relationship between a single ruler and subjects in a monarchy. "Analogies and patterns of these relationships can be found in the household. The association of a father with his sons has the form of monarchy, because he is concerned for the welfare of his children" (VIII, 10, 1161a 1). Father-son affection is rooted in the desire of the father to protect his children from harm. Similarly, the good monarch exercises his authority not for self-aggrandizement, as would a tyrant, but for the common good of the people he must govern and assist toward their moral perfection in virtue.

In the affection typical of husband and wife, the civic amity typical of an aristocratic regime emerges. A certain division, indeed partition, of duties in the governance of the family characterizes their amicable compact with each other. "The association of husband and wife is clearly an aristocracy. The man rules by virtue of merit, and in the sphere that is his by right; but he hands over to his wife such matters as are suitable for her" (VIII, 10, 1161a 3). Similarly, in an aristocracy, a small group of rulers shares the tasks of the governance of society through an equitable and differentiated share of the key political tasks. It is cabinet government rather than rule by the many. A respect for the specialized privileges of other members of the aristocratic class complements the friendly affection for the masses governed by the small elite. Tellingly, Aristotle condemns the tendency of the husband to usurp the prerogatives of the wife in an unbalanced marriage along with the tendency of unbalanced aristocratic governments to deteriorate into oligarchies no longer solicitous of the common good of the citizens under their command.

Affection among siblings most clearly parallels the mutual esteem that characterizes thriving democracies. It is the apprenticeship of affection for equals in a family that clearly parallels the respect for political peers that typifies a proper democratic regime. "The association of brothers resembles timocracy, because they are equals except insofar as they differ in age. Hence if the difference is great their friendship ceases to be brotherly. Democracy is most completely expressed in households where there is no master, for in them the members are all on an equal par" (VIII, 10, 1161a 5–7). It is this affection for one's political peer precisely as an equal in terms of civic dignity and governance that parallels the affection of siblings for each other. Unlike the strict if benevolent line of command that characterizes monarchy and the more subtle pattern of mutual deference that typifies aristocracy, the peer affection that marks healthy sibling relationships mirrors the egalitarian friendship that marks a thriving democratic *polis*. Aristotle's reference to the "households where there is no master" suggests how freewheeling and anarchic this affection among peers can be.

Aristotle's intertwining of the virtues typical of affectionate family relationships with the civic virtues essential to particular types of regime is not a simple exercise in analogy. As in the *Politics,* where Aristotle defends the primacy of the family in fostering the moral virtues essential to political life, the *Nicomachean Ethics* indicates how the virtuous friendship typical of domestic interrelationships can prepare the individual for the moral challenges of civic life. These challenges pivot around the capacity to manifest an affectionate loyalty toward other members of the *polis* as one pursues the work of justice. The experience of friendship in family life is propaedeutic to successful political interaction. Experiences of benevolence in the parent-child relationship sculpt a citizen ready to command and obey; experiences of mutual deference in the spousal relationship deepen the capacity to share power; experiences of sibling affection shape the ability to show respect toward one's fellow citizens as the peers they are. On the contrary, hateful or mediocre experiences in these central domestic networks of power create the conditions for political descent into tyranny, oligarchy, and the chaos of mob rule.

II. Critical Evaluation

Aristotle's conception of friendship as a central political virtue challenges certain presuppositions of contemporary democratic order. Unlike the Lockean-Hobbesian model of politics, in which individual self-interest is protected by the political order, Aristotle's conception of political order insists that the communal pursuit of justice requires the cultivation of specific moral virtues by each citizen. Love of one's political community and affectionate respect for the members of each community in which one functions are essential virtues of the citizen in any well-ordered state. In the pivotal analogy between the family and the state, the successful ordering of a given political community depends on the degree to which a critical mass of the members of the community has perfected the virtues of being a parent, a spouse, and a sibling. In other words, the capacity to act as a friend, bearing the affection toward others that transcends simple respect of their rights, is a necessary condition for the ability to act as a citizen in the promotion of the common good.

Aristotle's emphasis on the centrality of friendship in civic life also indicates how civic education, what is often called education for democracy in the United States, is rooted in the apprenticeship of the virtues of amity acquired in family life. A sense of civic duty emerges not primarily through the study of the laws of a particular community or of its history or of its current pressing problems. Rather, it emerges primarily in the experience of devotion toward the good in the parental exercise of authority, in the spousal exercise of consultation and deference, and in the sibling exercise of conflict resolution among peers. It is practical devotion toward the common good, and not a theoretical comprehension of the common good, that characterizes proper citizenship. The loyalty to one's fellow citizens, rooted in a sense of common source and end, can only surface through an apprenticeship in the varieties of friendly affection and commitment conducted in the family cell. It is here that the basic human relationships of power manifest their moral *telos* and their affective charge of mutual sympathy.

Finally, Aristotle's stress on the centrality of friendship in the political order challenges the distinction between the private and the public that typifies the politics of modernity. In this modern conception of the well-ordered state, the government occupies a public realm where the external actions of citizens are measured and judged by a set of public laws and institutions. The moral and emotive lives of citizens are largely confined to the private sphere of religion, family, nonpolitical associations, and networks of friendship. On the affairs of moral character, the modern state must remain largely agnostic. For Aristotle, such a dichotomy is untenable. The fortune of the state is largely built on the existence of a critical mass of citizens who have acquired the virtues of loyalty, devotion, and sacrifice in their interaction with others. Only such an ethical friendliness can motivate the willingness to give one's life for one's nation or to help one's neighbor in need beyond the strict minimum of the law. It is in the intimate circle of the family and of one's immediate friends that such civic virtues emerge. Rather than being separate from or opposed to the public sphere of the *polis*, the allegedly private spheres of the family and friendship networks fashion the virtues essential to civic society's moral grandeur, indeed to its very survival.

WILLIAM SWEET

Love and Dignity

Near the beginning of Jacques Maritain's essay "Amour et amitié," in a section on "the different kinds of human love," Maritain writes that truly human love—a love "in which the spirit is engaged"—is a "love on a level with man and human dignity."[1] That there is a connection between love and dignity is surely not surprising, but what that connection is may not be evident.

Maritain does not dwell on the issue of dignity in this essay on love and friendship. Yet this brief reference reminds us that when we ask what love requires of us, the answer is that 'practical love,' the 'doing good' which we are commanded to do in Matthew 5:44,[2] involves treating others with dignity and as beings of dignity.

The concept of 'dignity' has been recognized by many as a key moral, legal, and political notion. It is a notion, however, that has been increasingly contested by academics. It is on this aspect of practical love—on the dignity that *we all* are called on to recognize and to respect—that this paper focuses.

I begin with some brief comments about the place that the concept of dignity has had in ethics, law, and politics, and how dignity relates to individual freedom. I next indicate a few issues that have led some to argue that the concept of dignity is problematic and ought to be abandoned. In response, I provide a description of what dignity means and an explanation

1. Jacques Maritain, "Amour et amitié," *Notebooks* [*Carnet de notes*], trans. Joseph W. Evans (New York: Magi Books, 1984), 222.

2. "But I say to you, Love your enemies: do good to them that hate you." *Douay-Rheims*, Challoner version.

of different ways in which one might defend it. This will show, in conclusion, how the concept is essential to ethical and political decision-making, to expressing the proper limits of individual freedom, but also to understanding civic friendship and the love that we are called on to show towards one another.[3]

I

Dignity is a foundational principle of a number of charters and declarations of human rights and freedoms. We see it employed *explicitly* in the *Universal Declaration of Human Rights* [*UDHR*] (1948), in the 3rd and 4th Geneva Conventions (on the treatment of prisoners of war),[4] and, *implicitly*, in many bills and charters of rights, such as the *Canadian Charter of Rights and Freedoms* (1983). For example, the Preamble to the *UDHR* states that "recognition of the inherent dignity and of the equal and inalienable rights of all members of the human family is the foundation of freedom, justice and peace in the world," and the first article affirms that "All human beings are born free and equal in dignity and rights." There are references throughout the *UDHR* to dignity, and one might see all of the rights that it enumerates as aimed at ensuring it.[5]

The notion of dignity is also important because it often lies at the basis of our calls to act as autonomous beings—to have our freedom respected, and to restrict others from infringing on it. For example, when we look at the arguments of those defending "the right to die" (and hence for the legalization of euthanasia and physician-assisted suicide), they often refer to 'dying with dignity.' Appeals to dignity arise, of course, in other areas besides bioethics. In a recent case in Canada, where a young Sikh student had initially been forbidden from wearing his kirpan at school, the claim was made that schools had to "accommodate factors related to the unique capabilities and inherent worth *and dignity* of every individual, up to the point of undue hardship."[6]

3. In the discussion that follows, I draw on my paper "Whose Dignity is it Anyway?" presented at the Breakfast on the Hill lecture series, Parliament Hill, Ottawa, May 10, 2007. See *http://old.fedcan.ca/english/pdf/advocacy/BOHSweet0507.pdf.*

4. The (1949) *Convention*. Pt. I, Art. 3 prohibits "at any time and in any place whatsoever," any "Outrages upon personal dignity, in particular, humiliating and degrading treatment."

5. See, in particular, Articles 22 and 23.

6. Emphasis mine. *Canadian Human Rights Commission*, Balvir Singh Multani and Gurbaj

Dignity has a central place in law and politics as well—particularly because of its relation to our sense of identity as individuals but also as members of cultural, ethnic or religious groups. When our character, religion, or ethnic or cultural heritage is attacked, we see this as an attack on our dignity, and perhaps even on the dignity of others. We accept that others may rightly question our actions, but not our dignity.

Dignity is also important because of its place in our relations to others. Respect for another's dignity is part of the love (as Maritain puts it) "in which the spirit is engaged."[7]

Dignity, then, is a key, if not a fundamental ethical notion, underlying many of our claims to rights and to respect, as well as our life together in the state. If we are not more conscious of this, perhaps it is because we often take the recognition of our dignity for granted; as Thomas De Koninck notes, it is perhaps only when dignity is tested that we are most aware of it.[8]

II

Despite the wide recognition of dignity in ethics, law and politics, an increasing number of authors have found the concept, and its relation to individual freedom, perplexing and troublesome. Consider some of the recent debates in bioethics. On the one hand, we have appeals to 'death with dignity.' Here, individuals claim a right to do with their lives as they choose. To restrict a person's freedom here, it is argued, is to challenge her dignity as an autonomous rational being who can make informed decisions about her own life. On the other hand, we have restrictions concerning cloning or commercial surrogate motherhood; here, people *do not* have a right to do with their lives or their bodies as they choose, and one reason given is that to use one's body in such ways is inconsistent with human dignity. The source of this puzzle seems to lie within the notion of 'dignity' itself. Determining whether and when a person's life has dignity, and dying in a way that allegedly preserves one's dignity, seem to be matters that only the individual involved can judge; surely, it is said, the individual alone is the only and ultimate judge of the quality and dignity of her life. Yet, when we

---

Singh Multani v. Commission scolaire Marguerite-Bourgeoys and Attorney General of Quebec. See http://www.chrc-ccdp.ca/legislation_policies/factum/multani_toc_tdm-en.asp.

7. Maritain, *Notebooks*, 222.

8. *La dignité humaine*, ed. T. De Koninck and G. Larochelle (Paris: PUF, 2005), 19.

look at the wish of some women to engage in surrogate motherhood for profit, opponents—and the law in Canada—insist that human dignity is *not* an individual matter, but one which concerns society as a whole.

Thus, appeals to dignity are sometimes made when people seek to justify a freedom to make certain choices, but they are also sometimes made in order to limit them. Again, dignity is sometimes regarded as something that individuals determine for themselves, but at other times it is not.

Bioethics is not the only area where appeals to dignity seem to lead to problems or puzzles. Consider the issue of the treatment of prisoners and the morality of torture. One objection to torture is that it degrades people, treats them as objects, and robs them of their dignity. But is torture wrong if the stakes are high, and the chances of getting important information are good? As former US judge and Attorney General Alberto Gonzales famously wrote, in a 2002 memo to then President George W. Bush, the necessity of combating terrorism "renders obsolete Geneva's [i.e., the Geneva convention's] strict limitations on questioning of enemy prisoners."[9]

There seem to be other problems with the notion of human dignity as well. Some see it as simply too abstract and unverifiable—it cannot be observed or empirically tested, and appeals to it have no weight independent of pre-existing social consensus or the law. More radically, some have argued that the notion of dignity is an arbitrary cultural construction,[10] that there is nothing about human beings that justifies it, that it can and does vary from culture to culture, and that it need not always be respected. Finally, some hold that the term 'dignity' is too often used in partisan sloganeering[11]—generating more heat than light—and, so, is unhelpful in clarifying or resolving controversial issues.

It is, then, because appeals to dignity seem to be problematic or puzzling, or do not give us any "clear and unambiguous guidance" in difficult situations, that some, like the British bioethicist, Ruth Macklin, have ar-

9. See Michael Isikoff, "Memos Reveal War Crimes Warnings," *Newsweek*, May 17, 2004.

10. See Arthur L Caplan, "Dignity is a social construct," *British Medical Journal* 327 (2003) (24 December) http:// *www.bmj.com/cgi/eletters/327/7429/1419#44646*.

11. See, for example, Julie Mertus, "Mightier than the Sword: The Bush Administration's Flagging Human Rights Rhetoric," *Harvard International Review: Development and Modernization* 25 (2003). Mertus writes: "Equally troubling for those who support multilateral approaches to security and safeguarding justice is the document's replacement of human rights with the watery notion of "human dignity." … The White House's message is clear: the United States does not seek to champion human rights, but instead promotes an abstract substitute."

gued that the concept of dignity is vague and useless.[12] This is a position echoed by Harvard professor of psychology, Stephen Pinker.[13] These critics conclude that we simply ought to abandon the notion of dignity altogether in favour of other, presumably less ambiguous notions, such as 'respect for persons,' 'autonomy,' and 'human rights.' More and more people appear to be taking this advice. Despite the presence of the concept of dignity in many codes of ethics for healthcare professionals, in some of the standard textbooks in Canada on nursing ethics, dignity is neither discussed nor even included.[14]

III

Where does this leave us? Is dignity an important human value, or is it just a term, rooted in archaic theologies and philosophies, that has no place in contemporary ethics? Does it bear on our regard or love for one another—and for ourselves? Or is it just a piece of rhetoric?

The principal reason why the term 'dignity' has been problematic, I would suggest, is that it has been used carelessly, and confused with notions like 'autonomy,' 'respect for one's choices,' and 'pursuing one's own good in one's own way.' Because of the problems and puzzles noted above, then, we need to look more closely at the concept of dignity. To do this, I want to outline more carefully what dignity is and to whom it applies. Second, I want to comment on its source—i.e., where dignity is supposed to come from. Finally, I want to say something about what respect for dignity, clearly understood, requires of us.

IV

What is dignity? For an answer, it may be useful to examine a few of the contexts in which the term has had a place.

Dignity is, fundamentally, an ethical term used to indicate "the quality

12. According to Macklin, dignity means nothing "over and above respect for persons and their autonomy." "Dignity is a useless concept" *British Medical Journal* 327 (2003): 1419–20 (20 December).

13. Stephen Pinker, "The Stupidity of Dignity. Conservative bioethics' latest, most dangerous ploy," *The New Republic*, May 28, 2008.

14. For example, *Concepts and Cases in Nursing Ethics*, ed. Anne Moorhouse and Michael Yeo, 2nd Edition (Peterborough, Ontario: Broadview Press, 1996).

of being worthy or honourable."[15] So far as it is present today in philosophical anthropology, moral discourse, law and constitutions, and so on, it is something that is egalitarian and universal.

1. In his *Commentary on the Sentences* of Peter Lombard, St Thomas writes: "'Dignity' signifies the goodness of something for its own sake [*propter seipsum*];"[16] for human beings, it signifies that moral worth which all possess. This worth is a 'trump'; that is, it is a value that overrides many, if not all, other values. Consider codes restricting the wearing of religious symbols or dress in schools. It may well be that it is efficient (a value) or useful (another value) to impose such codes, and it would be a hardship (another value still) to define and make exceptions to the rules. Yet sometimes this hardship simply must be accepted if it is necessary to respect the dignity of a person, given her ethnic identity or religious traditions.

2. Dignity distinguishes human beings from commodities or mere objects. Some philosophers have taken dignity, then, as a sign of being an end in oneself—that we cannot be used just as instruments or means to some other end. Thus, even when we are punished, and even when the punishment is to be a deterrent to other potential offenders, it ought not be degrading; there can be no "cruel and unusual treatment or punishment."[17] To withhold certain constitutional or civil rights from prisoners would normally be violations of this dignity as well.

3. Dignity is rooted in what it is to be a human person. In the *Summa theologiae*, St Thomas writes: "dignity is something absolute, and pertains to the essence"[18]—to what it is to be a human person, with its distinctive character, function, and natural teleology. It is, in this sense, intrinsic and inherent. Thus, human persons are, by their nature, worthy of a special level of respect.

As an illustration of this, consider the following example from Ronald Cole-Turner. He writes that we would find it fundamentally morally objectionable if someone were to attempt to engineer a child who was somehow less free, or who, like a well-behaved dog, wanted to do nothing but make

15. *Oxford English Dictionary* (1989), 656–57.

16. *Super Sent.*, lib. 3 d. 35 q. 1 a. 4 qc. 1 co.; my translation.

17. *Canadian Charter of Rights and Freedoms*, sec. 12; see the Eighth Amendment to the *United States Constitution* (1787) and the *Universal Declaration of Human Rights*, art. 5.

18. Thomas Aquinas, *Summa theologiae* (hereafter *ST*) I, q. 42, a. 4 ad 2; *Basic Writings of Saint Thomas Aquinas*, Vol. 1, trans. Anton Charles Pegis (Indianapolis: Hackett Publishing, 1997), 407.

his parents happy and serve them as his masters.[19] The reason, surely, is that this is, in a very deep sense, a violation of something about the essence of the child—its dignity—and an offence not just against that one child, but against humanity. Yet people likely wouldn't find this as objectionable if we were to carry out such engineering on non-human animals or plants—and probably not at all on machines.

To say that dignity is intrinsic, then, is to say that it depends on what human persons are, and is not based on what a particular individual may will, wish, or feel. Nor is it anything that someone or some society can give to a person. (The *recognition* of one's dignity does depend on one's relations with other human beings, but that is another matter.) Strictly speaking, human dignity cannot be gained or lost—though, when one is being degraded, there is an effort to subvert the recognition of one's dignity. It is because we are human persons who have dignity that others *ought* to recognize it. This also means, however, that we cannot deny *our own* dignity; we have dignity, regardless of how or what we feel about ourselves.

4. Dignity is an objective characteristic. While one can refuse to recognize another's dignity, doing so is to refuse to recognize something that exists—and the fact that it exists is the basis for the demand that it ought to be respected, and ought *not* be denied. (Being unaware of one's dignity does not mean that it does not exist.) Consider the example of the happy or contented slave; it has been estimated that there are some 25 million slaves in the world today, and not all of them are dissatisfied with their status.[20] The fact that a slave accepts, perhaps even prefers, this slavery, however, does not mean that there is no violation of dignity. Similarly, while a person at the end of life may find himself isolated and abandoned, with a low estimation of quality of life, it does not follow that he has lost his dignity; rather, and more tragically, his dignity may simply be being ignored.

5. Dignity, in the sense that I describe it here, is something possessed universally and equally, and applies to all members of the human species as members of the human species.[21] (We see this reflected in principles

19. Cited in Heather J. Ciras, "Customized kids may be the wave of the future," *Science and Theology News*, June 9, 2005.

20. See Tom Masland, Rod Nordland, Melinda Liu, and Joseph Contreras, "Slavery," *Newsweek*, May 4, 1992, 30–39.

21. Martin Hailer and Dietrich Ritschl, "The General Notion of Human Dignity and the Specific Arguments in Medical Ethics," in *Sanctity of Life and Human Dignity*, ed. K. Bayertz (Dordrecht: Kluwer, 1996), 91–106, at 104: "the mere belonging of a human being to the species

such as 'equality before the law.') Some hold that dignity is possessed by all because it involves a relation to an ability held collectively—"the ability of human kind to collectively understand compassion and collectively understand the need for justice to remedy unnecessary suffering.... [Thus, t]he fact that all humans belong to the human collectivity gives them the inherent right to human dignity."[22] It is because dignity is a characteristic of humanity that an offense against one person's dignity is an offense against human dignity in general. This is also why violations of someone's dignity should, and normally do, matter to each of us.

Reference to the universal and egalitarian character of human dignity reflects the view that dignity is not based on the possession, by each and every human individual, "of certain functional capacities such as intelligence, abstract reason, language, creativity, ability to feel pain, empathy, awareness of personal biography over time, health, or beauty."[23] As William Cheshire notes, "functional capacities accrue with age and by degrees, many people possess them in slight degree, and others may lose some of them altogether." If the possession by an individual of all such capacities were essential to the existence of dignity, then it would also be essential to one's status as a person—and that would imply that someone could be more or less a person. If this were so, "then we could instrumentalize and commodify human beings, deny them individuality, and treat them as products to be designed and manufactured"—and even disposed of—"according to another's specifications."[24]

Of course, characteristics like "self-consciousness," "the capacity to express needs and desires," or "the capacity to feel pain"—or some combination of them—*can* be signs of the presence of a being with dignity, but they are not decisive in establishing it. Young children—not to mention infants, those with serious developmental delays, and those suffering from advanced Alzheimer's—are beings of dignity even though they do not possess all of the preceding functional capacities. In this respect, then, digni-

---

suffices to speak of a legitimate and necessary axiom that whoever deals with this being is to impart Human Dignity upon it...."

22. Errol P. Mendes, "Taking Equality into the 21st Century: Establishing the Concept of Equal Human Dignity," *National Journal of Constitutional Law* 12 (2000); *http://www.cdp-hrc.uottawa.ca/publicat/dignity.html.*

23. William P. Cheshire, Jr., "Toward a Common Language of Human Dignity," *Ethics Medicine* 18 (2) (2002): 7–10 at 8.

24. Cheshire, "Toward a Common Language," 8.

ty is quite distinct from the contemporary conception of autonomy. For, while the preceding characteristics are characteristics of autonomous beings, they are not necessary for human dignity.

6. Dignity, as a value, is incommensurable; it cannot be measured against, or somehow exchanged for, some other value. This is reflected when we talk about the 'infinite value,' or the 'pricelessness,' or the 'sacredness' of human life. This may seem a strong claim, but to abandon it would be inconsistent with some of the characteristics noted earlier (especially in 2 and 3, above).

7. Dignity is, finally, the basis for human rights.[25] As Jacques Maritain put it: "If the affirmation of the intrinsic value and dignity of man is nonsense, the affirmation of the natural rights of man is nonsense also."[26]

The preceding description of dignity summarizes how it has long been understood. Some of these features have, admittedly, been contested—even by those who appeal to dignity today—and the result is that we end up with confused, if not contradictory, statements of what dignity involves or requires.

To return, then, to the question 'What is dignity?', we see that the term means 'the intrinsic moral worth of human beings, possessed by all human beings equally, and present in humanity as a collectivity, regardless of the capacities and of the specific relations of any member of that collectivity to others.' This is why human beings are worthy of respect, why they have human rights, and why people insist on the recognition of these rights. Dignity is a basis for civic friendship, but it is also one reason why we are called to love one another. When an individual or a community uses, or degrades, or humiliates a person—when it violates her dignity—it undermines all this.

Dignity, however, can be violated when we treat *ourselves* in certain ways; there are, then, limits on what we can do to or with ourselves. Some would say that, by extension, we have to treat our bodies in certain ways as well. This point is crucial to understanding dignity. For while dignity obviously involves respect for the human being as a free being, it is not reducible to deferring to individual freedom to pursue one's own 'good' in one's own way.

25. According to Hailer and Ritschl, "Human Rights are a juridical concretization of the more general concept of Human Dignity" ("General Notion of Human Dignity," 93).

26. See Jacques Maritain, *Natural Law: Reflections on Theory and Practice*, ed. William Sweet (South Bend, Indiana: St Augustine's Press, 2003), 62.

In reply to critics such as Ruth Macklin and Stephen Pinker, then, dignity is *not just* respect for beings who are autonomous (in our ordinary sense of the term)—"free, independent, able to make a decision and act, self determined," and capable "of deliberating or acting on the basis of his or her own plans." Autonomy in this sense is a value, of course, but it is not a fundamental value, and it is not the same as dignity. As we have seen, not only does autonomy presuppose the possession of certain functional properties and characteristics, but to overemphasize it (particularly, in the popular sense, above) marginalizes other values, such as beneficence and the common good. There are a number of reasons why we should not overvalue autonomy and certainly not confuse it with 'dignity.'

Neither is dignity reducible to "a duty to respect the person." We may have a duty to respect nature, but this does not prevent us from using nature as a means to our purposes. Nor is the recognition of dignity just a recognition of human rights; if dignity disappears, human rights become simply a series of civil liberties recognized or granted by public authority—and there can be no protest that one's human rights have been violated if the agency that grants them, takes them away.

In short, the notion of dignity clearly has had, and has, a distinctive and crucial place in our moral vocabulary.

V

More, however, needs to be said. What is the evidence for human dignity as something real, universal, and objective? There have been a number of different explanations of how dignity can be said to exist and why it ought to be recognized and respected. Perhaps no one of the explanations that follow is necessary, but together they show a broad consensus on the existence and importance of this notion.

1. The first piece of evidence for the existence of human dignity as objective, real, and universal, is that dignity is recognized by cumulative human experience. One of the most influential documents declaring the fundamental place of dignity is the *Universal Declaration of Human Rights*. World War II exhibited, in a clear and unequivocal way, how far human beings can be degraded and mistreated, and so, in response, the *UDHR* declared—it did not create the claim—that dignity is a fundamental moral principle.

This "recognition" of the "inherent dignity … of all members of the human family," is also found in jurisprudence around the world. For example, in one of the landmark cases on bioethics in Canada, *Rodriguez v. British Columbia (Attorney General)*, the justices speaking both in the majority and in the minority recognized the importance of basic human dignity, as "one of the underlying principles upon which our society is based."[27]

2. Human dignity has been long recognized in religious traditions, both east and west. In Judaism, Christianity, and Islam, the notion of human dignity is rooted in scriptural texts which record that men and women are special and unique creations of the divine.[28] We can find this notion as well in the major religions of Asia, where it underlies such a value as compassion.[29]

3. Still, dignity is neither dependent on, nor presupposes the truth of, any religion. The Stoic philosophers of ancient Rome recognized the dignity of the human person, seeing it as based on humanity's rational faculty as employed in the pursuit of truth.[30] Dignity was also emphasized by the most important philosopher of the Enlightenment. For Kant, morality requires not mindless obedience to law, but one's own recognition that the moral law is something that must be respected. In this sense, we are 'self-legislators,' giving universal and objective moral law to ourselves. This is what Kant means by autonomy (in a sense quite distinct from the contemporary usage). It is the possession of autonomy in this specific sense that is, for Kant, the basis of the "dignity of human nature and of every rational nature"[31] and why human beings are worthy of respect.

4. More recently, a number of philosophers see human dignity as implied by the very concept of what it is to be a human person. Some—for example, the late Alan Gewirth—focus on the fact that beings who are agents can be morally praised or condemned, and it is this capacity to act

27. *Rodriguez v. British Columbia (Attorney General)* [1993] 3 *S.C.R.* 519. The majority opposed physician-assisted death, despite acknowledging personal autonomy (at least with respect to the right to make choices concerning one's own body).

28. See Genesis 1:26, 9:6. In Islam, see also al-Hijr 15:29: Saad 38:72.

29. See Qianfan Zhang, "The Idea of Human Dignity in Classical Chinese Philosophy," *Journal of Chinese Philosophy* 27 (2000): 299–330.

30. See Cicero, *De officiis*, I. 30: "Man's mind … is developed by study and reflection … ; sensual pleasure is wholly unworthy of the dignity of the human race." Cited in Charles Trinkaus, "Renaissance Idea of the Dignity of Man," in *The Dictionary of the History of Ideas: Studies of Selected Pivotal Ideas*, ed. Philip P. Wiener (New York: Charles Scribner's Sons, 1973–74), vol. 4, 136.

31. Immanuel Kant, *Groundwork of the Metaphysics of Morals*, trans. Mary Gregor (Cambridge: Cambridge University Press, 1997), 436.

morally (and immorally) that distinguishes human beings from all other things and, therefore, is the basis of their moral worth and dignity.[32] Others would add to Gewirth's account, as noted earlier, that dignity is not contingent upon any functional capacities which vary in degree. While evidence of personhood may be found in such capacities as abstract reasoning, use of language, and a desire to determine elements of our lives as we choose, personhood is not reducible to them.

5. Even though it has had formulations in philosophy and in religious traditions, some regard dignity as just a fundamental moral fact. Thomas De Koninck sees it as "a requirement that is prior to all philosophical formulation" that has been expressed, in varying degrees, in cultural traditions from antiquity.[33] Even Ronald Dworkin, in *Taking Rights Seriously*, points out that "anyone who professes to take rights seriously" must accept—though not necessarily in any foundational way—"the vague but powerful idea of human dignity."[34]

6. Recognition of and respect for dignity can also be seen in feminist ethics, and specifically in the ethics of care that is central to many feminist views. Idris Baker, a worker in palliative medicine, notes: "When we toilet and wash dying people rather than leaving them dirty, when we moisten their mouths rather than leaving them dry, when we lay them out carefully after death, it is their dignity that we are respecting."[35] It is the recognition of 'something' about others—something that indicates they are the kinds of beings with whom we *can* enter into a relationship, even though we may not in fact do so—that undergirds the love we are called to show them. This 'something' is their dignity.

7. We may say, as well, that dignity is something that is *connaturally* recognized—a point attested to by Maritain and, earlier, by Aquinas—of which we become aware directly through our experience of ourselves and others.[36] We see the fact of the humanity of another being—of the other as

32. Alan Gewirth, "Dignity as the Basis of Rights," in *The Constitution of Rights; Human Dignity and American Values*, ed. M.J. Meyer and W.A. Parent (Ithaca: Cornell University Press, 1992), 10–28 at 18–19.

33. Thomas De Koninck, *La dignité humaine*, 15

34. Ronald Dworkin, *Taking Rights Seriously* (Cambridge, Massachusetts: Harvard University Press, 1977), 198.

35. "Rapid Responses for Macklin," *British Medical Journal* 327 (2003): 1419–20 *www.bmj.com/cgi/eletters/327/7429/1419*.

36. Cheshire writes: "One comprehends dignity less through reason and more through in-

human or as another self—and recognize the moral claim that is made on us at the same time. This *sense* of dignity is also a characteristic of who we are, and distinguishes human beings from non-human animals.

The preceding list of explanations is not exhaustive, nor may any one of them be strictly necessary. Still, they point to the large number of ways in which, throughout the lengthy history of the notion, people have understood dignity, recognized it as characteristic of human persons, and regarded it as a fundamental value.

VI

What, then, does dignity imply concerning how we are to respond to others and concerning the love that we are commanded to show them, but also to show to ourselves? Applications obviously require knowing the particulars of concrete cases. We can, however, identify some general guidelines.

First, because dignity has a foundational role, other values—including social and political freedoms—derive their moral weight from it. The reason why people ought not lie to others, or degrade or humiliate them, or ignore them when they are in serious need, and so on, is because to treat persons in these ways is ultimately to violate their dignity.

Second, because dignity is an essential characteristic of human personality, it provides a moral basis for a critique of those attitudes and practices that attack or attempt to undermine it. Because it is objective, it does not depend on one's own feelings about oneself or about one's judgment of the quality of one's own life; it is not simply left up to each individual to determine when his or her dignity is involved or at stake. Dignity does not mean, or depend on, autonomy in today's sense of 'being free to do what one wants,' even if what one wants to do putatively affects only oneself.

Third, because dignity involves recognizing that persons are not just commodities or things that can be used, people cannot legitimately be exploited by others as a mere means to their, or even society's, ends.

Thus, when we are confronted with the issue of commercial surrogacy, we have to ask whether this commodification of the person and use of

tuition, in a way that is comprehensible to human reflection universally" ("Toward a Common Language," 8).

one's body are consistent with dignity. We also have to ask whether claims to autonomy, in the sense of having a right to do as we will, are consistent with the dignity that is in us. (Note that, if dignity is put aside, and if our bodies can be used as commodities, then perhaps a case can be made for the expropriation and public ownership of our reproductive capacities—and even ourselves.) Or again, when we are confronted with the claim of a 'right to die,' we have to ask whether the implication that our bodies are our property—that each of us can do with it as we choose—is consistent with human dignity.

On the preceding account of dignity, individuals cannot be used merely as objects or means to others' interests. Yet neither can individuals use themselves as mere means to their own ends. When it comes to actions that may degrade an individual, it is irrelevant whether a person consents to be treated in these ways.

These may be difficult guidelines to follow, particularly in those contexts where dignity is not recognized as a basic value, or where individualism and autonomy (in the popular sense) are deeply rooted within a political or legal system. Such difficulties do not, however, count against the moral weight of the demands dignity places on us.

VII

It is because of the confusions in contemporary ethical discourse concerning the notion of dignity and, perhaps, also because of the infiltration of alien ethical values, that we find a number of puzzles concerning how human dignity is determined, what it entails, what its relation is to individual freedom, and how it bears on issues such as practical love and civic friendship. As the notion of dignity becomes clearer, however, we should be better able to see how it applies to a range of ethical, social, legal, and political issues.

The concept of dignity gives us an explanation—a strong secular explanation—for human value, for respecting others and ourselves, and even for why we should value autonomy, identity, and individual consent. It also explains why and when we need to show respect for diversity. (This does not mean always deferring to, or declining to challenge, difference, though it may mean that we do need to make attempts to understand and appreciate it.) We need to insist on the respect of our dignity, but we must also treat others with respect; we must not lose sight of the fact that, as human persons, they have dignity, even if they threaten or seek to destroy us.

This emphasis on dignity supports the deeply held conviction that human beings cannot be owned and should not be used, or use themselves, in certain ways—and that human life is, in a profound sense, priceless. This bears on how to respond to the non-medical use of drugs, pornography and prostitution or the sex trade, those who suffer painful, terminal illness, and so on. It reminds us, as well, not only how the exercise of freedom is a sign of our dignity, but how the exercise of this freedom is conditioned by that dignity. As a moral imperative, dignity calls us out of the tendency to fixate on our private interests and wishes and wills.

Furthermore, I have argued that dignity undergirds our life in community and the civic friendship on which it depends. Fundamentally, dignity lies at the root of practical love—the doing good, the loving of enemies, the praying for their persecutors that people of faith are called to do.

Dignity is something that each human person has, and which ought to be respected. At the same time, it is not just up to each of us to determine what our dignity is and what it licenses us to do. It is only when we fully appreciate this that we will be able to see how to extricate ourselves from some of the puzzles and paradoxes that we are confronted with on ethical, social, and political issues. It is also only when we appreciate this that we can show, not only practical love, but genuinely human love—that love "in which the spirit is engaged"—of which Maritain reminds us.

FRANCISCO PLAZA

Yves R. Simon's Metaphysics of Love

A Hidden Treasure

In a short article entitled "Progress in Metaphysics,"[1] Simon addressed the need to develop a metaphysics of love as a "new center of organization" for a more profound and living understanding of the system of being. This was the leading theme of the course he gave at the University of Notre Dame during the summer of the year 1945, the typewritten transcripts of which, over two hundred pages long, will hopefully someday be edited for publication, along with his articles on the nature and dynamics of ecstatic, disinterested love.[2] Developing Maritain's reflections on the "basic generosity of existence,"[3] Simon dedicated this course to exploring the indissoluble ontological complementariness between the "in-itself" and the "towards-others" dimensions of being.

The implications of Simon's metaphysics of love soon found their place in his political philosophy. In a series of lectures delivered in the 1950s, Si-

1. Yves R. Simon, "Progress in Metaphysics," *The Commonwealth* XLII, no. 1 (April 1945): 5–6.

2. "Lecture on Metaphysics of Love: Notre Dame" (1945), TMs [typed manuscript], Simon Papers, Box 12, Folder 22, Hesburgh Memorial Library, University of Notre Dame, South Bend, Indiana. Other very relevant unpublished texts include "Mexico: Lectures on Metaphysics of Love" (1942–1943), TMs, Simon Papers, Box 12, Folder 29; "Five lectures on the Metaphysics of Love" (1944)," TMs, Simon Papers, Box 12, Folder 30; "The Metaphysics of Disinterested Love" (N.D.), TMs, Simon Papers, Box 12, Folder 01; "Love and Freedom" (N.D), TMs, Simon Papers, Box 12, Folder 13.

3. Jacques Maritain, *Existence and the Existent* (Garden City, New York: Doubleday, 1957), 90.

mon focused on the intimate relationship between justice, authority and love.[4] Gradually, the subject of love became the anchor for his analyses of the issues of order and freedom. This article, therefore, explores the relevance of Simon's unpublished texts on the metaphysics of love for a deeper understanding of central themes in his political thought. I will first identify some fundamental concepts in Simon's meditations on the relationship between love and freedom. I will then discuss the connection between Simon's reflections on love and his understanding about the true meaning of the common good in the life of democratic societies. I will conclude with some reflections about the importance of these unpublished texts to uncover essential themes in Simon's political philosophy.

I

Beyond the more benign drive towards natural spontaneity that Simon found in the most uninhibited expressions of the modern consciousness of freedom, he identified the sources of a deeper spiritual disorder in the modern demand to link freedom to the prerogative of choosing evil. For Simon, the modern vision of freedom involves a spirit of rebelliousness against anything that may stand as a sort of impediment to its absolute exercise, as well as a refusal to recognize the limitations on its unbounded existence that derive from human nature. Modern man, Simon insisted, claims for himself the infinite existence of freedom. The Romantic rejection of "the will to refrain" is undoubtedly a manifestation of this drive. For Simon, however, the deepest drive behind the modern quest for absolute autonomy comes from the idea that the capacity to choose evil is essential to freedom. By rebelling against the indefectible adherence of the will to the comprehensive good (*bonum in comuni*), which serves as the ground for authentic freedom, the modern consciousness of freedom claims for itself the autonomy to decide whether to repress its love for the supreme good.[5]

4. For example, Simon's lectures at the Newman Center of the University of New Mexico in 1956. See "Justice, Authority and Love, (1956)," TMs, Simon Papers, Box 29, Folder 16, Hesburgh Memorial Library, University of Notre Dame, South Bend, Indiana.

5. For Simon's reflections on the modern consciousness of freedom, see especially Yves R. Simon, *Freedom of Choice*, ed. Peter Wolf, with a foreword by Mortimer J. Adler (New York: Fordham University Press, 1969, 1987, 1992); and *Freedom and Community*, ed. Charles P. O'Donnell (New York: Fordham University Press, 1968).

Simon linked this disorder of the modern world to the existential drama involved in the ultimately Gnostic opposition between immanence and transcendence.[6] In his diagnosis of the spiritual revolt of the modern world, Simon continuously returned to those passages in *Integral Humanism* where Maritain describes modern rationalism as raising "a proud and splendid image of the personality of man, jealous of his immanence and his autonomy," while condemning "any intervention from the outside into this perfect and sacred universe, whether such intervention would come from revelation and grace, from a tradition of human wisdom, from the authority of a law which man is not the author, from a Sovereign Good which solicits his will, or finally, from an objective reality which would measure and rule his intelligence."[7] Simon saw at the core of the existential drama of the modern soul the belief that man is unable to develop in freedom unless he first breaks with the Transcendent Being. He recognized a deep spiritual rebellion which leads man to reject the Truth and the Good in order to set himself up as an absolute principle unto himself. This rebellion is a focal point in Simon's reflections on the problems of political order. For Simon, the rupture of the essential link between freedom and truth is the source of the greatest weakness of the liberal democratic order. To the extent that the liberal-democratic order allows this cleavage between human freedom and the transcendent source which alone sustains it, it grows vulnerable to the anthropocentric distortion that threatens to deprive men of their authentic humanity.

Simon recognized that a philosopher cannot withdraw from this existential struggle in his effort to recover the sources of order. Political theories that look for neutral, non-controversial solutions are as ineffective as moral exhortations seeking to rescue the values of tradition. Both perspectives ignore the dynamics of a spiritual struggle that affects a liberal society ready to stand "unflinchingly" for its values and yet, paradoxically, inclined to deny truth in order to preserve freedom.

Avoiding dogmatic formulations that are foreign to the modern liberal

6. See, especially, Yves R. Simon, "Le problème de la transcendence et le défi de Proudhon," *Nova et Vetera* 9 (1934): 225–38; English translation by Charles P. O'Donnell and Vukan Kuic, "The Problem of Transcendence and Proudhon's Challenge," *Thought* 54, no. 1 (1979): 177–85; and "Notes sur le fédéralisme proudhonnien," *Esprit* no. 5 (April 1937): 53–65; English translation by Vukan Kuic, "A Note on Proudhon's Federalism," *Publius* 3, no. 2 (1973): 19–30.

7. Jacques Maritain, *The Collected Works of Jacques Maritain*, ed. Otto Bird, vol. 11, *Integral Humanism* (Notre Dame, Indiana: University of Notre Dame Press, 1996), 169–70.

consciousness, Simon realized that the means for recovery are only those that remain embedded in the living practice of a liberal-democratic society. Anticipating a leading theme in Pope John Paul II's Encyclical *Veritatis Splendor*, Simon recognized that it is freedom itself that needs to be set free, that freedom must go from self-possession to openness to all that exists, from passing beyond self to knowledge and love of the other. In other words, human freedom, rooted in the truth of human existence, is ultimately directed towards communion.[8] This is the problem that guided Simon's reflections on the spiritual dynamism at work in modern culture and the challenge that led him to explore the political implications that the ecstatic nature of love—the state of being that is placed outside of itself—has in the life of individuals and communities.

Drawing from the immediate data of concrete human experience, Simon insisted on the fact that man behaves as if transcending his own needs were the deepest of all his needs. Reflecting on this reality, Simon recognized that through the element of self-determination, the human self is revealed to itself, not only as self-possession and self-governance, but also as a tendency toward self-fulfillment. Neither self-consciousness nor self-possession, therefore, encloses the human self within itself as a subject. For Simon, quite the opposite is true. The whole "turning toward itself" that modern consciousness works to bring about is ultimately a source of the most expansive openness of the subject toward reality.[9] In the human self as a personal subject, self-fulfillment and transcendence are inseparably connected. "The true notion of transcendence," Simon explained, "in no way excludes immanence; on the contrary, it calls for it and is alone able to give it meaning."[10] The modern myth of immanence, Simon concluded, is destructive of the real values of immanence.

This perspective allowed Simon to articulate the essential unity between freedom, truth, and love in a way that could resonate with the modern demand for absolute autonomy. In order to explain the relationship between immanence and transcendence in the experience of personal freedom, Simon described the different ways in which this relationship holds,

8. See John Paul II, Encyclical Letter, *The Splendor of Truth* (Washington, D.C.: United States Catholic Conference, 1993), 131, par. 86.

9. See Karol Wojtyła, *Person and Community: Selected Essays*, trans. edited by Theresa Sandok (New York: Peter Lang, 1993), 233.

10. Simon, "The Problem of Transcendence and Proudhon's Challenge," 183.

respectively, for physical objects, the life of the senses, and intellectual perception. In nature, every gain is balanced by a loss and every loss by a gain. For physical objects, to be acted upon means the substitution of one form for another. In the case of the senses, however, the change in quality involved is not replacement or destruction. For the senses, to be acted upon "represents the actualization of the senses themselves."[11] The same occurs, Simon argued, with intellectual perception. The change of quality that occurs in the knower does not change his being or nature. On the contrary, the soul is perfected when acted upon by the objects of understanding. Simon used the relationship between immanence and transcendence in intellectual perception to argue, by way of analogy, that the autonomy of free creatures is safeguarded precisely by the infinitely strong influence God exercises. Divine transcendence, accordingly, not only respects the autonomy of creatures but is, moreover, "the authentic source of their autonomy and at the same time the principle of its limits."[12] It is the wonder of human freedom that man finds its perfection by surrendering his subjectivity through the gift of self to the glory of truth and love.[13] This is the problem that Simon explored at length in his unpublished texts on the metaphysics of love, and one that allows us to appreciate better the enormous implications of the passage he wrote in his *The Metaphysics of Knowledge*, very early in his philosophical career, about the need to transcend subjectivity in order to reach true freedom:

Indeed, between the laws of progress in knowledge and the supreme law of salvation there is a striking analogy. In both cases we are confronted with an interest that needs and desperately wishes to be preserved but can be preserved only by total disinterestedness. The drama of thought is like that of destiny. A nature that does not possess its supreme perfection by self-identity has necessarily an interest in its perfectibility, and in one sense only divine love is totally disinterested. Man cannot not desire happiness, the subjective beatitude of what is called the ego: but he will find happiness only when he turns away from himself and his happiness to

11. Ibid., 184.

12. Ibid., 184–85.

13. See Simon, *Freedom of Choice*, 119. As Maritain explains, the accomplishment of freedom in the spiritual progress of the soul involves "the obligation of passing freely (through all the misfortunes and the accidents that follow our fragility) from a freedom of choice between good and evil (which marks the imperfections of the creature as such) to a freedom always to choose the good, which is the work of the Divine nature and which presupposes the transformation of the soul by Grace and Love": *The Collected Works of Jacques Maritain*, ed. Otto Bird, vol. 11, *Freedom in the Modern World*, (Notre Dame, Indiana: University of Notre Dame Press, 1996), 18.

lose himself in God. Similarly, our created intelligence cannot not desire the subjective qualification and enrichment that ideas bring to it, since it is by means of such qualification that the object of knowledge is delivered to it. But as soon as the mind goes after the ideas themselves, instead of the object, the ideas conceal the object by taking its place, and the thinker who wanted to know and conquer the world is left with but a system of thought of his own making. To grasp the object of knowledge, our thought must die to itself, just as love must die to reach the true good. In one case, we overcome selfishness; in the other we transcend subjectivity. This ascetic requirement of our intelligence, bound by its own law that alone can lead us to objective knowledge, is just like the denial of oneself that leads to God. Happy, therefore, is he who seeks the truth in charity; his scientific asceticism will be mixed with his human righteousness and he will move with undivided effort toward both intellectual and personal salvation.[14]

II

Simon's unpublished texts on the metaphysics of love are also invaluable sources to better understand Simon's reflections on the meaning of community and the common good. Men are bound together by their determination to be just and by their willingness to obey government. However, Simon observed, even though justice and authority indeed are indispensable forces to insure the constitution and operation of human communities, of their living and acting together, they are simply insufficient. Not only do injustice and disobedience bring about the dissolution of human communities, but also hatred, division, and, most importantly, indifference to achieve communion in truth. Hence, Simon insisted on the need to reflect also on the benevolence, friendship, and love that the members of a community must have for one another if they are to remain together. Loving by way of legal fulfillment is not enough, Simon warned. There is an essential tendency of love to transcend the law, without being at variance with it.

Simon, of course, realized that this perspective went against the liberal myth that plainly states that "disinterestedness is impossible, and further it is not relevant, for the best that anyone can do for his neighbor and for the common good is to seek his own interest with intelligence, i.e., with foresight and a sense of balance."[15] This utilitarian philosophy is led to treat

14. Yves R. Simon, *The Metaphysics of Knowledge*, English edition and translation by Vukan Kuic and Richard J. Thompson (New York: Fordham University Press, 1990), 21.

15. Simon, "The Metaphysics of Disinterested Love," 1.

cient that it concerns several persons. Rather "it is necessary that it be of such a nature as to cause, among those who pursue it and in so far as they pursue it, a common life of desire and action."[25] Acting "together" (i.e. "in common") does not mean engaging in a number of activities that somehow go along side by side. Rather, it means that these activities, along with the existence of those many I's, are related to a single value, which, therefore, deserves to be called the common good. The relation of many I's to a common good seems to be the very core of social community. By virtue of this relation, the people involved in it, while experiencing their personal subjectivity, are aware that they form a specific We, and they experience themselves in this new ecstatic dimension.[26]

The principle of the primacy of the common good is often misunderstood and yet its powerful hold on man's conscience remains a fact: "[even] people of debased conduct and skeptical judgment still find it natural to die for their country."[27] In the social life of human beings, it is also true that beyond the lust for individual sovereignty in the exercise of freedom, the true dignity of each man's uniqueness lies in the mystery that links human liberty with the transcendent significance of man's existence in love.

III

Simon's unpublished texts on the metaphysics of love unveil the deeper implications involved in the commitment of the liberal political order to protect the conditions for the authentic exercise of individual freedom. The will to preserve our autonomy, Simon explained, does not exhaust the deepest drive behind our desire to preserve our freedom, because this will coexists with another fundamental drive in moral action: concrete human experience shows that the will to preserve what is most intimate in ourselves goes together with the need to move towards others, a will to self-transcend and self-communicate precisely what is most interior and sacred of ourselves. Thus, the original division that leads the self to preserve his intimacy yields to the more profound reality of self-giving as a fundamental dimension in the person. In these texts, Simon meditated on the fact that love is what makes possible this polarity in a way in which it is no

25. Ibid., 49.
26. See Wojtyła, *Person and Community*, 247.
27. Simon, *Philosophy of Democratic Government*, 50.

longer unbearable but, rather, the very condition for the growth and plenitude of the person. These ideas are crucial for a deeper understanding of Simon's philosophy of democratic government as a whole. They allow us to recognize perhaps one of the most fundamental ideas in Simon's political philosophy, namely, that beyond the tensions that beset democratic societies in matters of truth, the liberal-democratic order will only rediscover its spiritual foundations to the degree that human beings find in the disinterested gift of themselves the true meaning of their quest for freedom. This is what we find at the core of Yves R. Simon's philosophy of democratic government.

V

THE LOVE OF BEING AND THE BEING OF LOVE

CHRISTOPHER S. MORRISSEY

The Intuition of Being

Guardian of Metaphysics in a Time of Unbelief

Hans Urs von Balthasar learned something important from his philosopher friend Gustav Siewerth:[1] namely, a positive evaluation of Heidegger as "the most fertile" resource for any future Thomistic metaphysics.[2] More than any other Thomist, Siewerth sought to explain in painstaking detail how Thomas Aquinas escapes Heidegger's critique of Western philosophy as wholly forgetful of Be-ing.[3]

All beings have their various natures (e.g., "rock," "tree," "cat"), but to this may be contrasted Be-ing, which is the "pure positivity" of existence, realized as it passes historically into the *actus essendi*[4] (the act of existence) that shines forth in various natures. Unlike these various natures (e.g., "rock," "tree," "cat"), Be-ing cannot become an "object" for thought. Hence

1. See his eulogy, Hans Urs von Balthasar, "Abschied von Gustav Siewerth," *Hochland* 56 (1963/64): 182–84. English translation available in Andrzej Wiercinski, *Inspired Metaphysics? Gustav Siewerth's Hermeneutic Reading of the Onto-Theological Tradition* (Toronto: The Hermeneutic Press, 2003), 19–23. See also their correspondence, Andrzej Wiercinski (ed.), *Between Friends: The Hans Urs von Balthasar and Gustav Siewerth Correspondence 1954–1963* (Konstanz: Verlag Gustav Siewerth Gesellschaft, 2005).

2. Hans Urs von Balthasar, *The Glory of the Lord*, Volume V (San Francisco: Ignatius Press, 1991), 449.

3. "Be-ing" is my preferred English rendition of the Latin *esse*. The hyphen highlights the verbal action of the participial expression ("-ing") of existing, thus emphasizing the dynamic act of existence; whereas the capitalization of the "b" is a sop to the lamentable convention of rendering the Latin *esse* or German *Sein* as "Being." The purpose of my rendition is to encourage the reader always to think of *esse* as a dynamic, non-subsistent act, rather than as a subsistent static identity.

4. Wiercinski, *Inspired*, 32.

forgetfulness about Be-ing now reigns, because modern thought in general, and scientists in particular, tend to dismiss from thought what cannot be grasped as an "object" by the modern scientific method:

> The modern forgetfulness of Be-ing begins with Scotus, for whom Be-ing is exhausted in *essentia*. The Scotistic denial of the real distinction of *essentia* and *existentia*, and the related denial of the inconceivability of God in the notion of *univocatio entis*, gives birth to the essentialism of modern philosophy and the subjectivism of German idealism. Against this trend Siewerth unfurls a set of hermeneutically revised Thomistic concepts. He shows how Aquinas distinguishes Be-ing (*esse*) from beings (*entia*) on the grounds that the latter possess *essentia, quidditas*, which can be abstracted and conceptualized, where the former is pure nonessential act. The "existentialist" formulation of the *distinctio realis*, however, is not enough to meet the challenge of Heidegger, for both whatness (*essentia*) and thatness (*existentia*) belong to the being of substance. Siewerth argues that, in order to answer Heidegger's critique, we must retrieve Aquinas's distinction between act and subsistence: the former is the pure, nonsubstantive, dynamic energy of coming into presence; the latter is the stasis of that which has come to be. The act of Be-ing subsists in a being while remaining distinct from it. The distinction underscores Aquinas's often overlooked distinction between the Be-ing of God (*ipsum esse subsistens*) and the Be-ing of beings (*ipsum esse non-subsistens*). The Being of a being is a nonsubsistent act, the event of the sheer upsurge of beings from nothingness. It cannot be abstracted into a concept. As Siewerth says, it can be thought (there is a *conceptio entis*) but not abstracted (there is no *conceptus entis*).[5]

This thinkable but un-definable *conceptio entis* is implicitly found at the pre-scientific root of all cognition (within that which Aquinas calls *ens ut primum cognitum*: "being as first known").[6] But this *conceptio entis* can be expressly appreciated in philosophy by means of the so-called "intuition of Be-ing," something about which Jacques Maritain has written so carefully in his expositions of Aquinas.[7] The analogical naming of Be-ing across mul-

5. Sean McGrath, review of Andrzej Wiercinski, *Inspired Metaphysics? Gustav Siewerth's Hermeneutic Reading of the Onto-Theological Tradition*, in *The Thomist* 69 (April 2005): 332–35, at 334. (Note: whenever I quote McGrath's review, to avoid confusion, I have modified the quotation so that "being" is capitalized and hyphenated as "Be-ing" whenever McGrath is clearly referring, in context, by the word "being," to *esse*.)

6. Cf. John Deely, *Four Ages of Understanding* (Toronto: University of Toronto Press, 2001), 347–50. Cf. also Josephus Gredt, *Elementa Philosophiae Aristotelico-Thomisticae* (Herder, 1961), §619.

7. Jacques Maritain, *Existence and the Existent*, trans. Lewis Galantiere and Gerald B. Phelan (New York: Pantheon, 1948), 19–35, and Jacques Maritain, *A Preface to Metaphysics: Seven Lectures on Being* (New York: Sheed and Ward, 1962), 48–64. Cf. John P. Hittinger, "Maritain on the Intuition of Being," in *Liberty, Wisdom, and Grace: Thomism and Democratic Political Theory* (Lanham, Maryland: Lexington Books, 2002), 203–12.

tiple judgments of beings happens all the time in human cognition (e.g., "cats are furry," "rocks are hard"). But when this analogical naming *itself* is viewed by cognition, then we can have the *conceptio entis* by which we see (i.e., have the intuition of) Be-ing as something different from beings (i.e., we see the ontological difference). Cats are different from rocks, but both beings are different from their Be-ing (e.g., they pass into and out of their existence).

Siewerth helps us appreciate this by maintaining that there is "no concept of Be-ing but only an understanding of Be-ing ... [that] takes place in 'judgment' ... whose nature it is not to 'combine concepts with each other' but rather to reveal 'realities', that which 'is', in their obviousness, i.e., to reveal them as 'true' and to confirm them."[8] When we view the analogical deployment of Be-ing across a range of judgments about beings, this "judicious intuitive knowledge of the truth of Be-ing"[9] is called an "intuition" because its "cognition of a being (*ens*) based on, and secured by, judgment" is precisely an "eidetic visualization" (as Maritain put it). That is, it is an intellectual visualization that Siewerth notes "stays close, in all directions, to the mediating rational discourse,"[10] namely, to the vast range of various judgments themselves about various beings (e.g., "cats are furry," "rocks are hard," etc.). Judgments therefore permit "a judgmental apprehension of Be-ing (*conceptio entis*)."[11] In other words, judgments about beings (e.g., as being "hard" or "furry") yield "a judgmental understanding"[12] in which Be-ing is also predicated of a being, so that the result of our "search for a description of Be-ing"[13] results in a *conceptio* of Be-ing (intuited across many judgments) rather than a *conceptus* of a being (abstractly considered in isolation, as in one judgment): e.g., we can catch sight of Be-ing when existence itself becomes the predicate, when we can say "the cat is" or "the rock is," however different those respective existences may be (e.g., "furry"

8. Gustav Siewerth, "Die Abstraktion und das Sein nach der Lehre des Thomas von Aquin," *Gesammelte Werke* 1 (Düsseldorf: Patmos Verlag, 1975), 586–87; translated at Wiercinski, *Inspired*, 189. (I have inserted the hyphen into Being, here and elsewhere in quotations from this same work.)

9. Siewerth, "Abstraktion," 588; translated at Wiercinski, *Inspired*, 190.

10. Ibid.; *Inspired*, 189.

11. Gustav Siewerth, "Das Sein als Gleichnis Gottes," *Gesammelte Werke* 1 (Düsseldorf: Patmos Verlag, 1975), 660; translated at Wiercinski, *Inspired*, 190, n. 101.

12. Gustav Siewerth, "Das Schicksal der Metaphysik von Thomas zu Heidegger," *Gesammelte Werke* 4 (Düsseldorf: Patmos Verlag, 1987), 660; translated at Wiercinski, *Inspired*, 189, n. 95.

13. Wiercinski, *Inspired*, 189.

or "hard"), i.e., however variegated Be-ing itself, as actually manifested in a "cat" and in a "rock," may be.

This judgmental understanding, "the intuition of Be-ing," is the explicit unfolding in consciousness of what is implicit in *ens ut primum cognitum*: a being as what is first known.[14] In it, we come to an explicit grasp of the ontological difference (beings and Be-ing) implicitly structuring the identity of the *ens* (as "a being Be-ing"): i.e., any given being will be an "essence exist-ing"; e.g. "a rock is," "a cat is." Now, because of what is proper to its method, modern science prefers to focus on the essential nature or properties of the substance (whether rock or cat), rather than to focus on unfolding the difference structuring "the disclosure of a being, which has substance and which is present."[15] Again, this difference is the difference between the essence and its act of existence. It is the very ontological difference that is enfolded in the "being Be-ing," i.e., in the cat that exists, or in the rock that exists.

Yet it is here, where science resists thinking the ontological difference (considering it inconsequential), that Siewerth's articulation of the Thomist distinction between act and subsistence can be of service. It can serve to remind us of "the basis for cognition," which "is always the relationship between Be-ing and thought,"[16] namely, the prior relationship that guarantees that the scientific method can in principle and in fact arrive at truth: *ens ut primum cognitum*. Something first has to exist (whether as cat or rock or otherwise) for it to be studied by science. What is first known of the *ens* (i.e., as it first appears to cognition as "an essence exist-ing") is the identity of knowing thought with known Be-ing. The implicit act of knowing thought is identical with the inner act of what is being known.[17] This implicit, prior relationship of identical act is what becomes explicitly unfolded in the scientific (or even the everyday) mental grasp of the substance's essence. But the subsistence of the nature as a substance is made possible by the prior *esse*, "the *actus essendi*, the act of an essence, that is, the act of subsisting."[18] In sum, act is prior to subsistence, not temporally, but as the

14. Cf. John Deely, *Four Ages*, 347–50. Cf. also Josephus Gredt, *Elementa Philosophiae*, §619.

15. Wiercinski, *Inspired*, 189.

16. Ibid.

17. Aristotle, *De Anima* III, 5; cf. Aquinas, *Summa Theologiae* I, q. 79, a. 3: *in anima est aliquid quo est omnia fieri.*

18. Sean McGrath, "Heidegger's Approach to Aquinas: Opposition, *Destruktion*, Unbelief," in Conor Cunningham and Peter M. Candler, Jr. (eds.), *Belief and Metaphysics* (SCM Press, 2007), 288.

condition for the possibility of knowing thought becoming identical with actual, known Be-ing.

Siewerth explains: "This Be-ing is therefore the reason for the possibility of any knowledge of a being";[19] yet "the Be-ing of a being can only come to perception in a being."[20] The mental grasp of essence is the mental grasp of Be-ing and non-Being in the being (e.g., "it *is* a cat" and "it *is not* a dog"), what Siewerth calls the "identity of identity and non-identity," a Thomistic understanding of the "ideality" of the relationship between Be-ing and beings, between identity and difference, which he terms "exemplary identity," articulated in opposition to the Hegelian "dialectical identity."

Andrzej Wiercinski has argued (in an argument that may be put in contrast with Balthasar's appreciation) that Siewerth's appropriation of these Heideggerian insights for Thomistic metaphysics is untenable. Because Siewerth, appropriating Hegel for "an idealistic exposition of Thomism," did not appreciate the radical role of Scotus and phenomenology in Heidegger's thinking on nature, the consequence is (in Wiercinski's blunt assessment): "Siewerth does not understand the early Heidegger."[21] In reply to Wiercinski's carefully considered judgment, however, I would wish to note two things.

First, assume for the sake of argument that Siewerth's focus on explicating the *actus essendi* is a Neothomist misunderstanding of Heidegger's *Sein*,[22] a misunderstanding that fails to comprehend the virtues of Scotus,[23] and fails to appreciate the role of phenomenology in Heidegger, in which the Be-ing "proper to things existing as known"[24] (*ens logicum*) is pursued as the true focus. Assume, for the sake of argument, that Heidegger's true position is "a Scotistic position," "privileging possibility over actuality"[25] and hence fundamentally at odds with Aquinas. If so, then this misunderstanding shall have been a blessing. Even if Siewerth thought it "possible to reconcile the Christian history of salvation with the fate of the forgetfulness of Be-ing"[26] and had to misinterpret Heidegger to do so, then I would say he was right: not right about Heidegger, but rather about the truth of the matter. The misunderstanding shall have been a blessing.

19. Siewerth, "Schicksal," 76; translated at Wiercinski, *Inspired*, 42.

20. Wiercinski, *Inspired*, 42. Cf. Josephus Gredt, *Elementa Philosophiae*, §619.

21. Ibid., 213.

22. Cf. Deely, *Four Ages*, 290–97, on "A Note on the Distinction Between Essence and Existence."

23. Cf. Wiercinski, *Inspired*, 63–78.

24. Deely, *Four Ages*, 290.

25. Wiercinski, *Inspired*, 212.

26. Ibid., 129.

Second, I would defend Balthasar's assessment of Siewerth's promising work, for the truth of the matter is that Siewerth, *pace* Wiercinski,[27] has the right solution to the deleterious theological ramifications of the Scotistic univocity of Be-ing which is apparently a fundamental feature of Heidegger's Lutheran "phenomenology for the godforsaken."[28] The right solution is Siewerth's articulation of Be-ing as likeness of God:[29] "Act and potentiality constitute Be-ing as likeness of God."[30] "Be-ing itself cannot ... be understood as part of the Be-ing of a being. It shows itself as a whole in relation to God, and can only be His image."[31] Be-ing as likeness of God is understood by Siewerth in this way as the "exemplary identity" in Be-ing itself of identity and difference: "Thought thinking itself is the ground of reality. The Be-ing of a being comes into existence as the other of thought in the depths of divine Be-ing. The Be-ing of a being is difference, that which is other, yet at the same time identical, with absolute thought."[32]

Neither a being nor God, the Be-ing of beings is the perfect image of God, a pure reflection of divine kenosis. It empties itself into beings and comes to realization in them. Hence it depends upon the subsistent Be-ing of God as much as beings depend upon it. By distinction, the Be-ing of God is subsistent act, that which resides in itself, infinite, eternal, self-sufficient, excluding all potency and requiring nothing else in order for it to be. As the first creation, the Be-ing of beings is horizoned by the nothingness of primordial potency; it is "complete and simple, but not subsistent." Just as the triune God is a mediation through otherness (the Father is Father by virtue of the relation to the Son, etc.), Be-ing is an identity-in-difference, an identity that realizes itself through its other.... In the act of creation, the self-emptying Trinity images itself in that which only exists insofar as it empties itself into a being. Be-ing is kenosis. As nonsubsistent, Be-ing is not identical with itself: it is only real insofar as it has poured itself out and allowed a being to be.[33]

27. Cf. Ibid., 211–14.

28. Cf. Sean McGrath, *The Early Heidegger and Medieval Philosophy: Phenomenology for the Godforsaken* (Washington, DC: Catholic University of America Press, 2006).

29. Andrzej Wiercinski, *Philosophizing with Gustav Siewerth: A New German Edition with Facing Translation of "Das Sein als Gleichnis Gottes"/ "Being as Likeness of God," And A Study, "From Metaphor and Indication to Icon: The Centrality of the Notion of Verbum in Hans-Georg Gadamer, Bernard Lonergan, and Gustav Siewerth"* (Konstanz: Verlag Gustav Siewerth Gesellschaft, 2005).

30. Wiercinski, *Inspired*, 29.

31. Ibid., 184.

32. Ibid., 86.

33. McGrath, review of Wiercinski, 334–5.

I maintain that this solution of the "exemplary identity" in Be-ing, as likeness of God, addresses the Lutheran contradictions in Heidegger's "phenomenology for the godforsaken." Heidegger "poses as one who is theologically neutral, when in fact, unlike Husserl, he has made concrete decisions about what is and what is not possible in phenomenology."[34] In his 1927 lecture "Phenomenology and Theology,"

> Heidegger declares that a union between phenomenology and theology is not possible for two reasons: (1) because phenomenology alone is ontological, while theology is merely ontic; and (2) because in its declaration of "faith in the crucified," theology shows itself to be the mortal enemy of phenomenology, which has facticity as its theme. That (2) is in tension with (1) is one of the curious inconsistencies emerging out of this muddled lecture.[35]

The "exemplary identity" in Be-ing, as likeness of God, can resolve such Lutheran contradictions in Heidegger because Siewerth's "exemplary identity" addresses the problem with the "dialectical identity" in Hegel's metaphysics, which attempted "a philosophical grounding for Lutheran theology."[36] Hegelian metaphysics was a "hymn of praise to contradiction."[37]

Moreover, with this solution, Siewerth also solves the problem of the Scotistic univocity of Be-ing in Heidegger to which Siewerth was perhaps blessedly blind. Siewerth, unlike Heidegger or Hegel, "sees the Nothing as a condition of knowing Being"; for Siewerth, the Nothing is "not as primordial as the difference of Being and being."[38] In Hegel, the *Science of Logic* begins with the unity of Being and Nothing: "Being, the indeterminate immediate, is in fact *nothing*, and neither more nor less than *nothing*.... *Pure being* and *pure nothing* are, therefore, the same."[39] Yet Heidegger's insistence on the finitude of Be-ing is "a repetition of Hegelian dialectics."[40] Heidegger writes: "This proposition of Hegel's ... is correct. Being and Nothing hang together ... because Being itself is finite in essence and is

34. Sean McGrath, "Alternative Confessions, Conflicting Faiths: A Review of *The Influence of Augustine on Heidegger*," *American Catholic Philosophical Quarterly* 82.2 (2008): 334.

35. McGrath, "Alternative Confessions," 334.

36. Wiercinski, *Inspired*, 101.

37. Ibid., 102.

38. Ibid., *Inspired*, 122.

39. Hegel, *Science of Logic*, trans. A.V. Miller (Atlantic Highlands, NJ: Humanities Press International, 1989 [1969]), 82.

40. Wiercinski, *Inspired*, 126. Cf. Michael Schulz, "Being, World, and Man: Images of the Triune God in Gustav Siewerth's Trinitarian Ontology," *Communio: International Catholic Review* 29.2 (2002): 397–423, esp. "6. What we can learn from Hegel, and where it is necessary to keep a distance," 412–17.

only revealed in the Transcendence of *Da-sein* as projected into Nothing."[41] Siewerth intentionally avoids this dialectical mistake of Hegel's, and blessedly, if unwittingly, avoids this similar mistake of Heidegger's (i.e., finitizing Be-ing with the Nothing). Siewerth instead recognizes the "exemplary identity of absolute and finite Being,"[42] rather than a dialectical identity: "If God were identical with non-Being, it would be impossible to think finite entities. Again we are forced by the contingency of a being to think the fathomless unity and difference within God."[43]

For Siewerth, non-Being is "the constitutive measure for every perception of Being itself;"[44] "reason fashions non-Being in itself without thereby conveying it into Being"[45] because "there is no transition from non-Being to Being in the act of Being."[46] "Reason is necessarily able to produce" non-Being; hence the nothing is a principle "that emerges from reason."[47] "From the beginning, thinking is only possible within Being and is also initially cognizable only in Being. Being reveals itself in original thinking as pure mediation."[48] Accordingly, for Siewerth, Be-ing is "ideally mediated finiteness"[49] because the "exemplary identity is grounded only in the 'relational' variety of ideas, whose simple oneness is the archetypal contemplation of God."[50] "Being is … an 'idea,' whose reality belongs to divine thought.… Its structure is to be the ideal mediation."[51]

Sean McGrath, imagining what Heidegger's rejoinder to Siewerth would be, points out that Heidegger's insistence on the finitude of Be-ing would mean his refusal to allow his thought to be integrated into a Christian metaphysics of creation, since McGrath rightly imagines Heidegger would argue that Aquinas de-temporalizes *esse*.[52] In reply, I would argue that, in fact, Aquinas does not de-temporalize *esse* because of his explicit qualification:

41. Martin Heidegger, "What is Metaphysics?" in *Existence and Being* (Chicago, Illinois: Henry Regnery Company, 1949), 355–99; quotation at 377.

42. Wiercinski, *Inspired*, 37.

43. Ibid., 155.

44. Gustav Siewerth, "Der Thomismus als Identitätsystem," *Gesammelte Werke* 2 (Düsseldorf: Patmos Verlag, 1979), 76; translated at Wiercinski, *Inspired*, 40.

45. Siewerth, "Identitätsystem," 78; *Inspired*, 41.

46. Wiercinski, *Inspired*, 180.

47. Siewerth, "Identitätsystem," 81–82; *Inspired*, 181.

48. Wiercinski, *Inspired*, 141.

49. Siewerth, "Identitätsystem," 215; *Inspired*, 182.

50. Ibid., 308; *Inspired*, 183.

51. Ibid., 121; *Inspired*, 141.

52. McGrath, "Heidegger's Approach to Aquinas," 284–90.

i.e., that *esse* is "something fixed and at rest [only when having become subsistent] *in a being*" (*aliquid fixum et quietum in ente*).[53] True, "The primary meaning of *esse* is verbal but the present tense of the verb takes pre-eminence,"[54] but not because Aquinas valorizes constant presence, but rather because it is only *the finite actuality* of what is presencing that is accessible to our senses and which is cognized by us first as *ens* (a being Be-ing, an essence exist-ing), from which we can then proceed to a judgmental understanding of the Be-ing of this being when it is compared analogically with all other beings: i.e., we can proceed from the sensory multiplicity of the acts of various subsistent beings to the intellectual intuition of non-subsistent Be-ing.

Therefore Siewerth's exposition of Be-ing as "ideally mediated finiteness"[55] can validly baptize Heidegger, i.e., in a way that removes the deleterious theological ramifications of Heidegger's "pagan" thought (which Hans Jonas has so vividly identified in his chapter on "Heidegger and Theology," his bold challenge to Heidegger in *The Phenomenon of Life*):

> My theological friends, my Christian friends—don't you see what you are dealing with? Don't you sense, if not see, the profoundly pagan character of Heidegger's thought? ... Being—i.e., the Being of the beings—*reveals itself*, by *its initiative*, in experience, in the encounter of beings (human) with beings (things); i.e., that revelation is immanent in the world, nay, belongs to its nature; i.e., that the world is divine.[56]

I would argue that Jonas' critique of Heidegger is in fact suitably addressed by Siewerth's Thomistic distinction between act and subsistence.

So let us continue McGrath's thought experiment of Heidegger replying to Siewerth. Were Heidegger to argue that, despite this distinction that accommodates Heideggerian *physis* at the center of Thomistic thinking on act, Heideggerian thought on its own insistence takes a stand refusing to be thus baptized, I would note that that would be as decisively willful as Heidegger's 1927 lecture and its contradictory declaration of a Lutheran disjunction between phenomenology and theology. The baptism would still be valid. But would Heideggerian thought, especially when baptized

53. My translation and my emphasis. Cf. McGrath, "Heidegger's Approach to Aquinas," 288.
54. McGrath, "Heidegger's Approach to Aquinas," 289, n. 85.
55. Siewerth, "Identitätsystem," 215; *Inspired*, 182.
56. Hans Jonas, *The Phenomenon of Life: Toward a Philosophical Biology* (Evanston, Illinois: Northwestern University Press, 2001 [1966]), 248.

thus against its own will, still be Heideggerian? I would argue so, since Be-ing as "the first creation"[57] of God is still *finite* in a way that God is not: *Be-ing itself* does not subsist.

It is this, Siewerth's Thomistic distinction between act and subsistence, that allows us to think of Be-ing as the "original emanation of God," "the idea of all ideas,"[58] an "ideally mediated finiteness"[59] to replace Heidegger's (apparently univocal) notion of finite Be-ing that in temporality exalts possibility over act. To the contrary, Siewerth, refuting not just Hegel but (even if unwittingly) also Heidegger, argues that "the highest and first clear difference *is not that of Being and essence (potentiality [Potenz]) but that of 'act' and 'subsistence'.*"[60] "Because of its non-subsistence this emergence [of act in the potency of essence] as pure [finite] act is always [potentially] non-Being. But its power is operative in relation to Being and can only be nullified by Being."[61]

McGrath himself observes the consequences of Siewerth's Thomistic distinction between act and subsistence, and how this "transfigures" Heidegger's thought:

> The Be-ing of beings is the condition of the possibility of time. The Be-ing in which all things participate, the Be-ing the horizon of which is time, to speak Heidegger's language, is not the Be-ing of God, but the first act of God, the donation of the energy of his presence in the othering by which creation becomes possible. It is the simple unlimited Be-ing of every thing that exists.... However near to us, it is "a profound mystery," for it includes within itself all possible conceptual determinations, while remaining "uncircumscribed" by any concept. It is the act that actualizes every thing that is, but is "captured and consumed" by none of them.[62]

Nevertheless, McGrath also observes, "Siewerth refers to many texts of Aquinas in constructing his central points. One might question whether this metaphysics is true to Aquinas."[63] However that may be (and to settle such a general question is beyond the scope of this brief presentation), I would still argue that on this particular point, with the distinction between

57. McGrath, review of Wiercinski, 334.

58. Gustav Siewerth, "Die Differenz von Sein und Seiend," *Gesammelte Werke* 3 (Düsseldorf: Patmos Verlag, 1971), 128–9; translated at Wiercinski, *Inspired*, 155.

59. Siewerth, "Identitätsystem," 215; *Inspired*, 182.

60. Siewerth, "Schicksal," 367; *Inspired*, 165.

61. Wiercinski, *Inspired*, 156–57.

62. McGrath, review of Wiercinski, 336.

63. Ibid.

act and subsistence, Siewerth's metaphysics is true to Aquinas.[64] In any case, whether it is true to the man or not is beside the point, if indeed it is true to the matter at hand, as I think it is.[65]

In sum, this is Siewerth's vision, his own articulation of the "intuition of Be-ing": Divine providence, by thinking the divine "ideas," "brings forth a being into occurrence" as Be-ing itself is thereby "*the event* of subsistence": "The not-being-God of Be-ing makes divine self-mediation possible,"[66] and this "mediating mediation" of Be-ing is "not revealed but rather hidden by the light it sheds,"[67] "in the immediately revealed reality of a being."[68]

I think Balthasar is right to commend to us Siewerth's emphasis on the Thomistic distinction between act and subsistence,[69] a distinction of which Christian metaphysics must be the guardian in a time of unbelief. For Siewerth is correct to observe that, for the most part, in modernity, "We can no longer reach out to God by means of our reason, because we no longer differentiate between Be-ing and a being."[70] But as Balthasar himself writes, "without a philosophical mediation," theology will fail in its dialogue with the sciences.[71] In short, without the mediation that metaphysics offers, a theology oblivious to "the intuition of Be-ing" is destined to fail.

64. For clear textual evidence supporting this point, see Aquinas, *ST* I q. 4, a. 2 and ad 3; *ST* I q. 11, a. 4; and *ST* I q. 12, a. 4 and especially ad 3.

65. Cf. McGrath, *Early Heidegger*, 234 n. 57.

66. Wiercinski, *Inspired*, 154. I have italicized "the event" for emphasis on the non-subsistent dynamism of Be-ing.

67. Ibid., 202.

68. Ibid., 141.

69. Thus "this nonsubstantive notion" of Be-ing (i.e., of Be-ing as non-subsisting act) neatly accommodates "Heidegger's retrieval of the pre-Socratic notion of physis, 'self-blossoming emergence,' while preserving the Scholastic principle of the subsistence, eternity, and infinity of God. The First and Absolute Being remains the eternal ground of all that is; it excludes time": McGrath, review of Wiercinski, 336.

70. Wiercinski, *Inspired*, 212.

71. Balthasar, *Glory of the Lord* Volume V, 449.

BRYAN R. CROSS

St. Thomas Aquinas on Unity as an End of Love

In his work titled "Love and Friendship," Jacques Maritain discusses Raïssa's distinction within disinterested love between friendship and love. The essence of friendship, claims Raïssa, is "in desire for the good of one's friend, strong enough to sacrifice oneself for him."[1] The essence of love, by contrast, is "in the communication of oneself, with fullness of joy and delight in possession of the beloved."[2] Both friendship and love, according to Jacques, are gifts of self, but the difference between them is one of "intrinsic quality," not merely of degree. Friendship is a gift of self in an *indirect* manner through giving to the beloved something that one has, even up to one's physical life itself. Love, however, is a gift of self in a *direct* manner, by giving to the beloved one's very own person, directly disclosing one's own subjectivity in an open and "naked" manner.[3]

1. Jacques Maritain, *Notebooks*, trans. Joseph W. Evans (Albany, New York: Magi Books, 1984), 220.

2. Maritain, *Notebooks*, 220.

3. *L'amour de dilection*, when mutual, is what St. Thomas Aquinas calls *amor amicitiae*. This is from Aristotle's claim in *Nichomachean Ethics* VIII, 2 that friendship is "goodwill when it is reciprocal." *Nicomachean Ethics* VIII, 2, 1155b 33, trans. W.D. Ross, in *The Complete Works of Aristotle: Revised Oxford Translation*, J. Barnes, ed., Bollingen Series, (Princeton, New Jersey: Princeton University Press, 1984), 1826. St. Thomas draws from Aristotle to make a distinction between *amor amicitiae* and what he calls *amor concupiscentiae*, i.e. love of concupiscence. Cf. Thomas Aquinas, *Summa theologiae* (hereafter *ST*) II-II, q. 23, a. 1; I-II, q. 26, a. 4; I-II, q. 27, a. 3. Here and throughout, quotations of the *ST* are taken from *The Summa Theologica of St. Thomas Aquinas*, translated by the Fathers of the English Dominican Province (Westminster, Maryland: Christian Classics, 1981). Latin excerpts are from the *Textum Leoninum* (Rome, 1888).

Raïssa's distinction within disinterested love between friendship and love rests on the philosophical background of St. Thomas's distinction between the love of concupiscence and the love of friendship. These two forms of love aim at unity with the beloved in different ways. The sort of unity pursued by the love of concupiscence is relatively straightforward. But why does the love of friendship seek union of lover and beloved? To answer this question I examine here the unitive aspect of love in St. Thomas, with respect to these three loves: the love of concupiscence, friendship, and love in the sense that Raïssa and Jacques use the term 'love' in this essay. I argue that the unity resulting from the love of friendship takes up into itself and thus does not lack the unity resulting from the perfected love of concupiscence, because the love of concupiscence as taken up into the love of friendship produces an internal union.

I. Two Fundamental Types of Love in St. Thomas Aquinas

St. Thomas distinguishes between two fundamental kinds of love, and the kinds of unity to which they are ordered. In his answer to the question "Whether in God there is love," he writes the following:

> An act of love always tends towards two things; to the good that one wills, and to the person for whom one wills it: since to love a person is to wish that person good. Hence, inasmuch as we love ourselves, we wish ourselves good; and, so far as possible, union with that good. So love is called the unitive force.... And by the fact that anyone loves another, he wills good to that other. Thus he puts the other, as it were, in the place of himself; and regards the good done to him as done to himself. So far love is a binding force [*vis concretiva*], since it aggregates another to ourselves [*quia alium aggregat sibi*], and refers his good to our own. And then again the divine love is a binding force, inasmuch as God wills good to others....[4]

This consideration of the nature of love reveals the basis for St. Thomas's distinction between the love of friendship and the love of concupiscence.[5] He refers here to Aristotle's statement that "to love is to wish good to someone." From this statement St. Thomas draws the conclusion that love by its very nature has a twofold tendency: "towards the good which

4. Aquinas, *ST* I, q. 20, a. 1 ad 3.
5. cf. Aquinas, *ST* I-II, q. 26, a. 4.

a man wishes to someone (to himself or to another) and towards that to which he wishes some good." This twofold tendency intrinsic to love makes possible the difference between the love of friendship and the love of concupiscence. The difference between these two kinds of love is that "man has love of concupiscence towards the good that he wishes to another, and love of friendship towards him to whom he wishes good."[6]

If we love something with the love of concupiscence, and thus as a good-for-ourselves, such love is unitive in that we seek to be united to that good so that it becomes our good and we are perfected by it. If I am hungry and I see an apple, I seek the sort of union with that apple by which the apple contributes to my perfection; in this case, it is a union of consumption, so that the apple provides the goods of nourishing my body, satisfying my hunger and pleasing my palate. Thus, the type of unity aimed at by the love of concupiscence is a sort of *having* of the beloved good by the lover. *Having* here is an extrinsic union. In order to have something other than oneself, that something must be extrinsic to the one having it.

In what way then, does the love of friendship aim at unity? Given what we have considered so far concerning the manner in which the love of concupiscence is unitive, it may seem that the love of friendship is unitive only in the sense that the lover wishes that what is good for his friend be united to his friend. The unity brought about by the love of friendship, it might seem, would be equivalent to that brought about by mere good will. But that cannot be because St. Thomas, following Aristotle, maintains that friendship requires not only mutual benevolence, and mutual awareness of mutual benevolence, but also mutual communication.[7]

II. Unity as Cause and Effect of Love

To show how the love of friendship also seeks the union of the lover and the beloved, we must consider how unity is both a cause and an effect of love. According to St. Thomas, union is a cause of love in two general ways. The first type of union that causes love is the union that causes the love with which one loves oneself; this is substantial union.[8] St. Thomas writes, "[E]verything has this aptitude towards its natural form, that when it has it not, it tends towards it; and when it has it, it is at rest therein. It

6. Ibid.

7. Cf. Aquinas, *ST* II-II, q. 23, a. 1.

8. Aquinas, *ST* I-II, q. 28, a. 1 ad 2.

is the same with every natural perfection, which is a natural good."[9] The transcendental relation of being, unity, and goodness entails that insofar as each thing is naturally inclined to its perfection, so it is naturally inclined to its being and unity, for a thing's greatest unity is found in its greatest perfection. Thus St. Thomas writes elsewhere, "[H]ence it is that everything guards its unity as it guards its being."[10] In all things, the natural appetite for their perfection is their self-love, and this self-love seeks their perfection and unity.

The second way in which unity causes love, according to St. Thomas, is by unity of likeness. The principle of movement in the appetite is the subject's connaturality with the appetible object, and connaturality is a kind of likeness of natures. But there are two types of likeness between things, and each causes a different type of love, and thus a different type of unity. One type of likeness is between two things having the same quality actually. The other is between two things wherein one thing has "potentially and by way of inclination, a quality which the other has actually."[11] The first type of likeness, that is, the type of likeness between two things having the same quality actually, is the cause of the love of friendship. St. Thomas writes:

> For the very fact that two men are alike, having, as it were, one form, makes them to be, in a manner, one in that form: thus two men are one thing in the species of humanity, and two white men are one thing in whiteness. Hence the affections of one tend to the other, as being one with him; and he wishes good to him as to himself. But the second kind of likeness causes love of concupiscence, or friendship founded on usefulness or pleasure: because whatever is in potentiality, as such, has the desire for its act; and it takes pleasure in its realization, if it be a sentient and cognitive being.[12]

Thus we can be caused to love through likeness in two general ways. We may apprehend in the other an actual good that we also have actually, or we may apprehend in the other an actual good that we have potentially. In the latter case, we love the other with the love of concupiscence as a means to the actualization of our potentiality.[13] But when we apprehend in the other

9. Aquinas, *ST* I, q. 19, a. 1, 103. See also *ST* I, q. 60, a. 1.

10. Aquinas, *ST* I, q. 11, a. 1: *"Et inde est quod unumquodque, sicut custodit suum esse, ita custodit suam unitatem."*

11. Aquinas, *ST* I-II, q. 27, a. 3.

12. Ibid.

13. Or we love the other as a pleasing subjunctive depiction of what we would be were our potentiality actualized.

an actual good that we also have actually, love is caused directly by apprehended likeness of actuality to actuality. According to St. Thomas, love of this sort is the love of friendship.

This does not yet explain why we would seek unity with a friend whom we love with the love of friendship. It seems rather that the love of friendship is based on an already existing and apprehended unity between friend and friend, and that the unity that the lover [in the love of friendship] pursues subsequently is not the union of himself with the beloved, but rather to effect the unity between his friend and what is good for his friend. To show how that picture is deficient, we have to consider the ways in which the lover and beloved are united, according to St. Thomas.

In answering the question, "Whether union is an effect of love?" St. Thomas claims that the union of lover and beloved is of two sorts. "The first is real union (*secundum rem*); for instance, when the beloved is present with the lover. The second is union of affection (*secundum affectum*)."[14] St. Thomas explains that *real union* is caused *effectively* by love, because "love moves man to desire and seek the presence of the beloved as of something suitable and belonging to him (*quasi sibi convenientis et ad se pertinentis*)." Union of affection, however, is caused *formally* by love, for "love itself is this union or bond."[15] Union of affection moves man to desire real union.

Why does union of affection move man to desire real union? St. Thomas explains that this union which is essentially love itself is a union "according to a bond of affection" (*secundum coaptationem affectus*), and is "likened to substantial union, inasmuch as the lover stands to the object of his love, as to himself (*ut ad seipsum*), if it be the love of friendship; as to something belonging to himself (*ut ad aliquid sui*), if it be the love of concupiscence."[16] The object loved is loved by way of a participation in the subject's self-love. This participation can take place in two ways. It occurs when the object is apprehended as *good for* the subject, and thus the object loved is caught up, so to speak, as a means of advancing the subject's self-preserving and self-perfecting activity. But the participation in the subject's self-love

14. Aquinas, *ST* I-II, q. 28 a. 1.

15. "*quia ipse amor est talis unio vel nexus.*" Here St. Thomas quotes St. Augustine, writing, "love is a vital principle uniting, or seeking to unite two together, the lover, to wit, and the beloved"; to which he adds, "For in describing it as 'uniting' he refers to the union of affection, without which there is no love: and in saying that 'it seeks to unite,' he refers to real union": Aquinas, *ST* I-II, q. 28, a. 1.

16. Aquinas, *ST* I-II, q. 28, a. 1 ad 2.

can also take place when the object is apprehended *as another self*. In this case as well, the beloved is caught up, so to speak, in the lover's self-love, but not as something perfecting the self, but as self. The lover's self-love is extended in scope, applying to other persons apprehended, as it were, as other instances of oneself.

Both these types of union of affection seek real union of lover and beloved, but the types of real union they seek are different, for the types of union they apprehend with the other are different. St. Thomas writes,

> Now love being twofold, viz. love of concupiscence and love of friendship; each of these arises from a kind of apprehension of the oneness of the thing loved with the lover. For when we love a thing, by desiring it, we apprehend it as belonging to our well-being (*quasi sibi convenientis et ad se pertinentis*). In like manner when a man loves another with the love of friendship, he wills good to him, just as he wills good to himself: wherefore he apprehends him as his other self (*vult ei bonum sicut et sibi vult bonum, unde apprehendit eum ut alterum se*), in so far, to wit, as he wills good to him as to himself. Hence a friend is called a man's "other self" (*Ethic.* ix, 4), and Augustine says (*Confess.* iv, 6), "Well did one say to his friend: Thou half of my soul."[17]

The kind of unity that, when apprehended, gives rise to the love of concupiscence is one in which the lover stands to the beloved as to something belonging to himself (*ut ad aliquid sui*). This unity is apprehended as a *potential* unity, until real union takes place. By contrast, the kind of unity that when apprehended gives rise to the love of friendship is one in which the lover *already* stands to the beloved as to himself (*ut ad seipsum*).[18] So this unity is apprehended as an actual unity. That is what makes pursuit of unity with the beloved seem superfluous in the love of friendship, for unity seems already to be accomplished. But importantly, the unity apprehended in the love of friendship is not necessarily apprehended as having no potency for further union. This potency leaves open the possible discovery and dynamic creation of further actual unity, as well as the mutual apprehension of potential unity. Real union is what union of affection seeks to effect, all other things being equal, because real union of the self with itself is what self-love already seeks both to preserve and advance, in the perfection of the lover.[19]

17. Aquinas, *ST* I-II, q. 28, a. 1.

18. Aquinas, *ST* I-II, q. 28, a. 1 ad 2.

19. St. Thomas writes, "Moreover this [real] union is in keeping with the demands of love (*convenientiam amoris*: for as the Philosopher relates (*Polit.* ii, 1), 'Aristophanes stated that lovers would wish to be united both into one,' but since 'this would result in either one or both being

But the beloved as an object of the love of friendship does not cease to be apprehended as a good any more than in self-love the self ceases to be apprehended as a good. Rather, just as the self is apprehended as a qualitatively greater good than all self-perfecting goods, so likewise the beloved as an object of the love of friendship is apprehended as a qualitatively greater good than all those goods perfecting either oneself or the beloved, God excepted. In the love of friendship, the beloved is apprehended as a good to be, not only as a mere good for me.

III. Mutual Indwelling and Dynamic Union

To understand the union of subject with subject in the love of friendship we need to examine what St. Thomas says about mutual indwelling. When he considers whether mutual indwelling is an effect of love, he describes three ways in which mutual indwelling occurs. In the *apprehensive* power, the beloved is in the lover as that which is known is in the knower. The beloved in this way dwells in the lover's heart. At the same time, the lover, through his apprehensive power, is in the beloved, "inasmuch as the lover is not satisfied with a superficial apprehension of the beloved, but strives to gain an intimate knowledge of everything pertaining to the beloved, so as to penetrate into his very soul."[20] By this penetration, the lover acquires an interior point of view in the beloved, and thus the lover, through his apprehensive power, is in the beloved.

In the *appetitive* power, mutual indwelling differs in the case of the love of concupiscence from the case of the love of friendship. In the love of concupiscence, the object loved is in the lover's affection by a kind of complacency (*per quandam complacentiam*) such that it causes him to take pleasure in its presence, and long for it in its absence. But, in the love of friendship, the beloved is in the lover's affection such that it causes him both to take pleasure in the beloved's good when the beloved's good is present, and, by his longing, to tend towards the good that he wills to the beloved, in the sense of seeking to effect the union of the beloved's good with the beloved such that the beloved has that good.

---

destroyed,' they seek a suitable and becoming union—to live together, speak together, and be united together in other like things" Aquinas, (*ST* I-II, q. 28, a. 1 ad 2). In seeking real union, love does not seek to destroy its own possibility, but seeks rather that which preserves its own actuality. Both types of love seek real union of the lover with the beloved.

20. Aquinas, *ST* I-II, q. 28, a. 2.

Similarly, in the love of concupiscence, the lover is in the beloved such that, as St. Thomas says, the lover "is not satisfied with any external or superficial possession or enjoyment of the beloved; but seeks to possess the beloved perfectly, by penetrating into his heart, as it were."[21] The lover, in this case, is present in the beloved in a certain manner, namely, the manner of *possession*, a possession that penetrates by desire even to the heart of the beloved. In the love of friendship, by contrast, the lover is in the beloved, as St. Thomas says,

> inasmuch as [the lover] reckons what is good or evil to his friend, as being so to himself; and his friend's will as his own, so that it seems as though he felt the good or suffered the evil in the person of his friend. Hence it is proper to friends "to desire the same things, and to grieve and rejoice at the same," as the Philosopher says (*Ethic.* ix, 3 and *Rhet.* ii, 4). Consequently in so far as he reckons what affects his friend as affecting himself, the lover seems to be in the beloved, as though he were become one with him: but in so far as, on the other hand, he wills and acts for his friend's sake as for his own sake, looking on his friend as identified with himself, thus the beloved is in the lover.[22]

This is a kind of spiritual union, made possible by intellect and will, because both by knowledge and appetite, the lover truly comes to be within the beloved such that the lover does not merely have the same abstracted knowledge ("knowledge that") and the same general appetite (general desire for the good) that the beloved has, but also the same particular knowledge, and the same particular appetite for the good of the beloved. The lover comes to occupy the same internal point of view, the same "perch," so to speak, from which the world discloses itself to the beloved, and thus the lover participates in the same particular appetites of the beloved, not in competition for the beloved's good, but sharing in the same appetites had by the beloved for the beloved's good.

But, for the purpose of this paper, the most important part of St. Thomas's discussion of mutual indwelling is the third way of mutual indwelling to which he devotes only one sentence. He writes: "In yet a third way, mutual indwelling in the love of friendship can be understood in regard to reciprocal love: inasmuch as friends return love for love, and both desire and do good things for one another."[23]

Mutual indwelling only by way of the apprehensive and appetitive pow-

21. Ibid.

22. Ibid.

23. Ibid.

ers would, by itself, be static, at least in humans. It would not be identical to goodwill, because goodwill does not include union of affection.[24] But an increase in mutual indwelling in the apprehensive and appetitive powers can only take place through a dynamic reciprocity of ever-deepening acts of self-donation and reception of the other. In humans this is an organic process requiring some kind of shared life. Here we find the locus for the love about which Jacques and Raissa have written, because the self-donation intrinsic to friendship and love finds its place in the dynamic reciprocity of a shared life between friends.

Is shared life a mere necessary condition for friendship, or is it truly a third form of mutual indwelling? For St. Thomas, the primary reason why goodwill is insufficient for friendship is that goodwill does not necessarily include mutual communication. He writes: "Yet neither does well-wishing suffice for friendship, for a certain mutual love is requisite, since friendship is between friend and friend: and this well-wishing is founded on some kind of communication."[25]

Communication provides the self-disclosure by which the beloved is apprehended by the lover, and comes to abide in the appetite of the lover. This is why the love of friendship cannot be had with non-rational animals.[26] But in humans, this is a temporal process, and so involves a shared life. By engaging in shared activities together, we effect a kind of mutual indwelling in our respective life stories. But the mutual indwelling is not merely that of intertwined life stories; it is also constitutive. That is because humans are temporal in our formation; we come to be who we are through a process in time.

This opens up a way to see a genuine third possibility for mutual in-

24. "But the love, which is in the intellective appetite, also differs from goodwill, because it denotes a certain union of affections between the lover and the beloved, in as much as the lover deems the beloved as somewhat united to him, or belonging to him, and so tends towards him. On the other hand, goodwill is a simple act of the will, whereby we wish a person well, even without presupposing the aforesaid union of the affections with him. Accordingly, to love, considered as an act of charity, includes goodwill, but such dilection or love adds union of affections, wherefore the Philosopher says (*Ethic.* ix, 5) that 'goodwill is a beginning of friendship'": Aquinas, *ST* II-II, q. 27, a. 2.

25. Aquinas, *ST* II-II, q. 23, a. 1.

26. "Friendship cannot exist except towards rational creatures, who are capable of returning love, and communicating one with another in the various works of life, and who may fare well or ill, according to the changes of fortune and happiness; even as to them is benevolence properly speaking exercised": Aquinas, *ST* I, q. 20, a. 2 ad 3.

dwelling. The lover does not merely seek the good of the beloved, for the person with goodwill might do the same. The lover seeks to make himself become, insofar as possible, the good of the beloved. He can do this in two general ways. These two general ways correspond to the extrinsic union of the love of concupiscence, and the intrinsic union of the love of friendship. The extrinsic form of self-donation is a giving of oneself indirectly by giving what one has. This is the kind of self-donation involved in what Raïssa calls friendship. The intrinsic and direct form of self-donation is a giving of one's very self, one's very heart. This is the kind of self-donation that Raïssa calls love, whether it be romantic love, *bel amor*, or, if given absolutely, mad boundless love.

Consider the following example of mutual indwelling through self-donation. The lover enjoys cooking for his beloved. He does so not only because he is nourishing the beloved and bringing gustatory pleasure to the beloved. He does so also because in preparing the meal, he puts something of himself into the food through his art, albeit indirectly, and thereby puts himself not only into the life experience of the beloved, but into the very being of the beloved. He himself becomes, in this indirect way, part of the good of the beloved, part of her perfection. His wanting to be part of the good of the beloved is not at all to the detriment of the good of the beloved. He wants this, insofar as the good of the beloved is open to his self-donation. So this shows us more clearly the nature of this third form of mutual indwelling. This is not mutual indwelling by apprehensive or appetitive power; this is mutual indwelling by acts of self-donation and acts of reception in which the acts of self-donation are received into the heart and life of the recipient.

Why does the lover want to be, or be part of, the good of the beloved? It is because donation of self into the very being and perfecting of the beloved creates a greater and, therefore, more perfect union of lover and beloved. And love seeks the greatest possible union with the beloved, all other things being equal. This is the nature of love, found fundamentally in self-love, from which come both the love of concupiscence and the love of friendship. In the love of friendship among humans, the lover apprehends not only the static connaturality of the beloved with the lover, but also the potential substantial ontological union of the lover with the beloved through the donation of the lover himself into the being of the beloved.

IV. The Three Unities

We can now say something about the three types of unity resulting from the three kinds of love. The love of concupiscence effects an extrinsic unity of having; the object loved is united to the lover in apprehension, appetite, and real union as a means of perfecting the lover. The love of friendship is based on an apprehension of an already existing unity of likeness. This apprehension produces a union of affection in which the beloved is united internally (that is, in spirit) with the lover such that the beloved comes to participate in the lover's self-love as another self. Union of affection seeks real union, and real union is not just in place and time, but also in activity, and, insofar as possible, in being. The lover seeks to make himself part of the good of the beloved. If he does this only through what he has, this is (within the love of friendship) what Raïssa calls friendship. But if he does this directly, giving his very self, this is what Raïssa calls love. In this way the friends, or lovers, seek real union through mutual self-donation.

Why then does the love of friendship seek union of lover and beloved, and not merely the union of the beloved's good with the beloved? It is because the self naturally seeks its own unity as it seeks its own perfection. The self seeks to be with itself, united to itself. Therefore, insofar as the other is apprehended as another self, the lover will seek through union of affection to be one with the beloved in real union. This real union involves not only mutual indwelling in the apprehensive and appetitive powers; it also involves a shared life together in which the lover and beloved place themselves into each other's lives through mutual acts of self-donation. In this shared life, the lover desires that the beloved, whom the lover loves as another self, becomes, without any detriment to the good of the beloved, also the good of the lover. And in this way the love of concupiscence is taken up and perfected within the love of friendship.[27]

27. I am especially grateful for the stimulation and creative suggestions, questions and objections of my students in my Philosophy of Human Nature class at Saint Louis University, in the Fall of 2008. Their gifts of self-donation helped shape the thesis and content of this paper.

PETER FELDMEIER

Maritain on Eros and Agape

Entering the Paradox

I. The Problem of Eros and Agape

Renowned ethicist Gene Outka marks 1930 as a turning point in theology and ethics, since this was the year when Swedish theologian Anders Nygren published the first of his three-volume opus *Eros and Agape.*[1] Outka argues that from this point on the nature, role, and analysis of the concept of love takes on a new prominence. Regarding Nygren, Outka writes, "His critics have been legion, but few have ignored or been unaffected by his thesis. Thus, whatever the reader may think of it, one may justifiably regard his work as the beginning of the modern treatment of the subject."[2] What is this thesis that has so marked modern discourse on love? In brief it is this: there are two kinds of love that ground two kinds of cultivation of the soul and generate two kinds of religiosity. One is *eros,* which is a drive for union that is self-interested and ultimately self-absorbed. While *eros* could merely point to the sexual drive, Nygren understands it as potentially representing the highest, most virtuous expression of Platonism, and the energy for the ascent to God. The other kind of love is *agape,* the biblical term for love, which represents self-denial and self-offering. In *agape,* one renounces oneself for the sake of the other, making the other singularly

1. This was initially published as *Den kristna kärleskstanken* between 1930 and 1936 and quickly translated into English, the first volume coming out in 1932, the second in 1938, and finally the third in 1939 under S.P.C.K. House. The volume I am relying on is a revised translation by Philip Watson, *Agape and Eros* (Chicago: University of Chicago Press, 1982).

2. Gene Outka, *Agape: An Ethical Analysis* (New Haven: Yale University Press, 1972), 1.

important. Jesus Christ represents the paradigmatic expression of *agape*, as one who came to serve (Mk 10:45) and whose glory is in self-emptiness and self-offering (Phil 2:5–11). In his famous juxtaposition, he makes clear the distinction between the two:

Eros is acquisitive desire and longing.	*Agape* is sacrificial giving.
Eros is an upward movement.	*Agape* is God's way to man.
Eros is man's effort: it assumes that man's salvation is his own work.	*Agape* is God's grace: salvation is the work of Divine love.
Eros is egocentric love, a form of self-assertion of the highest, noblest, sublimest kind.	*Agape* is unselfish love, it *seeketh not its own*, it gives itself away.
Eros seeks to gain its life, a life divine and immortalized.	*Agape* lives the life of God, therefore dares to lose it.
Eros is the will to get and possess which depends on want and need.	*Agape* is freedom in giving which depends on wealth and plenty.
Eros is primarily *man's* love; God is the object of *eros*. Even when it is attributed to God, *eros* is patterned on human love.	*Agape* is primarily *God's* love; God *is agape*. Even when it is attributed to man, *agape* is patterned on Divine love.
Eros is determined by the quality, the beauty, and the wealth of its object; it is not spontaneous, but *evoked* and *motivated*.	*Agape* is sovereign in relation to its object and is directed to both *the evil and the good*; it is *spontaneous, overflowing, unmotivated*.
Eros recognizes value in its object and loves it.	*Agape* loves and *creates value* in its object.[3]

Other critical and influential studies have followed Nygren here. Gene Outka's classic text, *Agape: An Ethical Analysis*, describes *agape* as the necessary move to Christian universality, a love that does not depend on the qualities of the one loved, a love that is unconditional.[4] Reinhold Neibuhr, following Nygren, challenges the Christian to conform to God's love, which is *agape*, and express one's own life as an act of self-abnegation. For Neibuhr, sacrificial love marks and uniquely distinguishes the Christian.[5] And finally, Karl Barth argues that in the end the soul must radically choose loves and

3. Nygren, *Agape and Eros*, 210.

4. Outka, *Agape: An Ethical Analysis*, 12ff.

5. Reinhold Neibuhr, *The Nature and Destiny of Man*, vol. 2 (New York: Charles Scribner's

the manner of life they direct; it is either *eros* or *agape*.[6] In light of this contrast between *eros* and *agape*, Nygren sharply criticizes the tradition of *caritas* as constructed by Augustine. He argues that Augustine created an amalgamation of these two inimical postures, the result of which compromises Christianity's unique and singular witness. *Caritas* becomes then a synthesis of what should forever be antithetical.[7] That Augustine was a Neo-Platonist buttresses Nygren's complaint.[8] So disturbing is this conflation that he even suggests that Augustine is a corrupter of Christian morality. In no way, of course, is Nygren suggesting that Augustine promotes immorality, but rather that Augustine grounds his moral vision with values that appeal to human happiness and flourishing; these undermine *agape*.[9] One could only wonder what Nygren would have done with Thomas Aquinas had Thomas been a subject in this famous study. Among other things, Thomas argues for pursuing a love that is attractive to the soul, satisfies it, and betters it.[10] All these are characteristics of *eros*, and Thomas was unapologetic for asserting that the soul is duty-bound to pursue its obvious good. Tellingly, Edward Vacek calls Thomas the "apostle of *eros*."[11]

More recently it has been demonstrated that *agape* is used in the Bible (both Septuagint and New Testament) to represent a variety of loves that are much wider than simply self-offering, and indeed that the bibli-

---

Sons, 1964), 82. I was led to this text by Bernard Brady's *Christian Love* (Washington, D.C.: Georgetown University Press, 2003).

6. Karl Barth, *Kirchliche Dogmatik* (Zollikon-Zurich, 1955), vol. 4, pt. 2, 835 as cited in Joseph Pieper, *Faith, Hope, Love*, trans. Richard and Clara Wilson (San Francisco: Ignatius Press, 1997), 223.

7. Nygren writes, "The streams of Eros and Agape meet in Augustine; yet he does not receive passively what they bring to him. He lives actively in both worlds and with his whole soul, so that the two motifs are brought into a mutual relationship which is far from superficial.... If the Agape motif gains ground as Augustine develops, the Eros motif is not correspondingly set aside. On the contrary, both assert their influence through his development.... This meeting of the Eros and Agape motifs produces a characteristic third which is neither Eros nor Agape, but Caritas" (*Agape and Eros*, 449–52).

8. See Nygren, *Agape and Eros*, 458–463. Augustine being identified as a Neo-Platonist is standard. Peter Brown writes that Neo-Platonism was "grafted almost imperceptibly into his writings as the ever present basis of his thought" (Peter Brown, *Augustine of Hippo* [Berkeley: University of California Press, 1969], 123).

9. Ibid., 458–59. In this latter claim, Nygren is citing approvingly Karl Holl.

10. This includes, for Thomas, both *caritas* and *amor*. See *ST* II-II q. 28, a. 5; *ST* II-II q. 27, a. 5; and *ST* II-II q. 26, a. 7. I was led to Thomas's material by Brady, *Christian Love*, 164ff, and am following him herein.

11. Edward Vacek, *Love, Human and Divine: The Heart of Christian Ethics* (Washington, D.C.: Georgetown University Press, 1994), 244.

cal witness is much more complex than Nygren's account suggests.[12] Still, his point, echoed by many others, appears salient. How could *eros* ever be considered noble or spiritual when it is by definition self-seeking? Isn't loving another for one's own sake an inherent contradiction? By definition it seems that one is really loving oneself, and the other is valuable only to one's own personal end. Indeed, Pope John Paul II describes engaging another in terms of utility as the opposite of true care for the other.[13]

II. Maritain's Solution

Jacques Maritain's analysis of love provides a nuanced construction of how the soul relates to God, self, and others that, I believe, provides an answer to the problem of the relationship between *eros* and *agape*. While Maritain does not use the terms *eros and agape* in his essay "Love and Friendship," he deals with their dynamic throughout. Interestingly, one could be tempted to align him with Nygren. For example, he clearly distinguishes *amor concupiscentiae*, love for the good of the lover, from *love of dilection*, unselfish love for the good of the beloved.[14] In fact, it appears that *amor concupiscentiae* is so grounded in narcissism that Maritain spends scant time on it, and it is virtually dismissed after definition. But Maritain is no unwitting defender of Nygren's position, which itself is an implicit critique of the Catholic tradition. Rather, Maritain's exposition of the kinds and qualities of love points to the actual necessity of uniting love as self-interest (*eros*) with love as self-offering (*agape*).

Let us look at three kinds of loving relationships from this seminal work to understand how, for Maritain, it is necessary to unite *eros* and *agape*. One typical kind of loving is that of friendship, *amor amicitae*, which Maritain believes one can have with a typical friend, with one's spouse, and even with God. If one were to embrace Nygren's distinctions, then Maritain's understanding of *amor amicitae* is confused. On the one hand, it is a love characterized as a "joy and delight in the possession of the beloved."

12. See Vacek's correctives, 158ff. It is also the case, as D'Arcy points out, that *agape* only appears twice in the whole of the synoptic gospels. See M.C. D'Arcy, *The Mind and Heart of Love: Lion and Unicorn—A Study in Eros and Agape* (New York: Henry Holt and Company, 1947), 55.

13. Karol Wojtyła [Pope John Paul II], *Love and Responsibility*, trans. H.T. Willets (San Francisco: Ignatius Press, 1993), 31–34.

14. See Jacques Maritain, "Love and Friendship," in *Untrammeled Approaches*, ed. Bernard Doering (Notre Dame: University of Notre Dame Press, 1997), 166.

Clearly this is *eros*. On the other hand, its essence is "the deep desire for the good of one's friend." It is a real, albeit indirect, gift of oneself.[15] Clearly this is *agape*. Can it be both? Thomas Aquinas, whom I briefly alluded to earlier, assumes that one ought to be attracted to what one loves, and that there is a kind of possession of the one loved. In contrast to undifferentiated love that does not seek value in the other (*agape*), love of friends intentionally seeks a good inherent in another, recognizes the good shared, and bonds to the other through this good. Indeed, the more good engaged in the relationship the stronger the bond and the deeper the love.[16] Presuming the love is ordered and the good pursued is a *bona fide* good (not just an apparent good), this kind of bonding and possession betters both friends.[17] Maritain follows Thomas here: the natural end of friendship is mutual perfection.[18] Does the dynamic of *eros* then undermine *agape*? For Maritain, like Thomas, the deeper one bonds with another via *eros*, the more easily and purposefully one can give oneself to the friend. One gives his possessions, his care, and "in a certain way, what he is, his own person or his very subjectivity . . . he can even go so far as to give up his very life."[19]

A second kind of love that Maritain treats is that of married love. Here *eros* takes initial center stage. If it is purely carnal *eros*, what Maritain calls *passionate love*, then it is no more than a mirage of actual love.[20] But prudently ordered sexual desire and passion do have a necessary place if this is to become an authentic marital love.[21] This is instructive, since *eros* becomes the foundation of, and the condition of possibility for, *agape*. From these beginnings, love's challenge is to create "a love that is radically free of all self-centeredness, which by no means excludes sensual desire and passion, but which in itself and by its essence is principally spiritual—a complete and irrevocable gift of one to the other, for the love of the other."[22] This *spiritual companionship*, as he calls it, transforms and transcends sexual love (*eros*), not by denying it or superseding it but by engaging it directly, "in such a way that in this love, where sensual desire is present with all its power, a tenderness or *dilection* takes a very real precedence over any selfish considerations."[23] Interestingly, Maritain's understanding of this marital

15. Maritain, "Love and Friendship," 166–67.
16. *ST* II-II, q. 26, a. 7.
17. *ST* II-II, q. 28, a. 5.
18. Maritain, "Love and Friendship," 179.
19. Ibid., 166–67.
20. Ibid., 168.
21. Ibid., 184.
22. Ibid.
23. Ibid.

love anticipates Vatican II, where married love is understood as grounded in utterly human affection and intimacy that is simultaneously a spiritual union and an authentic expression of holiness.[24]

The third kind of relationship of love that Maritain addresses is love of God. But to understand the possibilities of such a love, we must step back slightly. Maritain describes three kinds of human love: *passionate love,* by which he means mere carnality; *authentic love that is not given absolutely,* which is normal, healthy self-gift brought on by tested, mature companionship; and *authentic love that is absolutely given,* which expresses radical self-gift. There is a paradox to this latter form of love, Maritain argues, in that one experiences both a duality of lover and beloved and a kind of fusion of identities. This pursuit of radical unity is what Nygren means by *eros.* For Maritain, those who have such a love experience *amour fou* (mad love).[25]

One can have a relationship with God as one of friendship, *amor amicitae.* In such a love one knows and enjoys God, and gives oneself to God in an analogous way that one would to a dear friend. But the kind of love where one enters what Maritain calls "the habitual regime of the Gifts of the Holy Spirit" is the mystical life.[26] This is *amour fou* for God. Here Maritain speaks in even greater paradox than what we have seen above. One is full of desire, one is *intoxicated* by God, and one seeks to possess the divine Beloved. This is full-fledged *eros.* On the other hand, the soul discovers that it only loves for God's sake and not for its own. That is, it loves as *agape.*[27] Such an *amour fou* for God is the premier relationship and one, Maritain claims, every saint embraced.[28]

In each of these three relationships (friend, spouse, and God) we see a fundamental dynamic regarding *eros* and *agape,* which is that they are by no means antithetical, but rather imply and require each other. It is not merely that one begins with *eros* and progresses to *agape.* Such a schema would be easy to imagine. Here one is attracted to a good and pursues that good for one's own sake. As one unites with the beloved, such a motivation is purified over time so that one seeks the good of the other over one's own good, which had been one's initial motivation. A more accurate depiction of what Maritain has in mind sees that these loves mutually condition each

24. See *Gaudium et Spes,* #48–49, and *Lumen Gentium,* #41.
25. Maritain, "Love and Friendship," 168–70.
26. Ibid., 182.
27. Ibid., 171–75.
28. Ibid., 182.

other. Thus, *eros* becomes the condition of possibility for *agape*, and the expression of *agapic* love works to deepen *eros*. Such would be the teaching of Pope Benedict, who takes up the interrelationship between the two. In *Deus Caritas Est* Benedict writes, "Eros and agape ... can never be completely separated. The more the two, in their different aspects, find a proper unity in the one reality of love, the more the true nature of love in general is realized."[29]

While this is certainly right in and of itself, and indeed an excellent expression of the mutuality between *eros* and *agape*, even this latter formulation imagines that they are two different and possibly contrasting energies of the soul: one that seeks to possess and one that seeks to offer. I believe that Maritain supports a kind of mystical, paradoxical love that collapses both in a singular dynamic.

III. Love's Paradox in the Catholic Tradition

The Catholic tradition does know of this paradox. Bernard of Clairvaux, for example, witnesses it: "We must make this our desire: that as God himself willed that everything should be for himself, so we too will that nothing, not even ourselves, may be or have been except for him.... Of pure and sinless intention of the will—the more pure and sinless in that there is no mixture of self-will in it, the more sweet and tender in that everything it feels is divine."[30] Here Bernard suggests that the soul experiences the most sublime sweet possession in the context of self-offering. The soul, for Bernard, is simultaneously empty and divinely full. And one's passionate desire is simultaneously a form of emptiness. This dynamic does not suggest reciprocal movements in the soul. Rather, the paradox consists in both impulses conflating into something singular. Bernard again: "She loves with all her heart, nothing is lacking when all is given. So, as I have said, to love in that way is to be married, for a soul cannot love like this and not be loved in return. Full and perfect marriage consists in this."[31]

29. Pope Benedict XVI, *Deus Charitas Est*, #7; *http://www.vatican.va/holy_father/benedict_xvi/encyclicals/documents/hf_ben-xvi_enc_20051225_deus-caritast-est_en.html* (accessed 10 June, 2008).

30. Bernard of Clairvaux, *Bernard of Clairvaux: Selected Works*, trans. G.R. Evans (Mahwah, New Jersey: Paulist Press, 1987), 196.

31. Ibid., 274.

The Catholic paradox of simultaneous desire and selflessness, possession and self-offering, or fulfillment and self-abnegation is not easy to grasp. It does not mean that loving God is having it both ways as imagined by some. Irving Singer, for example, writes, "You get what you want by possessing the highest good and completing your nature in a world beyond this one. And you avoid the frustration of not getting what you want by no longer wanting it, by annihilating all inclinations other than those that God ordains and therefore protects."[32] This is not what I am arguing for, and Singer's version strikes me as more of a happy irony than an actual paradox. What the Catholic tradition is getting at more accurately claims that selfless detachment and passionate desire for unity represent a singular movement in the soul.

IV. Ontological Implications of the Paradox of Love

I see the paradox of simultaneously seeking union and self-offering to be tied to another question: what do we think we are in relationship to the rest of the world and to God? Are we really discrete individuals distinct from them? Or does love point us to an ontological vision that suggests that we are more like *beings-in-relation* or *interpenetrated beings*? Maritain does not flesh out such a question, but he does point us in that direction by arguing that love, particularly *amour fou*, is both a fusion and an offering. Pope John Paul suggests this reconsideration of identity in love in his work *Love and Responsibility*. "Love," he says, "finds its full realization not in an individual subject, but in a relationship between subjects, between persons. There is a transition from *I* to *we*."[33] In John Paul's theology, he is not suggesting that the marital partners now merely think in terms of a couple rather than each individualistically. For John Paul, this fusion is not a side-by-side bonding, but an interpenetration of persons that exist in a new *commmunio*.[34]

32. Irving Singer, *The Nature of Love: From Plato to Luther* (Chicago: University of Chicago Press, 1984), 361.

33. Karol Wojtyła, *Love and Responsibility*, 95. In *Familiaris Consortio* (#14), he describes the self-gift as creating the *one flesh* of marriage.

34. John Paul II, *Familiaris Consortio*, #33; see also *The Catechism of the Catholic Church*, #1623.

Interestingly, recent work in physiology and neurology support such an interpenetration. In *A General Theory of Love*, Physicians Lewis et al. describe the physiology of love in marriage as each partner having a dominant effect on the neural activity of the other. "Lovers," they write, "hold keys to each other's identity." They proceed to describe how the beloved conditions the lover's "emotions, neurophysiology, hormonal status, immune function, sleep rhythms, and stability." The loving relationship is not, they claim, 50–50, but 100–100 of concurrent reciprocity.[35] In short, medicine is beginning to realize that conceiving a person as a wholly discrete individual is an artificial construction.

So far we have been discussing the interpenetration of lovers. But could this point us to a deeper ontological level? The biblical witness has hints of this that point us to a fundamental unity we have with one another in God. St. Paul, for example, describes Christ as uniting all things in heaven and earth (Eph 1:10), filling all things (Eph 4:10), and indwelling through all things (Col 3:11). Indeed the *telos* of redemption is that "God may be all in all" (1 Cor 15:28). The Church fathers saw this as well. St. Augustine, for example, imagined those called by God (*societas sanctorum*) as an interpenetrating symphony.[36] Henri de Lubac sums up the patristic tradition in this regard: "Everything here below, including the Church herself, is for the elect, but the elect are not isolated beings.... The triumphant *Catholica* is not a mere addition, the sum total of the elect. She is a real unity, a trans-personal unity."[37]

Mystical literature is replete with this insight. Here are just a few soundings from various traditions: Martin Buber's famous book *I-Thou* was devoted to describing the paradox of interpenetration of identities. In an I-Thou relationship reality and relationality become "seamless, he is You and fills the firmament."[38] Such engagements represent not only the inter-subjectivity among creatures, but one with God as well. All relationships "intersect in the eternal Thou."[39] Such a vision has entered mainstream Judaism as well.

35. Thomas Lewis, Fari Amini, and Richard Lannon, *A General Theory of Love* (New York: Vintage, 2000), 207–08.

36. This citation is taken from Henri de Lubac, *Catholicism: Christ and the Common Destiny of Man*, trans. L. Sheppard and E. Englund (San Francisco: Ignatius Press, 1988), 118.

37. Ibid., 112–14.

38. Martin Buber, *I and Thou*, trans. Walter Kaufmann (New York: Simon Schuster, 1970), 59.

39. Ibid., 123.

Rabbi Lawrence Kushner writes, "There are invisible lines or threads that tie the universe to us and us to the universe.... [Y]ou must be willing to lose yourself; dissolve like a drop of water in the ocean—no longer understood as a separate or discrete thing.... The borders of yourself are erased. All that remains now instead is the unity of all being."[40] There is also a wonderful Islamic Sufi story that suggests this as well. The disciple knocks on the master's door. "Who is it?" he asks. "It is I, Sayeed," the disciple responds. There is no admittance. There is a second attempt with the same results. In the third attempt, however, to the question, "Who is it?" the response is, "It is you." The door opens.[41] Finally, what grounds Mahayana Buddhist anthropology is a concept called dependent co-arising, which asserts that our very natures are interpenetrated with all the beings of the universe. Thich Nhat Hanh describes Buddhist non-duality as "interbeing—the insight that everything is interconnected."[42] In examining a broad account of this insight from world religions, Paul Knitter writes, "'Every-thing' and 'every-body' are profoundly and dynamically interrelated, to the point that what a 'thing' or 'body' is, is constituted by its relationships."[43]

What may be ironic then, is that a principal criticism Nygren has with *eros*, and implicitly with the Catholic tradition, is that it is individualistic.[44] *Agape*, as Nygren presents it, is conceived of a separate entity applying value on another through love with no inherent interconnection between lover and the one loved. This is a radically individualistic ontology.

This same kind of interpenetration, now in its most profound form, can be said regarding *amour fou* with God. In commenting on the *Song of Songs* though the category of *amour fou*, Maritain says that the bride becomes so transformed in her Divine Bridegroom that she becomes entirely love herself.[45] This is the supernatural *telos* of the soul: to become di-

40. Lawrence Kushner, *Jewish Spirituality: A Brief Introduction for Christians* (Woodstock, Vermont: Jewish Lights, 2001), 34 and 68.

41. See a version of this told by Anne Twitty, "Opening One Eye at a Time," *Parabola* vol. 30, no. 1 (2005): 81–84.

42. Thich Nhat Hanh, *Anger: Wisdom for Cooling the Flame* (New York: Riverhead, 2001), 69.

43. Paul Knitter, *Introducing Theology of Religions* (Maryknoll, New York: Orbis Books, 2002), 10.

44. D'Arcy, *Mind and Heart of Love*, 66.

45. See John Dunaway, "Maritain on the Song of Songs," in *Jacques Maritain and the Ways of Knowing*, ed. Douglas Ollivant (Washington, D.C.: Catholic University Press, 2002), 315–23. Maritain also sees this bride as the Church, which, as the body of Christ, particularly reveals the both/and nature of this paradox of identity in relationality.

vinized, to become love itself.[46] St. John of the Cross, on whom Maritain principally relied regarding mystical theology,[47] describes the divinized experience insofar as one can on earth: "God will so communicate his supernatural being to the soul that it will appear to be God himself and will possess what God himself possesses ... both God and the soul become one in participant transformation" (*Ascent* II.5.7); "So great is this union that even though they differ in substance, in glory, and in appearance the soul seems to be God and God seems to be the soul" (*Spiritual Canticle*, 31:1).[48] In the context of such an exalted spiritual end to Christian love, we also find that the soul must live in perpetual poverty of spirit (*Ascent* II.6.1; 7.8; 24.8; *Spiritual Canticle* 34:5–6; *Living Flame* 3.47). Is the soul then emptied or glorified? The paradox remains.[49] In John of the Cross's famous sketch of Mount Carmel, he writes that the path to the top of Mount Carmel is

46. Jacques Maritain, *The Collected Works of Jacques Maritain, Vol. VII: The Degrees of Knowledge*, trans. Gerald Phelan (Notre Dame, Indiana: University of Notre Dame Press, 1995), 340.

47. See Maritain, "The Degrees of Supernatural Knowledge," in *The Degrees of Knowledge*, 263–410; Charles Fecher, *The Philosophy of Jacques Maritain* (Westminster, Maryland: Newman Press, 1953), 314ff; and Robert Delfino, "Mystical Theology in Aquinas and Maritain," in *Jacques Maritain and the Ways of Knowing*, 253–68.

48. I am using here and below *The Collected Works of St. John of the Cross*, revised, trans. Kieran Kavanaugh and Otilio Rodriguez (Washington, D.C.: Institute of Carmelite Studies, 1991). The most provocative expression I know of that encapsulates both *I-Thou* love and fusion of identities, comes from the medieval mystic Hadewijch: "The beloved and lover penetrate each other in such a way that neither of the two can distinguish oneself from the other.... They abide in one another in fruition, mouth in mouth, heart in heart, body in body, and soul in soul, while one sweet divine nature flows through them both, and they are both one thing through each other": Hadewijch, *Hadewijch: The Complete Works*, trans. Columba Hart (New York: Paulist Press, 1980), 66.

49. There have been attempts to break this paradox, given St. John's language of longing and desire. St. John teaches, for example, that which guides the soul is its heart's burning desire (*Dark Night* II.11.1-6; 25.4). Eugene Maio argues that, therefore, it is ultimately the appetite for the satisfaction of the soul that brings the soul to God. Maio sees this as pure neoplatonic ascent, and this in opposition to true Christian doctrine. See Eugene Maio, *St. John of the Cross: The Imagery of Eros* (Madrid: *Colleccion Plaza Mayor Scholar*, 1973), 61ff and 260. Interestingly, Elizabeth Wilhelmsen challenges this reductive interpretation by pointing out that Maio has too readily accepted Nygren's dichotomy between *eros* and *apage*. She argues that what St. John teaches is that in pursuing the ultimately desirable end for which it was created, the soul becomes stripped of its narcissism. If the soul wanted divinization as an end to itself, this would be a decisive impediment. The soul achieves divinization, when it wants only in simultaneously wanting nothing for itself, but everything for God's glory. See Elizabeth Wilhelmsen, *Cognition and Communication in John of the Cross* (New York: Lang, 1985), 184–85. She convincingly points to Jean Baruzi's classical study to support her interpretation. And interestingly Baruzi unwittingly anticipates Nygren's critique. See Jean Baruzi, *Jean de la Croix et le problème de l'expérience mystique* (Paris: Libraririe Felix Lacan, 1931).

"nothing, nothing, nothing, nothing, nothing, nothing, and even on the top of the Mount nothing." Above the peak in this sketch he wrote, "Only the honor and glory of God dwells on this mount."[50] Maritain describes this as *Todo Y Nada*.[51]

Ultimately, the nature of Christian love and our very identities as both lovers and those beloved find themselves in paradoxes. Christian love is *eros* and *agape* implying each other and indeed collapsing boundaries regarding each other. The problem cannot be properly solved conceptually since our love and our identity are grounded in God. This is something not communicable.[52]

Given that Maritain greatly admired Thomas Merton, let me close with several citations that reflect Merton's mystical anthropology:

> The secret of my full identity is hidden in him.... To say that I am made in the image of God is to say that love is the reason for my existence, for God is love. Love is my true identity. Selflessness is my true self. Love is my true character, Love is my name ... [one] lives in emptiness and freedom, as if he had no longer a limited and exclusive *self* that distinguished him from God and other men.... What happens is that the separate identity that is *you* apparently disappears and nothing seems to be left but a pure freedom indistinguishable from the infinite Freedom, love identified with Love.... He is the *I* who acts there. He is the one Who loves and knows and rejoices.[53]

50. See *The Collected Works of St. John of the Cross, revised*, 111.

51. Maritain, *Degrees of Knowledge*, 375–408.

52. Ibid., 329.

53. Thomas Merton, *New Seeds of Contemplation* (New York: New Directions, 1961), 33, 60, 210, 283, and 286–87.

BERNADETTE E. O'CONNOR

Toward a Metaphysics of Human *Amour Fou*

Jacques Maritain (hereafter JM), writing just two years after the death of his wife Raïssa (hereafter RM), and shortly after the publication of her *Journal*, tells us that in the chapter "Love and Friendship," in *Notebooks*, he speaks "neither as a philosopher . . . nor as a theologian" . . . but simply from "the experience of an old man who has seen many things." "It belongs to others," he stipulates, "to treat these questions in a systematic form and in the appropriate technical terms."[1] In this paper, I propose to make a contribution to a more complete understanding, in the appropriate technical terms, of one of the kinds of love Maritain discusses in that chapter, natural human *amour fou*, mad, boundless love. In this effort, I shall exploit understandings JM, himself, either develops or hints at in his great work, *Distinguish to Unite or The Degrees of Knowledge*.

JM describes human *amour fou* in detail in "Love and Friendship." *Amour fou* is the "extreme or entirely absolute form" (223) of authentic human love. *Amour fou* is a love of the properly human order that presupposes mutual willing of the good to the beloved. It is distinguished from friendship, and presumably from *bel amour*, inasmuch as *amour fou* "constitutes itself at a more profound—absolutely radical—level of the soul" (225).

In *amour fou*, the two persons or subjects mutually give themselves "*directly, openly*, or *nakedly*" (221). Here the gift of self to the beloved is abso-

1. Jacques Maritain, *Notebooks*, trans. Joseph W. Evans (Albany, New York: Magi Books, 1984), 219–20. (All references to this work hereafter are placed in the text, in parentheses.)

lute and preeminent. In *amour fou,* the communication of self is overt, not mediated by gifts-less-than-the-selves given. Here the lovers give them*selves,* "like Venus emerging from the sea" (227), "without any possible reserve" (221), in their "entirety" (224)[2] and "to the very end" (223). In *amour fou,* the lover ecstasizes himself or herself in the beloved; the lovers mutually give themselves to each other as to their "Whole," of which they make themselves parts (224, 228).

Because of the union of spirit and flesh in human nature, *amour fou* implies the willingness in its subjects, not only to give themselves spiritually to each other, but also to give themselves in their bodies to each other (225). One who loves with *amour fou* may freely choose to forego the physical expression of love, however, if the beloved asks it or if the two lovers discern this renunciation to be requested by God (225). *Amour fou,* arising "in response to a radical desire inscribed in the human being" (244), is an ontological perfection of human nature (221); it is "the summit and the perfection of love between Man and Woman" and therefore of that between spouses (224). *Amour fou,* as relating to the merely natural order, is available both "to the best and to the worst" human beings morally speaking (224). *Amour fou* for another human being is incompatible with *amour fou* for God, incompatible with a life lived in the mystical state (230), for "a human being cannot give himself [or herself] at the same time, to the very end, in an absolute manner, to two objects as each constituting his [or her] Whole" (228).

It is the nature of the Whole created by mutual human *amour fou* that I want to understand philosophically: what kind of being does it have; how does it exist? JM describes the Whole constituted by *amour fou* by borrowing the language in which St. John of the Cross speaks of the mystical union of the soul with God, which union is the full development of the supernatural life of grace, faith, and charity and the end to which, *de jure,* all Christians are called. Love "requires ... and *in its own* way accomplishes the unbroken unity, the actually consummated unity of these same persons ('in a single spirit and love')" (224). The Whole, the unity, created by love is then a unity in one spirit or, perhaps better, a spiritual unity. But, again, how does this spiritual unity exist, and what kind of being does it have? What is *amour fou's* "own way" of being?

2. Maritain, *Notebooks,* "totally": 225 and 228.

Whatever the nature of the unity of love, of the Whole created by *amour fou*, it is not a union that destroys the personal being of either lover. The lovers each remain "ontologically a person" (224). So the two lovers remain, as persons, as rational substances, discrete in their own beings. It is "the proper paradox of love," JM writes, that while, on the one hand, it constitutes the Whole, the spiritual unity of the lovers, on the other hand, it "requires the ontologically indestructible duality of persons" (224). When lovers ecstasize in each other as in their Whole and make themselves parts which no longer exist except through and in this Whole, they remain, nevertheless, ontologically persons and therefore wholes in themselves and, as such, cannot become mere parts of another whole (224).

To arrive at some understanding of the spiritual union of love, of this "unity in a single spirit," I believe we must, following JM, think in terms of two different kinds of analogy. The first analogy is that between the union of human love, on the one hand, and the union of the graced soul with God, on the other hand. The second analogy is that between *esse intentionale*, on the one hand, and what JM calls "*esse amoris*," on the other.[3] By means of these two analogies we can arrive at some understanding of the kind of being which the unity, the Whole, of love enjoys.

Concerning the first and inverse type of analogy, JM asserts that what "St. John of the Cross will say apropos of supernatural mystical union ... is already true, on an altogether different plane and in an analogical sense, of the natural union between man and woman" (224). I call this comparison of the unity achieved in human love to that achieved in the soul's union with God "inverse" because ordinarily we use analogy with human things to achieve some knowledge of divine things, but here, at least in "On Love and Friendship," JM, and we following him, are understanding the union of human love by reference to the soul's supernatural union with the divine. It may be that this inversion of the normal order of analogical knowledge is merely accidental, but it is the order JM follows in *Degrees* as well. There, in two footnotes to his discussion of the union of the graced and mystic soul with God, JM offers his hints about the kind of being love has, hints which I want to apply in understanding human *amour fou*.

In discussing the charity-based union of a soul with God, JM writes

3. Jacques Maritain, *Distinguish to Unite or The Degrees of Knowledge*, trans. under the supervision of Gerald B. Phelan (New York: Charles Scribner's Sons, 1959), 371. Hereafter, references to this text will be cited as *Degrees*.

that "from the point of view of entity, in the register of the proper being of things, there is always a duality, nay, an infinite distance, between the soul and uncreated love."[4] But the graced union of the soul with God overcomes this ontological distance. As JM writes:

> There is another order than that of entity, and it is to that order that St. Paul makes allusion in his words: "one spirit," he says, not "one single being." This is the order of love as love, considered not in its ontological constituents of essence and existence (for there it is considered as a being) but in the absolutely proper reality of the immaterial intussusception by which the other within me becomes more me than myself.[5]

And it is in this order of love that, in the spiritual marriage of the soul with God, the distance between infinite Love and the finite soul is overcome:

> In the spiritual marriage the created will and uncreated love remain entitatively, distant to infinity, yet the soul, in its supernatural activity of love, loses or alienates itself in God who, according to the being or actuality of love, becomes her more than herself and is principle and agent of all her operations.[6]

The union of the soul with God is not in the order of being, for in that order the soul remains infinitely distant from God.

Applying what JM has written about the nature of the union of the soul with God and, *mutatis mutandis*, we could say that in the union that is human *amour fou* the lovers, while remaining in their ontological duality as persons, lose or alienate themselves in each other, each becoming the other more than the other is himself or herself, each becoming thereby the principle and agent of the other's operations.

At this point the second type of analogy comes into play to help us understand the kind of being the union of love exercises. JM proposes in *Degrees*, but does not fully develop, an analogy between *esse intentionale* and *esse amoris*. *Esse intentionale*, a concept that appears in St. Thomas and is further developed by John of St. Thomas, is the "to-be" by which the thing known is present in the knower and the knower is the thing known.

JM treats of *esse intentionale* extensively in *Degrees*. *Esse intentionale* "is not the proper act of existing of the subject as such or of its accidents"; nor is *esse intentionale* the *esse naturae*, that is, "the being a thing possesses when

4. Maritain, *Degrees*, 368.
5. Ibid. The words of St. Paul are from 1 Cor. 6:17.
6. Ibid., 369.

it exists in its own nature."[7] *Esse intentionale* is that "to be" by which "the thing exists in the soul with an existence other than its own existence, and the soul is or becomes the thing with an existence other than *its* [the soul's] own existence."[8] Thanks to *esse intentionale,* the immaterial activity of intellectual knowledge consists in the mind's becoming "the other as other."[9]

JM proposes that we can understand the union of love, that transpersonal Whole, whose parts are human persons and who remain entitatively discrete, each with his or her own *esse naturae,* by analogy with the union between knower and known effected by *esse intentionale.* Still discussing the graced union of the soul with God, JM writes:

> The mystery of cognitive union and of the true compels the philosopher to conceive a "being of knowledge" and an *esse intentionale* which is not entitative being or being of nature. The mystery of the union of love and of the good compels … [the philosopher] to conceive an *intentional being of love* which is not entitative being either.[10]

Following our first and inverse analogy, we meet the idea of an *esse amoris* first in a consideration of the union of the graced soul with God.

JM explains that in heaven, in the light of glory, the soul "becomes God according to the intentional being of knowledge."[11] But this union by knowledge, "the payment which the intellect will receive," must wait till the next life, till the beatific vision, for the soul cannot be transformed in God until the soul sees God.[12] In the spiritual marriage, which, however rarely, takes place even in this life, union of the soul with God is achieved, not through knowledge but rather, through love: "for the soul to be transformed into God it is enough that the soul love God, but love Him so much as to separate the soul from herself."[13] It is probably impossible to know whether the language of "separation" of the soul from itself in the union of love, which JM uses here, or the language of "alienation" of the soul from itself in love, which JM uses in "Love and Friendship" (and there more frequently in connection with that degree of charity which is mad boundless love for God), arose first in his reflections on human love or on the love of charity.

At any rate, it is in the course of JM's discussion of the union of the

7. Ibid., 114.
8. Ibid.
9. Ibid., 368.
10. Ibid., 369.
11. Ibid.
12. Ibid., 370.
13. Ibid.

soul with God that he first brings up the concept of an "intentional being of love." Maritain indicates that this intentional being of love is intentional only "by analogy with the intentional being according to which the mental word proceeds."[14] JM finds a basis for making an analogy between *esse intentionale* and *esse amoris* in St. Thomas. In answering affirmatively the question whether there is in the Godhead any other procession than that of the Word, St. Thomas writes:

> we must observe that procession exists in God, only according to an action which does not tend to anything external, but remains in the agent itself. Such action in an intellectual nature is that of the intellect, and of the will. The procession of the Word is by way of an intelligible operation. The operation of the will within ourselves involves also another procession, that of love, whereby the object loved is in the lover; as, by the conception of the word, the object spoken of or understood is in the intelligent agent.[15]

Esse intentionale is the being that spiritually unites, in the order of knowledge, known and knower; *esse amoris* is the being that unites, in the order of love, the lover and the beloved. These two *esse*s are not univocally "intentional," because they perfect two different faculties, and surely it is the intellectual "superexistence"[16] by which the thing known becomes the knower and the knower becomes the thing known that is the prime analogate. But the volitional "superexistence" of love, by which the beloved is present spiritually in the will of lover and by which the beloved becomes more the lover than he or she, the lover, is himself or herself, is also "intentional" at least inasmuch as this presence is, like the *esse* of knowledge, a spiritual presence and not an entitative presence that would destroy the personal being, the personal whole, of each lover.

Esse amoris can, I believe, also be compared to *esse intentionale* in the sense that both acts of being are immanent to their subject in the sense of perfecting in some way the subject, himself or herself. It is the subject of knowledge or of love, himself or herself, who receives a further, superentitative perfection in virtue of the act itself of knowing or loving, not the

14. Ibid., 369, n. 5.

15. Thomas Aquinas, *Summa theologiae* (hereafter, *ST*) I, q. 27, a. 3, in *Summa Theologica*, trans. Fathers of the English Dominican Province (New York: Benziger Brothers, 1947), Vol. I, 149. All subsequent translations of the *Summa Theologiae* are from this edition and volume.

16. JM speaks of *amour fou*'s accomplishing "in the special order or, if you will, the magic and spiritual 'superexistence' of love" what is "impossible or insane in the order of mere [*sic*!] existence or simply of being" (*Notebooks*, 224).

real object known or loved. It is true, of course, that inasmuch as love wills the good of the beloved, the love can be a cause which moves the executive powers, the human powers of external activity, to transitive activities of which the beloved is the beneficiary and by which the beloved is changed for the better. But these transitive activities by which the beloved is benefitted are consequences of the union of love, not the union itself.

And, I believe, the comparison between *esse intentionale* and *esse amoris* can be extended further to the degree of intimacy of the union both create. In discussing the union of knower and known effected by the spiritual *esse intentionale*, JM writes:

> A material being can become *other*, i.e., it can change or be modified, but it cannot become *the other*. Whereas the knower, even while maintaining his own nature intact, becomes the known itself and identifies himself with it, the knower being thus incomparably more *one* with the known than the matter with the form.[17]

The union of matter and form in a physical thing is, of course, a very intimate union, but the union of knowledge is even more intimate.

Now we have already seen JM suggest the degree of intimacy of the union that love causes; *esse amoris* unites the lover and the beloved in a union, in an "immaterial intussusception by which the other within me becomes more me than myself."[18] One of the denotations of "intussusception" is the slippage of a length of intestine into an adjacent position. Étienne Gilson, in commenting on St. Thomas' treatment of the union of love, a treatment that JM follows closely, writes: "There is no juster epithet than *intimate* to characterize this invisceration [this emboweling] of the beloved in the lover."[19] So the intimacy of the spiritual union of lover and beloved in the lover's will created by *esse amoris* is similar in degree of intimacy to that union, more intimate than the union of matter and form, created by *esse intentionale*. And Gilson holds that the union made possible by *esse amoris* is even more intimate than the union made possible by *esse intentionale*, for the union of knower and known is by the species and by the "resemblance" of the species to the known thing, but "love, as it were, makes two things become a single thing."[20]

17. Maritain, *Degrees*, 112.

18. Ibid.

19. Étienne Gilson, *The Christian Philosophy of St. Thomas Aquinas*, trans. L. K. Shook (New York: Random House, 1956), 277; his italics.

20. Gilson, *The Christian Philosophy*, 276; *cf.* Aquinas, *ST*, I-II, q. 28, a. 1 ad 2 and ad 3.

I want to return for a moment to the new Whole that, JM tells us in "Love and Friendship," *amour fou* creates. We have made progress in understanding the kind of being this Whole exercises. The being of this Whole is a spiritual being, a spiritual oneness of lover and beloved in the order of will comparable to the spiritual oneness of knower and known in the order of the intellect. Again, adapting language Maritain employs to describe the graced mystical union of a soul with God,[21] we can say that in love the lover alienates himself or herself in the beloved, who, according to the being or actuality of love, becomes the lover more than he or she, the lover, is himself or herself. Thus the immaterial activity of love is to lose oneself in the other-as-self, to alienate oneself in the reality of the other, of the beloved, to the extent that the beloved becomes the lover more than the lover is himself or herself.

I want to suggest that, for JM, who follows St. Thomas[22] in this, the Whole that exists in virtue of *esse amoris* has the being of two vectors of ecstasis, two spiritual tendencies or stretchings out, which move in opposite directions. And we should note that these tendencies would be present in the lover even if the love of devotion, which is a condition for human *amour fou*, were not reciprocated.

The first tendency is that by which the lover goes out into the beloved, ecstasizes himself or herself in the beloved. Thomas speaks of this as the lover penetrating, so to speak, the beloved.[23] In the love of friendship, of which *amour fou* is a species, "the lover is in the beloved, inasmuch as … [the lover] reckons what is good or evil to his friend, as being so to himself."[24]

The second tendency is that by which the beloved becomes the lover more than the lover is himself or herself. Thomas speaks of this as the beloved's being contained in the lover "by being impressed on … [the lover's] heart and thus becoming the object of … [the lover's] complacency."[25] So even in unreciprocated love of friendship the tendential being that is *esse amoris* moves in two directions: out, inasmuch as the lover goes into the beloved, and in, inasmuch as it brings the beloved into the lover. I will not enumerate the four ecstases that exist when love is mutual, but just for a moment consider the tendential vibrancy that exists in spirit when the love

21. Maritain, *Degrees*, 369.

22. Aquinas, *ST* I-II, q. 28, a. 2.

23. Aquinas, *ST* I-II, q. 28, a. 2 ad 1.

24. Aquinas, *ST* I-II, q. 28, a. 2.

25. Aquinas, *ST*, I-II, q. 28, a. 2 ad 1.

is mutual, as it is in the *amour fou* we have been discussing; in this case, the lovers are doubly in each other by two immanent but mutual acts of the being of love.

This mutual indwelling by means of *esse amoris* is the means by which each of the lovers becomes, again adapting JM's language concerning the mutual indwelling in the mystical marriage of God and the graced soul, "the principle and agent" of the other's operations.[26] In this context, JM speaks of a "principle of gravity of a whole spiritual universe," the universe of the beloved, being "'transessentiated' into another spirit" while remaining whole and intact entitatively.[27] It would seem that the presence of the beloved in the lover by way of *esse amoris* is the principle and agent of all the lover's activities; the metaphorical "weight" that mention of gravity suggests is the trans-entitative presence of the beloved in the lover whom the lover loves as another self. When one loves another with *amor amicitiae,* the lover wills good to the beloved just as the lover wills good to himself or herself. The lover can do this by virtue of the *esse amoris* that makes the beloved another self.[28] This also helps us understand how each beloved becomes the principle and agent of the lovers' operations. The lover wills and acts for the good of the beloved, in whom he or she is ecstasized and who, in turn, is ecstasized in the lover, as the lover wills and acts in his or her own self-interest. It is in this sense that the beloved is the cause of everything the lover does.

And it is inasmuch as the being of the beloved is so intimately identified with the being of the lover that the existence of the beloved is, in a certain sense, the prime analogate of existence (pp. 222–223)[29]; there is a sense, from our personal interiority out, in which our own being is always the first, and the beloved shares in that primacy of being.

In a penultimate comment, I want to suggest that the progress we have made in understanding the nature of the Whole *amour fou* creates by making possible the mutual indwelling of the lovers in each other helps us understand better why, in "Love and Friendship," JM calls the attainment of mad boundless love "extraordinary luck" and "a special and gratuitous gift" (245). JM's words remind us of grace. However, I believe that it would not be fruitful to press that analogy. Inasmuch as sanctifying grace is an entita-

26. Maritain, *Degrees,* 369.

27. Ibid., 371.

28. Aquinas, *ST* I-II, q. 28, a. 1.

29. Maritain, *Degrees,* 222–23.

tive modification of the soul, it is not strictly analogous with *esse intentionale* properly considered or, by extension, with *esse amoris* properly considered, however gratuitous mad boundless love is.[30]

And, finally, in the weeks of studying "Love and Friendship" and of attempting to develop one of its principal concepts, I have tried to observe a strict intellectual custody of the eyes concerning (not to be idly curious about) the growth of Jacques' and Raïssa's love and their paths to God. But I cannot resist observing in conclusion that they both give evidence of intimate experience of human mad boundless love and, RM, especially, in her *Journal*, of mad boundless love for God. We have both of their searing words to remind us that the cost of the latter is the sacrifice of the former, a cost JM suggests is well worth paying.[31]

30. Maritain, *Degrees*, 113 and 116–17.

31. Maritain, *Notebooks*, 226 and 249–51; *Degrees*, 357; and Raïssa Maritain, *Raïssa's Journal*, presented by Jacques Maritain (Albany, New York: Magic Books, 1974), 239.

VI

THEOLOGICAL FOUNDATIONS: LITURGY, MARRIAGE, AND THE COVENANT

DONALD J. KEEFE, SJ

John Paul II on the Eucharistic Foundation of Marriage and the Marital Foundation of a Free Society

I. Introduction

Pope John Paul II's insistent emphasis upon the strategic importance of the marital family went back to the earliest days of his pontificate.[1] In *Veritatis Splendor,* he linked the Catholic tradition of liturgical, sacramental worship to our moral responsibilities as Catholics in such wise as to establish on that firm foundation all discussion of family life and of Catholic morality, for the two are intertwined at their very source, our creation to the image of God. As the Pope taught over and over again, from his early *Catechesis on the Book of Genesis,* to *Veritatis Splendor* and his "Letter to Families,"[2] creation is maritally or nuptially ordered "in the beginning," which is to say, primordially, antecedent to the Fall. Because of the Fall,

1. Earlier statements of John Paul II on the family include *The Original Unity of Man and Woman: Catechesis on the Book of Genesis,* trans. Donald W. Wuerl (Boston: St. Paul Editions, 1981); "The Apostolic Exhortation On The Family," *Origins* 11 (1981) 437–68; "Familiaris Consortio: Apostolica Adhortatio," AAS 74 (1982) 82–191; *Blessed are the Pure in Heart: Catechesis on the Sermon on the Mount and the Writings of St. Paul,* trans. *L'Osservatore Romano,* English Edition, Preface By Donald W. Wuerl (Boston: St. Paul Editions, 1983); *Reflections on Humanae Vitae: Conjugal Morality and Spirituality,* trans. *L'Osservatore Romano,* English Edition, Preface By Rev. Msgr. Donald W. Wuerl (Boston: St. Paul Editions, 1984); *The Theology of Marriage and Celibacy: Catechesis on Marriage and Celibacy in the Light of the Resurrection of the Body,* trans. *L'Osservatore Romano,* English Edition, Preface By Most Rev. Donald W. Wuerl, D.D. (Boston: St. Paul Editions, 1986); and "Christifideles Laici," *L'Osservatore Romano* 25 (1075) 6 February, 1989, 1–21.

2. "Letter to Families," *Origins* 23/37 (March 3, 1994) 637–59.

that good creation—fallen, redeemed in Christ, and raised in its Head to the right hand of the Father—is present in our history only in the sacramental signs of the Church's worship: primarily in the Eucharist, secondarily in marriage, which are to each other as cause to effect.

Therefore, it is finally the Church's Eucharistic worship that alone can sustain what in marriage parents have vowed to each other and to their prospective children: a participation in that more abundant life which Christ died that we might have. In fact, as John Paul taught in *Veritatis Splendor,* that Eucharistic worship is the foundation and sustenance of all exercise of free responsibility, which is to say, of the moral life as such. At the same time, that foundation has as its first storey, if we may continue the building simile, the institution of marriage. Marriage is the plenary exercise of moral, nuptial responsibility short of that transcendent nuptial responsibility for the Church which is Christ's, and which responsibility for the Church is exercised, and can be exercised, only in the Person of Christ: here we refer to the priestly offering in his Person of the Eucharistic sacrifice.

This One Sacrifice causes the Church to be. As the Fathers never tired of remarking, the Church emerges in the water and the blood of her sacraments of Baptism and Eucharist, as the second Eve from the side of the "sleeping" second Adam. It is thus that, in principle as in particulars, John Paul taught the uniquely important—in fact, the normative—role of marriage and the family in Catholic life from the beginning of his pontificate. There is simply no aspect of the Church's mission which this doctrine does not inform, and which this free exercise of nuptial responsibility does not order. Marriage, and the family it connotes, provide the irrevocable content of all the decencies by which our world is made habitable, and of all the responsibilities by which it is made free.

II. Sacramental Humanity: The Eucharistic One Flesh of Christ and the Church

The depth, the plenitude, of these papal documents is such as to place anyone who would speak to this topic quite simply in the position of holding a penny candle to the sun. Their implications are enormous; they require of Catholic theologians the articulation of a wholly new theology of man as sacramentally actual and objective in history: as primordially created—created "in the beginning"—in the image of God, and as fulfilling that image in the Eucharistic worship of the Church. This sacramental anthropology has resources so great as to beggar the contemporary theological imagination, so profound as to transcend entirely those philosophical notions of the "natural" human condition which have heretofore impeded rather than contributed to our Catholic discussions of, for instance, the natural law. In the *Catechism*, in *Veritatis Splendor* and in his "Letter to Families," Pope John Paul II made this pellucidly clear: our human "nature" is nuptially ordered from the beginning, from its creation in the image of God. Further, it can only be sacramentally realized and sustained. Consequently, none of the usual systematic analyses, whether philosophical or theological, can speak to this reality. It must be dealt with from the viewpoint of the Church's sacramental practice and doctrine.

In reminding us of this, John Paul recalled us to our birthright, to the truth of Christ, historically mediated in the Church through the sacramental worship of the Church, and to each of us through our personal participation in that sacramental worship. By recalling us to our familial heritage in Christ, John Paul delivered us from the poverty, from the tedium long drawn out, of pseudo-theological discussions about a nonsacramental humanity—e.g., as joined in "natural" marriage—and from what is worse, the futility of the quasi-scientific studies of the family whose stiflingly secular premises are pagan at best, and whose conclusions finally can only ignore our very reality, our sacramental imaging of God in the Church.

In short, we were reminded by John Paul, throughout his papacy, that there is one source by which our family life may be understood and our familial responsibilities measured: that source is simply the Church's worship in truth—a worship whose public impact, whose redemptive efficacy, is guaranteed not by any human competence or cleverness, but by the Eucharistic immanence to the Church of the sacrificed and risen Christ who is the light of the world, and whose light is mediated to the world only by the Church, by the Bride from whom he is never apart. This union of Christ with the Church, the New Covenant, the Eucharistic One Flesh of the second Adam and the second Eve, is at once the criterion and the sustenance of all that is Catholic, all that is Christian, all that is holy. By recalling the family to the recognition of its sacramental foundation, John Paul summoned us, who are familial and nuptial in our very creation, in our imaging of God, to the fulfillment of that image, of that good creation—which is to say, it is precisely as familial that we are called to sanctity.

Henceforth, and from the outset, we must regard marriage and the family that it grounds not as "natural" in some philosophical or empirical sense,[3] but as naturally because innately holy, as holy because created in the nuptial image of the Triune God. We must remember that it is in the historical exercise of our nuptial, marital, and covenantal responsibilities that we image God, and that in honoring each other in the possession of nuptial, covenantal dignity, and in the exercise of this nuptially ordered, familial responsibility, we honor the holy Trinity in whose familial image we are made.

III. The Nuptial Image of the Triune God

It was perhaps Pope John Paul's most profound, and certainly his central, insight that our imaging of God is nuptial.[4] This is a radical departure from the usual theological understanding of the *Imago Dei*, which has arisen out of a rationalization of the Augustinian "psychological analogy." Augustine's account of human consciousness distinguished memory, intellect and will. These in their unity are the mind, indeed are each identified with the entire mind, yet are each irreducible. Memory is not intellect nor will, *et ita porro*. In this differentiated unity of the mind, Augustine found a "psychological" analogy or image of the Trinity. However, this unity, as will be seen, is free, appropriated in the Eucharistic worship of the Church. But with the change in theological climate that finds its full expression in St. Thomas, the experiential approach to understanding gave way to the analytical. Under its thrust, the image of God became a matter of existing in an intellectual nature. We are thought to be images of God simply insofar as we each are intellectual creatures—insofar then as we subsist in intellectual natures, insofar then as we are "persons" in this Thomist sense of the term. St. Thomas went so far as to observe that angels, because they are more completely

3. The assigning of a nonsacramental and therefore nonhistorical meaning (i.e., either merely pragmatic, or merely ideal) to "nature" and "natural" is unfortunately the commonplace of much Catholic theological writing on marriage and the family. Edward Schillebeeckx's well-known work, *Marriage: Human Reality and Saving Mystery*, trans. N. D. Smith (New York: Sheed and Ward, 1965), offers a case in point.

4. John Paul II began his doctrinal development of our nuptial imaging of God, which theme pervades and controls his anthropology, in the weekly lectures which inaugurated his pontificate. They are collected in his *The Original Unity of Man and Woman: Catechesis on the Book of Genesis*. His "Letter to Families" merely resumes this doctrine, which has been perennial in his thought.

intellectual than men, are therefore better images of God.[5] This intellectualist approach to the imaging of God, which insists upon the substantiality of each such person, makes each person the complete image of the Trinity. Such a view of the image cannot be nuptial, nor can it be sacramental. John Paul would appear to have returned to the Augustinian view of the image as nuptial.

This may be accounted no small advantage, for the now commonplace nonsacramental view of human nature, and particularly of our imaging of God, at once privatizes and dehistoricizes our humanity, our personal imaging of God, depriving it of the historical and communal concreteness which John Paul II called our nuptiality, our personal ordering toward selfless union with another nuptially ordered person. It is therefore of the highest importance that John Paul restored the nuptiality of our imaging of God. He reaffirmed a truth long neglected, although it is inherent in the liturgy itself. As nuptially ordered to the marital union whose acme and criterion is the One Flesh of the Eucharist, the man, the woman, and the irrevocable marital covenant they have freely formed each possesses the fullness of the image, of the human substance, but does so *suo modo,* in a manner precisely analogous to the possession of the fullness of divinity, *suo modo,* by each of the divine Persons. It is also evident that this nuptial or marital imaging of God, and the human substance that it constitutes, have only a sacramental realization in a fallen world. Our imaging of God is our glory, and here that glory is veiled, given in the signs and symbols of the Church's worship, but as veiled, not as manifest. That there is no manifest human unity in history is sufficiently evidenced by the failure to provide any account of that unity: the problem of the one and the many has never been resolved, whether theoretically or empirically.

But, as sacramentally realized, as veiled yet objectively actual and efficacious in history, the free and covenantal and nuptial unity of our human imaging of God is nonetheless actual and concrete in history. Despite all the human failures that attend our sacramental worship in the Church of sinners, the sacrament of marriage has leavened the world, leaving it with a vision of human dignity, of human freedom, human community, and human responsibility elsewhere and otherwise inarticulate, whether in theory or in practice. For it is only in a nuptially ordered world, whose order is at once free and sacramentally objective, that the personal dignity of men

5. *Summa theologiae* (hereafter *ST*) I, q. 93, a. 3.

and women has an inviolable because sacramental expression, subject to no earthly authority but their own, which authority is explicitly, historically, and objectively exercised in their marriage. It is therefore understandable that Catholic marriage should be under attack in a secular world, for it is entirely incompatible with the monism of power that governs that world. Sacramental marriage, by reason of the free, public community it forms, is in a secular world a most profoundly counter-cultural act, for it is the exercise of an utterly independent personal responsibility, which seeks permission from no higher source of authority. It is therefore entirely understandable that marriage has been targeted by every social reformer from Plato to Dworkin[6] as a thing irrational, insusceptible to social control and the higher utopian wisdom. But such reformers have found themselves fighting reality itself. It is marriage, not utopia, that is objectively given in the world, and its free sacramental realization is more obdurate than anything that may be brought against it by any competing authority however despotically it may be exercised.[7]

IV. The Augustinian Source of the Papal Doctrine on the Nuptial and Sacramental Imaging of God

In fact, moreover, despite his evident departure from the usual conception of our imaging of God, John Paul II's equation of nuptiality with our imaging of God is entirely loyal to a more profound reading of Augustine's explanation of our imaging through his famous psychological analogy, than St. Thomas' dehistoricized interpretation of that analogy provides. For Augustine, the imaging of God is always free, and can be achieved only in and by our graced participation in the worship of the Church, the realism

6. Ronald Dworkin, successor to H. L. A. Hart as Regius Professor of Jurisprudence at Oxford, and, with John Rawls of Harvard, one of the most influential Anglo-American jurisprudents, is the author of *Life's Dominion: An Argument about Abortion, Euthanasia, and Individual Freedom* (New York: Knopf, 1993), in which he continues the rationalist dissolution of the nuptial order of the common-law tradition that alone underwrites the constitutionality of Anglo-American jurisprudence—and that has been waning since Henry VIII criminalized the assertion of that nuptiality. Not much remains of the common law and the freedoms it underwrote in England and the U.S.

7. The Gelasian summary of the Augustinian Church-State doctrine denies the legitimacy of such competition: the ecclesial *authority* and the regal *power* are irreducible. "*Duo sunt* quippe, imperator auguste, quibus principaliter mundus hic regitur, *auctoritas sacrata pontificum* et *regalis potestas*. . . ." Gelasius I, *Ep. "Famuli vestrae pietatis"* [DS 347]; my italics.

of whose sacraments he developed and defended against the Donatists throughout all his long contestation with that heresy.[8] Augustine is preeminently the theologian of grace. It is often forgotten that he is yet more obviously the adamantine defender of the sacramental realism upon which John Paul II so heavily relies, and upon which his doctrine of the family is so evidently dependent. Much of our understanding of Augustine's genius is obscured by a rather facile reading back into his thought of the Neo-Platonism from which his doctrine is in fact a continuing conversion.[9] While this is not the place to enter into the history of Augustinian scholarship, we wish to stress the loyalty of John Paul II's doctrine to the Augustinian development of the Catholic tradition that stems from the Pauline Letters, and to point out that its entire congruence with that tradition does not prevent it from being at the same time a most striking development of it. Henceforth, there must be in view a far more vigorous exploitation of sacramental realism, and particularly of the efficacy, both *ex opere operato* and *ex opere operantis*, of its nuclear nuptial symbolism, than has ever been attempted. John Paul made it more clear than it had been before that the Church, and all that is Catholic, is caused by that symbolism, by the One Flesh of the Eucharistic sacrifice, and that we enter into its unity, its truth and its salvation only by entering into its worship.

V. Augustinianism: A Phenomenology of Sacramental Experience *in Ecclesia*

Augustine's theology is uniquely pertinent today, for it is a theology of experience. Nowadays, it is a familiar demand that theology must begin

8. For accounts of the influence of this controversy upon Augustine's thought, see Gerhart B. Ladner, *The Idea of Reform: Its Impact on Christian Thought and Practice in the Age of the Fathers* (New York: Harper and Row, 1967, [1959]) at 303–15, and Wilhelm Gessel, *Eucharistische Gemeinschaft bei Augustinus*; ser. Cassiacum, Band XXI (Würzburg: Augustinus Verlag, 1966), 147 ff.

9. E.g., T. J. Van Bavel, in "God in between Affirmation and Negation," *Augustine: Presbyter Factus Sum*, ser. Collectanea Augustiniana, II, eds. J. T. Lienhard, E. C. Muller, R. J. Teske (New York: Peter Lang, 1993), treats Augustine's theological hermeneutics simply in terms of his supposed Neo-Platonism, in entire dissociation from Augustine's sophisticated Christology, although Van Bavel had himself earlier provided a brilliant exposition of that Christology. There is no reason to suppose Augustine to be thus schizophrenic. Gessel has pointed to Augustine's continual subordination of his Neo-Platonism to his Christian faith: *op. cit.*, 85–89. See L. Grandgeorge to the same effect in *Saint Augustin et le Neo-Platonisme* (Paris: Minerva, 1896) and also M. F. Sciacca, *Saint Augustin et le Neo-Platonisme: La Possibilité d'une Philosophie Chrétienne* (Louvain: Publications Universitaires de Louvain; Paris: Béatrice Nauwelaerts, 1956).

with experience. Unfortunately, the notion of experience generally in view in the theological academy is secular, "natural" in the sense of uninformed by the Church's worship. "Experience" in this nonsacramental guise then is given a secular account and analysis that are mistaken for theology, whereupon the Catholic magisterium is charged with intransigence and obstinacy insofar as the Church does not accept this pseudo-theological reading of "experience" as authentic. It should be obvious that the only experience that is theological is that which is *in ecclesia, in Christo:* experience that is informed by the Catholic tradition, by a Catholic consciousness.

Augustine's examination of experience is theological in that sense. He is concerned to give an account of his own ongoing conversion, which is to say, his experience of worship in the Church. Thus the experience that interests Augustine is anything but secular. It is ecclesial and therefore sacramental from the outset. The interrelation of Augustine's *imago* doctrine with his sacramental realism needs to be understood.[10]

During his twenty years of struggle with the Trinitarian faith, which issued in the *De Trinitate,* Augustine concluded to the tri-relational, substantial unity of the mind as at once memory, intellect, and will, and found in this unity of the human mind an analogue of the tri-relational substantial unity of God as at once Father, Son, and Spirit. For Augustine, the unity of the mind, viewed as the tri-relational circumincession of memory, intellect, and will, is simply authentic, human, historical, substantial existence as self-aware. With all of Greek philosophy, he supposed this substantial unity to be identical with the unity of person, whose mind is integrated by worshiping in the Church, and therefore is sacramentally and historically integrated. This freely integrated worshiping mind is for Augustine the human image of the Triune God.

However, Augustine did not perceive the nuptial implication of this sacramental imaging of God, and thus did not perceive the nuptial unity

10. Here the Trinitarian studies of Earl C. Muller, SJ, are invaluable. His meticulous structural analysis of the *De Trinitate* has established the Eucharistic ground of Augustine's Trinitarian theology, and thereby of his understanding of the imaging of God. See "Rhetorical and Theological Issues in the Structuring of Augustine's *De Trinitate,*" *Studia Patristica* 27, ed. Elizabeth Livingstone (Leuven: Peeters Press, 1993), 356–63, and the review article, "The Science of Theology: A Review of Catherine LaCugna's *God for Us,*" *Gregorianum* 75, 2 (1994) 311–41. A comparable development of the Eucharistic ground of Augustine's *imago* doctrine is set out in D. J. Keefe, SJ, *Covenantal Theology: The Eucharistic Order of History, II: The Metaphysics of the Covenant,* TWO VOLUMES IN ONE, REVISED EDITION, WITH AN APPENDIX (Novato, CA: Presidio Press, 1996), at 570ff.

of the human substance. Neither did he grasp directly the nuptial ordering of the free, Eucharistic integration of the worshiping mind, the image of God, whose unity is that of the Eucharistic worship of the Church. At the same time, he did perceive the Eucharistic sustenance of that imaging of God; from this all the rest follows as a necessary consequence. For the Eucharistic *anamnesis* is of the nuptial union of Christ and the Church, the One Flesh that is consummated on the cross, whereon the New Covenant is instituted and Christ is revealed as the image of the Father by reason of his being the source, the *arché*, the Head of the Church. As the Father is the Head of Christ, so Christ is the Head of the Church; as Christ is the glory of the Father, so the Church is the glory of Christ.

Therefore, Christ is the image not as the immanent Son, but historically, as nuptially and sacrificially ordered to the Church as to his body, his bride in the One Flesh that is the New Covenant. It is only as instituting this New Covenant, as the Head of the Church, that Christ is the image of the Father; it is only in virtue of his relation to the Church, of the covenant which is his union with the Church, that he is image. The image is at once substantial and Trinitarian, and is so only as nuptially ordered: the second Adam, the second Eve, the New Covenant. Christ, as image of the Father, cannot be dissociated from the image of the Trinity that is the *totus Christus*, the One Flesh, the New Covenant in his blood.

The Augustinianism of the psychological analogy is therefore the phenomenology of the Catholic consciousness, of the historical mind whose free *ordo* or dynamic unity of memory, intellect, and will can only be that of the sacramental *ordo* of the worship itself.

VI. The Eucharistic and Covenantal Integration of the Family

Augustine is the great theologian of the nuptial unity of Christ and his bridal Church in the Eucharist. Henri de Lubac has detailed this Augustinian insight, which named the Eucharistic food "Una Caro;"[11] it is the near-equivalent of the *pharmakos athanasias* of Ignatius Martyr.

The Augustinian doctrine of the imaging of God is of the highest pertinence to the role of the family in the Church. For, as John Paul II empha-

11. See H. de Lubac, *Corpus Mysticum: L'Eucharistie et l'Église au moyen âge. Étude historique*, 2nd ed., ser. Théologie 3 (Paris: Aubier, Editions Montaigne, 1949), 197–209.

sized in his "Letter to Families," the familial experience of familial disintegration has become a commonplace. Over and again, families confront the dichotomy that the Fall has placed between freedom and unity, and interpret it as an intolerable contradiction. Within the intellectual context provided by post-Enlightenment Modernity and post-Modernity, freedom is understood to be destructive of community, and community to entail the suppression of personal freedom. Thereby freedom is concretely exercised as alienation, dissociation from all that is not self, and community is concretely experienced as coerced submission to servitude, as alienation from the self. The family is caught up in this contradiction, and finds itself enlisted perforce in all the failed therapies—political, economic, psychological, ideological in any case—that cleverness can spawn and power impose. The consequences are disastrous. The family becomes a problem for which the solution is its elimination in favor of a more rational association of persons.

If the history of human thought proves anything, it proves that there is no logical resolution of or practical solution to this dilemma, long since classic, of the one versus the many: over and again, the alternative is posed in our everyday experience—either the jungle or the cage. The dilemma is encountered more starkly in family situations than anywhere else, for there the intimacy inseparable from familial life exacerbates the tensions of our fallen existence. Love is experienced as manipulative; familial intimacy is experienced as stifling. At the same time, the absence of love is unbearable, and the loss of familial intimacy is an anguish anticipating the loss of self. Yet the alienation of modern man from the family, from its burdens, its responsibilities, its support—in sum, the ideal of a personal existence apart from any familial frame of reference, without any inherent obligation to anyone—now very nearly typifies life in the modern world. It is a life increasingly atomized, increasingly irresponsible, increasingly feral, wherever it is not coerced into passivity before some *force majeure*.

A host of technical solutions have been brought forward to counter the social pathologies that are the symptoms of this alienation. That they have failed is nearly the single point of agreement among their several advocates. Over and again, the failure is ascribed to an insufficiently lavish application of the preferred remedy: typically education, or some other form of socialization. For the remedies offered more and more bespeak an uncritical reliance upon an "administered society." And more and more this impersonal and irresponsible paradigm becomes the surrogate for the marital family.

In fact, this has already gone very far even in some Catholic circles, where there is evinced a willingness to drop sacramental marriage as the foundation of the family, in order so to extend the range of "the family" or "household" as to leave no "relationship" outside it. The people composing these circles typically distrust the Church's involvement in "the church of the home." For them, the family has a natural—in the sense of secular—autonomy which has no sacramental ground, and concerning which the Church has no particular authority. This secularizing sociology, of late all too authoritative in Catholic discussions, is merely one more expression of that teleogism that John Paul II excoriated, that is radically incompatible with our imaging of God, and that accelerates rather than restrains the dissolution of the marital family.

As his "Letter to Families" made clear, Pope John Paul II was of an entirely different view. He insisted upon the sacramental foundation of the marital family, and he insisted as well upon its Eucharistic sustenance. In this fallen world, we exist, so Augustine's analysis of history insisted, in a tension between "two loves, which build two cities."[12]

One of these loves is specified as marital, for it is normed by the One Flesh of Christ and his Church. Thus normed, marital love underwrites all free society. The Western civilization was founded upon the dominical celebration of this nuptially-ordered love, apart from which the cultures of Europe and the Americas are unthinkable. For a single example of its impact, the sacramental praxis of love as nuptial is equivalently the acceptance of authority as nuptial, which is to say, as Trinitarian, in such wise that the effect *ex opere operato* of marriage is to establish personal freedom and personal responsibility as the very fabric of all law. It is not too much to say that the nuptial institution of feminine authority underlies all constitutional law, all limitation upon the otherwise despotic exercise of authority as mere coercive power.

The other love is not eucharistically normed, and so is not nuptial; it is then simply the rationalization of fallen *sarx* (the "flesh"), the reduction of love to the necessity which governs *sarx*, and so to immanence. As immanently normed, love becomes narcissism, the self-love that builds the "City of Man," the coerced existence in the cage that is the sole rational alternative to chaotic existence, to the jungle. Because the radical selfish-

12. See Ladner, *The Idea of Reform*, 265–66.

ness that norms it is the standing alternative to our sacramental and nuptial imaging of God, and to our consequent entry into the history of salvation, it deserves some examination, if only because it is the specific temptation offered contemporary Catholics by modernity.

VII. The Two Loves: the Nuptial vs. the Narcissistic and the Cities They Build—the Kingdom vs. the Cage

Let us recall that, in the first place, the only human love that is real, that is actual in history, and the only love that in the end is not hatred, is that which is nuptially ordered and sacramentally mediated, that which as free is graced: the love that is given and received in the Church. This love is "natural" in the sense of having been established primordially, "in the Beginning;" thus John Paul presents it, in all his writings on marriage and family, as established in Christ. In *Veritatis Splendor*, John Paul repeatedly called this primordiality of nuptial "human nature" to our attention.

Opposed to this nuptially ordered and sacramentally mediated love, the covenantal fidelity of the marital "one flesh" that is the graced recovery of the free unity lost by the Fall, is that "love" native to man simply as fallen into alienation, servility, and irresponsibility; it is the *aversio a Deo* that is *sarx*, man turned away from freedom, and toward death.

This false or surrogate love stands in the same symbolically effective relation to damnation and Hell as does our nuptial imaging of God to salvation and the Kingdom of God. More than ever, it is the love that builds the City of Man that tempts us who are in the Church; the temptation is to the irresponsibility of the New Age, the false historical consciousness, which constitutes the "New Manichaeism" of which the "Letter to Families" speaks.[13] This false love we have termed narcissistic. It is also atomistic, for it is a standing denial of any obligation to anyone, of any relation

13. Toward the end of §19 of the "Letter to Families," John Paul II writes of the atomization and depersonalization of humanity that results from the dissolution of the free unity of the marital family under the impact of the contemporary rationalism. Within a similar anthropological perspective, the human family is facing the challenge of a new Manichaeism, in which body and spirit are put in radical opposition: the body does not receive life from the spirit, and the spirit does not give life to the body. Man thus ceases to live as a person and a subject; regardless of all intentions and declarations to the contrary, he becomes merely an object. In the same context of the modern denial of the significance of the body, *Veritatis Splendor* §48 quotes the felicitous, "Corpore et anima unus," from the Second Vatican Ecumenical Council's Pastoral Constitution on The Church in The Modern World, *Gaudium et Spes*, §14.

to anyone. For this love, the self becomes absolute, which is to say, related to nothing whatever. Its prophet is Cain, who, rather than be his brother's keeper, became his murderer. Such a love is a hatred: finally a hatred of the self, for it works an isolation from God and man that is finally unbearable. Its final solace is extinction, nirvana, for it is a love of nothing and of nothingness, a hatred of whatever is.

Only a covenantal and nuptial love can build a free city. It is always the City of God whose cornerstone is the Christ, and whose freedom is that of the children of the one Father: "a chosen race, a royal priesthood, a holy nation."[14] There is no other free human unity, no other free personal existence, than that which is freed in Christ. All its surrogates are idolatries, demonic hatreds directed to what C. S. Lewis has termed "the abolition of man."

Our century, our modern world, has been drenched and is yet being drenched with the blood spilled by that hatred. It has a single remedy: the sacrificial love of Christ for his Church, and the nuptially ordered love which that worship alone sustains. That love is familial, marital, the one valid and authentic expression of human freedom, which is identically our imaging of God and our building of that City in which alone we can be human, in which alone, finally, we can live.

For the City of Man is merely the rationalization and the normalization of what Paul and John have called the flesh (*sarx*), and what Heidegger termed an existence toward death: *Sein zum Tode*. A generation earlier, Nietzsche's savage humor called it a Joyful Wisdom: the *fröhliche Wissenschaft* which knows that with the death of God, everything is permitted.

VIII. The Familial Role in Salvation History

The "holy society by which we belong to God" is first and foremost the One Flesh of Christ and the Church, which Paul called the "great mystery." Secondarily, it is that "society of love" that is the family. These are inseparable as cause and effect, as John Paul made clear beyond cavil.[15]

14. 1 Pet 2:9 (RSV).

15. For John Paul II, the "family" is grounded in the Church's sacramental worship: specifically in Baptism, in the Eucharist and in the sacrament of matrimony. See his "Letter to Families," §17, where we read that

> Marriage, which undergirds the institution of the family, is constituted by the covenant whereby "a man and a woman establish between themselves a partnership of their

By such statements, multiplied as we have seen with a richness of resource and application beyond any possible summary or adequate condensation, Pope John Paul II placed the family thus at the strategic center of human nature, of human society, of the public life whether as the nation or as the State—of morality and of history across the board—as to require of all subsequent Catholic intellectual life a renewal amounting to a total reform of its customary conceptuality, which has understood and appreciated little or nothing of the concrete impact of the Catholic sacramental tradition.

The Catholic affirmation of the familial foundation of society has long been reduced to an unreflected upon cliché, apart from the largely economic discussion of "natural" social justice generated by *Rerum Novarum* and its sequels down to *Mater et Magistra*. Only John Paul II's *Redemptor Hominis* departed from the nonsacramental notion of natural law which pervaded that discussion of Catholic social principles.[16] But if the family

---

> whole life," and which "of its own very nature is ordered to the well-being of the spouses and to the procreation and upbringing of children" (*Code of Canon Law*, c. 1055, §1; *Catechism of the Catholic Church*, no. 1061).
>
> Only such a union can be recognized and ratified as a "marriage" in society.

Further on in the "Letter to Families," in §19—entitled "The Great Mystery"—the dependence of marriage upon the spousal union of Christ with his Church, a union communicated in Baptism and the Eucharist and imaged by Marriage, is affirmed at length and in detail:

> This is unquestionably a new presentation of the eternal truth about marriage and the family in the light of the New Covenant. Christ has revealed this truth in the Gospel by his presence at Cana in Galilee, by the sacrifice of the Cross and the Sacraments of his Church. Husbands and wives thus find in Christ the point of reference for their spousal love. In speaking of Christ as the Bridegroom of the Church, St. Paul uses the analogy of spousal love, referring back to the Book of Genesis: "A man leaves his father and his mother and cleaves to his wife, and they become one flesh" (Gen 2:24). This is the "great mystery" of that eternal love already present in creation, revealed in Christ and entrusted to the Church. "This mystery is a profound one," the Apostle repeats, "and I am saying that it refers to Christ and the Church" (Eph 5:32). The Church cannot therefore be understood as the Mystical Body of Christ, as the sign of man's Covenant salvation, unless we keep in mind the "great mystery" involved in the creation of man as male and female and the vocation of both to conjugal love, to fatherhood and to motherhood. The "great mystery," which is the Church and humanity in Christ, does not exist apart from the "great mystery" expressed in the "one flesh" (cf. Gen 2:24; Eph 5:31–32), that is, in the reality of marriage and the family.

16. As his "point of departure," John Paul links his "Letter to Families" (§1) to the message of *Redemptor Hominis* [(4 March, 1979); AAS 71 (1979), 284ff.]—viz., that "man is the way of the Church"—by identifying the family as the first and most important of the paths comprising this human "way." Thus John Paul's social doctrine as spelled out in *Redemptor Hominis*, issued at the beginning of his reign (and, notoriously, without consulting the "theological community"), is

in its Catholic sacramental reality is truly the foundation of society, then it must be explicitly recognized and exploited as foundational, as constitutive of the entirety of public life, of public responsibility, public freedom, of culture, custom, and the public law. These, which have their sole ground in the sacramentally-instituted family, must reflect that foundation, that constitutionality, and any Catholic discussion of these subjects that would prescind from that foundation is quite frankly bogus, a false accommodation to the modernity that cannot bear to hear that the world is created in Christ and subsists in him. If, with John Paul, we seriously affirm the primacy of the One Flesh of Christ and the Church, and of the Catholic worship that has there its center and its sustenance, there can be no dimension of public or private life that is not freely to be informed and normed by the free, covenantal criterion that is the sacramentally-grounded family. That is to say, because the concrete and historical human condition is in fact covenantal in the sense spelled out with care in John Paul II's "Letter to Families" and therefore is sacramentally signed as a matter of objective fact, any social, political, economic and cultural establishment that does not reflect that sacramentality is false to reality and to history. For, apart from the covenanted good creation, there is no reality, and apart from the history of salvation, there is no history.

---

not so much discontinuous with that of his predecessors as a restatement of the foundations of the Church's social doctrine on the ground that cannot be transcended: the Church's sacramental worship, whose normative role he declared in this *Letter*, as in the many other documents that he published after *Redemptor Hominis*.

LAWRENCE FEINGOLD

The Vision of God in Christ, "Who Loved Me and Gave Himself for Me"

Jacques Maritain, in chapter 7 of the *Notebooks,* introduces the notion of "mad, boundless love," by which a person offers his gift of self "without any possible reserve, made to the beloved."[1] When given to God, this love is described as the "immediate mutual donation of person to person—as to the Bridegroom of their soul."[2] This mystical love is possible because Christ loved us first in an absolutely personal way with His human heart during His earthly life (see John 13:1 and 1 John 4:10).

But how did Jesus love us during His earthly life? If He loved us simply as members of a vast and anonymous humanity, that love would not be spousal; it would have been only *in potency,* a love of some possible human being. Is not the spiritual life based on the fact that Christ loved us with His human heart through an intimate knowledge of every aspect of our personal identity? Only such a personal and concrete love could properly be the absolute exemplar of spousal love.

A key text on the personal nature of God's love for us is given by St. Paul in Galatians 2:20: "I live by faith in the Son of God, *who loved me and gave himself for me.*"[3] To attain to this overflowing maturity of love, each one of

1. Jacques Maritain, *Notebooks,* trans. Joseph W. Evans (Albany, New York: Magi Books, 1984), 220–21.

2. Maritain, *Notebooks,* 241.

3. All Scripture citations are from the Revised Standard Version, Second Catholic Edition.

us must be able to say likewise: "Christ loved *me* and gave himself for *me*." This conviction is necessary so that "we may have power to comprehend with all the saints what is the breadth and length and height and depth, and to know the love of Christ which surpasses knowledge" (Ephesians 3:18–19).

The great theologians of the thirteenth century explain how Jesus could have loved in this personal and concrete way by distinguishing three kinds of knowledge in Christ's human intellect: acquired or experiential knowledge, infused or prophetic knowledge, and the vision of God face to face.[4] Experiential knowledge would not have enabled Jesus to know all human beings personally so as to love them personally. Even infused knowledge would be inadequate, for it implies separate intellectual ideas, which would not have enabled Christ to think of billions of distinct individuals at once. Only in the Vision of God could Christ have had all the members of His Mystical Body actually before His mind's eye at all times during His life.

I. Pius XII on the Vision of God in Christ

The Magisterium of the Church has dealt with the question of Christ's intimate human knowledge of the members of His Mystical Body in Pius XII's 1943 encyclical on the Church, *Mystici Corporis Christi*:

> All the treasures of wisdom and knowledge are in Him" (Colossians 2:3) abundantly. The knowledge which is called "vision" He possesses with such clarity and comprehensiveness that it surpasses similar celestial knowledge found in all the saints of heaven. So full of grace and truth is He that of His inexhaustible fullness we have all received (cf. John 1:14–16).[5]

Later in the encyclical, Pius XII shows how Christ's vision of God enabled Him to keep His entire Mystical Body before His eyes throughout His earthly life:

> But the knowledge and love of our Divine Redeemer, of which we were the object from the first moment of His Incarnation, exceed all the human intellect can

4. See William J. Forster, *The Beatific Knowledge of Christ in the Theology of the 12th and 13th Centuries* (Rome: Catholic Book Agency, 1958); John C. Murray, *The Infused Knowledge of Christ in the Theology of the 12th and 13th Centuries* (Windsor, Canada, 1963).

5. Pius XII, *Mystici Corporis Christi*, 1943, no. 48 (translation from the Vatican website: *http://www.vatican.va/holy_father/pius_xii/encyclicals/documents/hf_p-xii_enc_29061943_mystici-corporis-christi_en.html*).

hope to grasp. For hardly was He conceived in the womb of the Mother of God, when He began to enjoy the beatific vision, and in that vision all the members of His Mystical Body were continually and unceasingly present to Him, and He embraced them with His redeeming love.... In the crib, on the Cross, in the unending glory of the Father, Christ has all the members of the Church present before Him and united to Him in a much clearer and more loving manner than that of a mother who clasps her child to her breast.[6]

Pius XII is saying that the vision of God contributed in a crucial way to Christ's redemptive mission by enabling Him to see all the future members of His Mystical Body and unite Himself to them in love throughout His earthly life. The contact we have now with the mysteries of Christ's life in the sacraments presupposes a prior contact in the soul of Christ Himself. The sacraments bring Him to us in our time; His vision of God brought us to Him, in the time of His earthly life.

Pius XII also affirms the beatific vision in Christ in his 1956 encyclical on devotion to the Sacred Heart, *Haurietis aquas* 56, in which he says that the Sacred Heart is the "symbol of that burning charity which ... enriches the human will of Christ, enlightened and governed by the *most perfect knowledge* derived both from the *beatific vision* and that which is directly infused."[7]

Pius XII in these two documents is exercising the ordinary Magisterium of the Church, to which the faithful must respond with "*religious submission of mind and will.*"[8] Many contemporary Catholic theologians disagree, saying that we have no clear obligation to endorse this teaching, because it concerns a topic incidental to the theme of the encyclical (*obiter dicta*).[9] This opinion cannot be sustained, because Pius XII introduces this Christological theme precisely because of its *intimate connection with the mystery of the Church.* Pius XII clearly regarded the vision of God in

6. Pius XII, *Mystici Corporis Christi*, 75–76.

7. See also Pius XI, *Miserentissimus Redemptor*, May 8, 1928, no. 13: "Now if, because of our sins also which were as yet in the future, but were foreseen, the soul of Christ became sorrowful unto death, it cannot be doubted that then, too, already He derived somewhat of solace from our reparation, which was likewise foreseen" (translation from the Vatican website: http://www.vatican.va/holy_father/pius_xi/encyclicals/documents/hf_p-xi_enc_08051928_miserentissimus-redemptor_en.html).

8. *Lumen gentium* 25, in *The Sixteen Documents of Vatican II* (Boston: Pauline Books and Media, 1999), 152.

9. See, for example, Gerald O'Collins, SJ, and Daniel Kendall, SJ, "The Faith of Jesus," *Theological Studies* 53 (1992): 410.

Christ to have fundamental importance for a key question of ecclesiology: the *nature of the spousal union binding Christ to His Mystical Body*. Likewise, Christ's vision of God is essential for a proper understanding of the love of the Sacred Heart, and our devotion to it. Furthermore, the teaching contained in encyclicals and similar documents demands "religious assent of mind and heart" not directly because of the cogency of the reasons adduced, but because of the *authority* of the teaching office of the Roman Pontiff. Pius XII asserts this doctrine as something evident and accepted by Catholic theologians. Indeed, this teaching is in harmony with the entire theological tradition.

II. Christ's Vision of God according to the *Catechism of the Catholic Church*

The *Catechism of the Catholic Church* 473 teaches the same doctrine as Pius XII, speaking of the fullness of Christ's human knowledge of the Father:

> This truly human knowledge of God's Son expressed the divine life of his person. "The human nature of God's Son, not by itself but by its union with the Word, knew and showed forth in itself everything that pertains to God."[10] Such is first of all the case with the intimate and immediate knowledge that the Son of God made man has of his Father.[11]

The *Catechism* refers to Christ's knowledge of the Father as "intimate and immediate." All acquired or infused knowledge of God is mediated by created concepts and images. The only "immediate" knowledge of God is through the vision of God. "Immediate and intimate knowledge of the Father" is a non-technical way of referring to the beatific vision.

In no. 478, the *Catechism* speaks of Christ's human knowledge of each of us, citing Galatians 2:20: "*Jesus knew and loved us each and all during his life*, his agony and his Passion, and gave himself up for each one of us: 'The Son of God ... loved me and gave himself for me.' He has loved us all with a human heart."[12] A footnote refers to the above-mentioned texts of Pius XII,

10. Maximus the Confessor, *Questions and Doubts*, I, 67 (in PG 90:840a) in *St. Maximus the Confessor's Questions and Doubts*, trans. Despina D. Prassas (DeKalb, Illinois: Northern Illinois University Press, 2010), 149.

11. The footnote in the *Catechism* cites Mark 14:36; Matthew 11:27; John 1:18; 8:55; etc.

12. My italics.

Mystici Corporis and *Haurietis aquas*. Cardinal Ratzinger comments on this text of the *Catechism* in his work, *Gospel, Catechesis, Catechism*:

> Each one of us can and may apply to himself the dramatic personalization that Paul accomplishes in these words. Every man may say: The Son of God loved *me* and gave himself up for *me*.[13]
>
> Only with this statement does christological catechesis become gospel in the full sense of the word. We are not an indistinct mass before God. Christ does not and did not treat us as such. In all truth, Christ walked his path for me. This certainty is a grace given to accompany me in all the stages of my life.... He did all that he did for me and for every man who crosses my path in life.... When we have learned to believe this again, when we are able to announce it to others as the message of truth, evangelization takes place.... And this knowledge gives us the strength to live and act out of this nearness.[14]

As it is true that "we are not an indistinct mass before God," it is no less true that we were not an indistinct mass *to Christ's human soul*, while He lived, suffered, and died for us. It is for this reason that the traditional doctrine that Christ had the vision of God throughout His earthly life has such importance in catechesis and evangelization.

III. Scriptural Basis for the Vision of God in Christ

In Scripture we see that Christ, from the beginning, manifested an intimate knowledge of the Father and of His unique filial relationship to Him. The first example of this knowledge was when He was found in the Temple at twelve years of age and says to Mary and Joseph: "How is it that you sought me? Did you not know that I must be in my Father's house?" (Luke 2:49).

Jesus speaks of His intimate knowledge of the Father in Matthew 11:27–28: "All things have been delivered to me by my Father; and no one knows the Son except the Father, and no one knows the Father except the Son and any one to whom the Son chooses to reveal him."[15] When He says "all

13. See also the International Theological Commission, "The Consciousness of Christ concerning Himself and His Mission," proposition 4, in *International Theological Commission: Texts and Documents, 1969–1985*, vol. 1, ed. Michael Sharkey (San Francisco: Ignatius Press, 1989), 314.

14. Joseph Ratzinger, *Gospel, Catechesis, Catechism: Sidelights on the* Catechism of the Catholic Church (San Francisco: Ignatius Press, 1997), 71; italics original.

15. See Luke 10:22 and John 10:15. See also J. Mouroux, "Propositions sur la conscience du Christ et le temps," in *Problèmes actuels de christologie*, ed. H. Bouëssé and J.-J. Latour (Bruges:

things have been delivered" to Him, this refers above all to knowledge of divine mysteries, as the context makes clear.[16] Furthermore, this gift of knowledge of the Father must be in His human intellect, for the Son reveals the Father through His human soul. If Jesus did not have the vision of God, then "all things" would not have been delivered to Him. Furthermore, Jesus affirms that the Son's knowledge of the Father is on the same level as the Father's knowledge of the Son. Infused knowledge would not have enabled Him to say that He knows the Father as the Father knows Him.[17]

St. John tells us that "no one has ever seen God; the only Son, who is in the bosom of the Father, he has made him known" (John 1:18). When he says "no one has ever seen God," clearly the humanity of Christ alone is excluded, for He is the Son in the bosom of the Father, who "makes Him known." "In the bosom" indicates the intimacy of the knowledge that the Son has of the Father.[18]

Furthermore, "in the bosom" should probably be understood in contrast to the vision of God's back that was granted to Moses in Exodus 33:23. Joseph Ratzinger makes this contrast in *Jesus of Nazareth*:

> The saying at the end of the prologue is the decisive key to the image of Jesus in John's Gospel.... Only the one who is God *sees God*—Jesus. He truly speaks from his *vision of the Father*, from unceasing dialogue with the Father, a dialogue that is his life. If Moses ... could only show us ... God's back, Jesus, by contrast, is the Word that comes from God, from a *living vision* of him....[19]

Although *Jesus of Nazareth* is not a magisterial document, it has ecclesial importance, and it is worthy of note that the Pope endorses the traditional view that Jesus had the vision of God. One of the most fundamental and recurring themes of the book is that the face-to-face *vision* of the Father formed the center of Jesus' human life, from which His entire redemptive mission flowed.[20]

Desclée de Brouwer, 1965), 182–84; Karl Adam, *The Christ of Faith: The Christology of the Church* (New York: Pantheon Books, 1957), 128–33.

16. See also Matthew 28:18.

17. See 1 Corinthians 13:12.

18. See Lagrange, *L'évangile selon Saint Jean*, 7th ed. (Paris: J. Gabalda, 1948), 28; Feuillet, *Le prologue du quatrième évangile* (Brussels: Desclée de Brouwer, 1968), 131–34; "La science de vision de Jésus et les Évangiles: Recherche exégétique," *Doctor communis* 36 (1983): 158–79.

19. Joseph Ratzinger, *Jesus of Nazareth: From the Baptism in the Jordan to the Transfiguration*, trans. Adrian J. Walker (New York, Doubleday: 2007), 265–66 (my italics).

20. See Ratzinger, *Jesus of Nazareth*, 3–8, 23–24, 68, 95, 126, 181–82, 235–36, 340–42, etc.

The vision of God is also alluded to in John 1:14: "And the Word became flesh and dwelt among us, *full of grace and truth*." The fullness of grace and truth is understood here as belonging to Christ's humanity, and includes both the infinite grace of the hypostatic union and the fullness of Christ's "capital grace"[21] by which He received in His humanity all the graces to be distributed to His Mystical Body.

John is speaking of a fullness of truth that is absolute, for he also says that "*it is not by measure*" that Christ has received this fullness: "For he whom God has sent utters the words of God, for it is not by measure that he gives the Spirit; the Father loves the Son, and has given all things into his hand."[22] The fullness of grace and truth in Christ's humanity cannot be measured by any higher standard; rather, it is the measure of all of God's gifts to creatures, for "from his fullness have we all received, grace upon grace" (John 1:16).

A further implication of John 1:14 is that Christ's humanity was endowed with this fullness of grace and truth *from the beginning of His Incarnation*: "The Word was made flesh and dwelt among us, full of grace and truth." Since the infinite fullness of grace consisting in the hypostatic union was given in the instant of His conception, it would seem to follow that the fullness of truth likewise was possessed from the beginning. This could only be through the vision of God.

A similar text is Colossians 2:3, where St. Paul says that in Christ "are hid all the treasures of wisdom and knowledge." How could Christ's soul have all treasures of wisdom if He lacked the vision of God?

The fullness of Jesus' knowledge is also referred to in John 2:23–25 with regard to His knowledge of the human heart. John says that "Jesus . . . *knew all men* and needed no one to bear witness of man; for he himself *knew what was in man*."[23]

In John 3:10–13, Jesus explains that the basis for the authority of His revelation lies in the fact that He speaks of what He *sees* and *knows*:

> Truly, truly, I say to you, we speak of what we *know*, and bear witness to what we have *seen*. . . . I have told you earthly things and you do not believe, how can you believe if I tell you heavenly things? No one has ascended into heaven but he who descended from heaven, the Son of man (who is in heaven).

21. See Thomas Aquinas, *Summa theologiae* (hereafter *ST*) III, q. 8, a. 1.

22. John 3:34–35.

23. See Thomas Aquinas, *Commentary on the Gospel of St. John*, vol. 1, trans. James Weisheipl (Albany, New York: Magi Books, 1980), 177.

Jesus tells Nicodemus that He can give authoritative witness of heavenly things because He has known and seen them, and this is because He "descends from heaven." Jesus does not speak of heavenly things as "from below," by the power of human speculation or the acuteness of His religious sense. Rather, it has been given Him "from above" to *see* that of which He speaks. The phrase "ascended into heaven," does not refer to His Ascension, for that had not yet taken place. It could refer to His "spiritual ascension" into heaven, which would be the beatific vision.[24] This is reinforced by the last words of John 3:13 (imperfectly attested in the manuscript tradition), according to which the Son of man remains in heaven, although He has descended from heaven. This recalls John 1:18: the Son of man abides in the "bosom of the Father."[25]

This affirmation that Christ speaks of what He sees is repeated in John 3:31–33: "He who comes from above is above all; he who is of the earth belongs to the earth, and of the earth he speaks; he who comes from heaven is above all. He bears witness to what he has *seen* and heard, yet no one receives his testimony; he who receives his testimony sets his seal to this, that God is true."

In John 5:19–20, Jesus says to the crowd: "Amen, amen, I say to you, the Son can do nothing of his own accord, but only what he *sees* the Father doing; for whatever he does, that the Son does likewise. For the Father loves the Son, and shows him all that he himself is doing." This vision of the Father is reiterated in John 6:46, where Jesus says: "Not that any one has seen the Father except him who is from God; he has *seen the Father*."[26]

IV. Was Christ Ignorant of the "Day and Hour" of the Second Coming?

A very common objection to the doctrine that Jesus had the vision of God is based on Mark 13:32 in which Christ says that He does not know the "day and the hour" of the Second Coming: "But of that day or that hour no one knows, not even the angels in heaven, nor the Son, but only the

24. This is the interpretation of Suarez, *De Incarnatione,* disp. 25, no. 2; in *Opera omnia* 17:670.

25. See A. Feuillet, "La science de vision de Jésus et les Évangiles," *Doctor communis* 36 (1983): 165–69.

26. See also John 8:14, 38, 55 and 17:24, 25.

Father." This question was raised in the year 600 by a sect called the Agnoetae, who held that Christ's human soul contained some ignorance, at least of the day of the Second Coming.[27] The assertion of true ignorance in Christ's human soul was condemned at that time by the Catholic Patriarch of Alexandria, Eulogius,[28] and by the bishops of Jerusalem, Stephanus[29] and Sophronius.[30]

Eulogius communicated his condemnation to Pope St. Gregory the Great, who wrote back to him, authoritatively approving and confirming his action in the following words:

> The omnipotent Son says He does not know the day which He causes not to be known, not because He himself is ignorant of it, but because He does not permit it to be known at all.... The Only-begotten having been incarnate, and made perfect man for us, did indeed know the day and the hour of judgment *in* His human nature, but nevertheless He did not know this *from* His human nature.... But the fact is certainly manifest that *whoever is not a Nestorian, can in no wise be an Agnoeta*. For with what purpose can he, who confesses that the Wisdom itself of God is incarnate say that there is anything which the Wisdom of God does not know? ... It is written also: Jesus knowing, that the Father gave him all things into his hands [John 13:3]. If all things, surely both the day of judgment and the hour. Who, therefore, is so stupid as to say that the Son has received in His hands that of which He is unaware?[31]

Gregory the Great holds that Christ said that He did not know the day of the Second Coming because to make it known was not part of His mission. Gregory also explains that the Son does not know the day and the hour *through created reason*, but only through divine knowledge communicated to His human soul.

The *Catechism of the Catholic Church* 474 is in harmony with this interpretation: "By its union to the divine wisdom in the person of the Word incarnate, Christ enjoyed in his human knowledge the fullness of under-

27. Mark 13:32; see Acts 1:7.

28. See Eulogius, *Photius Cod.*, 230, in PG 103:1080–84.

29. See Stephanus, *Analecta patrística: Texte und Abhandlungen zur griechischen Patristik*, series Orientalia christiana analecta, ed. Franz Diekamp, vol. 117 (Rome: Pont. institutum orientalium studiorum, 1938), 156.

30. See Sophronius, *Epistola Synodica ad Sergium*, in PG 87:3192.

31. Gregory the Great, Epistle 39, *Sicut aqua frigida*, to Eulogius, Patriarch of Alexandria, PL 77:1096–99, in Denzinger, *The Sources of Catholic Dogma*, trans. Roy J. Deferrari (St. Louis: Herder, 1957), no. 248, 98–99. See also Thomas' interpretation of Mark 13:32 in *ST* III, q. 10, a. 2 ad 1.

standing of the eternal plans he had come to reveal. What he admitted to not knowing in this area, he elsewhere [Acts 1:7] declared himself not sent to reveal."

V. Brief History of the Development of This Thesis

The gradually more explicit theological explanation of the fullness of knowledge in Christ's human intellect provides a remarkable instance of development of doctrine in the Church. Among the Church Fathers, the dominant view was that no ignorance could be affirmed in Christ's human intellect. St. Basil (329–379) writes:

> He, indeed, is without deceit who said: "All things that the Father has are mine." But one of the things which He has is the knowledge of "that day and hour." ... But the saying of Mark ... we understand in this way: that no one knows, neither the angels of God, but not even the Son would have known, unless the Father had known, that is, the cause of the Son's knowledge is from the Father.[32]

St. Jerome is even more explicit, saying: "No man, except He who for our salvation condescended to take on flesh, had a fullness of knowledge and most certain truth."[33] With regard to Christ's knowledge of the Day of Judgment he writes: "What is greater, knowledge of the Father or of the judgment? If he knows the greater, how is he ignorant of the lesser? We read that it is written: 'All things that are the Father's have been given to me.'"[34]

In the sixth century, St. Fulgentius of Ruspa (468–533) maintained the position, based on John 3:34–35 and John 1:14–18, that Christ's human soul enjoyed a fullness "without measure" of the knowledge or vision of God.[35]

In the seventh century, St. Maximus the Confessor explained Christ's human knowledge with a profound analogy:

32. Basil, Epistle 236 to Amphilochius, PG 32:879, in *Saint Basil: Letters*, vol. 2, trans. Agnes Clare Way (New York: Fathers of the Church, Inc., 1955), 167–68.

33. Jerome, Epistle 36 to Damasus, n. 15, in PL 22:459. See Jean-Marie Salgado, "La science du Fils de Dieu fait homme: prises de position des Pères et de la Pré-scolastique (IIè–XIIè siècle)," *Doctor communis* 36 (1983): 225.

34. Jerome, *Commentary on Matthew*, trans. Thomas Scheck (Washington, D.C.: Catholic University of America Press, 2008), 278 (on Matthew 24:36, in PL 26:181).

35. See Fulgentius of Ruspe, Epistle 14 to Ferrandus 29–30, in *Fulgentius: Selected Works*, trans. Robert B. Eno (Washington, D.C.: Catholic University of America Press, 1997), 539–42.

And so, if, in the case of the holy prophets, distant things that are not dependent upon us were discerned by grace, how much more was the Son of God not cognizant of all things and thereby his humanity, too, not by nature but by union with the *Logos*? For just as iron having been heated in the fire has all the properties of fire—for it shines and burns—although, to be sure, it is not fire by nature but iron, so also the humanity of the Lord, inasmuch as it was united to the *Logos*, knew everything, and in it, clearly, everything worthy of God was revealed. But insofar as the nature united with human things, he is said not to know.[36]

The analogy of iron in the furnace is very apt in rendering the idea of the vision of God in Christ's human intellect. His human intellect remains human and finite, but receives a participation of the divine act of knowing, and thus seems to take on, by participation, the properties of the higher nature: knowing God as He knows Himself, and seeing creatures in the Word.[37]

In the eleventh century, St. Anselm, in *Cur Deus homo*, says of Christ's human soul: "If nothing is loved except as it is known, and there be no good thing which he does not love, then there can be no good thing of which he is ignorant."[38]

In the thirteenth century, theologians first began explicitly to distinguish the beatific vision in Christ's human soul from His infused knowledge. St. Thomas Aquinas affirmed with special clarity a threefold knowledge in Christ's human intellect: acquired knowledge, infused knowledge, and the vision of God.[39] Later theologians unanimously adopted the general solution of the thirteenth-century theologians exemplified by St. Thomas. Suarez, in his *De Incarnatione*, holds that to deny the vision of God in Christ from the first moment of His conception would be theologically erroneous and close to heresy.[40] He is followed in this by many other eminent theologians.[41]

36. Maximus the Confessor, *Quaestiones et dubia* I, 67 (PG 90:840) in *Questions and Doubts*, 149.

37. See also John Damascene, *On the Orthodox Faith* 3.21, in *Nicene and Post-Nicene Fathers*, Second Series (Peabody, Massachusetts: Hendrickson Publishers, 2004), vol. 9, 69.

38. Anselm, *Cur Deus homo?* 2.13, in *Saint Anselm: Basic Writings*, trans. S. N. Deane (La Salle, Illinois: Open Court Publishing Co., 1968), 260.

39. See Aquinas, *ST* III, qq. 9–10.

40. See Francisco Suárez, *De Incarnatione*, disp. 25, no. 6, in *Opera omnia* (Paris: Vivès, 1860), 17:672.

41. See, for example, Humbert Bouessé, *La Sauveur du monde*, vol. 2, *Le mystère de l'Incarnation* (Collège théologique dominicain de Chambéry-Leysse, 1953), 374–75; William J. Forster, *The Beatific Knowledge of Christ*, ix; Petavius, *Dogmata theologica Dionysii Petavii*, bk. 11, *De In-*

VI. Objections against the Traditional Doctrine that Jesus Had the Vision of God

Beginning with the Modernist crisis in the early twentieth century,[42] and especially from the 1960's, following Karl Rahner,[43] many theologians denied to Christ the vision of God, or strongly attenuated it, for the following reasons:

1. It is said that the vision of God would make it impossible for Christ to have led a life truly like ours.[44] Belief that Jesus had that vision would introduce a Monophysite tendency to divinize Christ's humanity[45] and destroy the reality of the self-emptying described by St. Paul in Philippians 2:6–11.[46] It is also said that the vision of God is not believable for contemporary man, who prefers to think of the incarnate Son of God in terms of what He "has in common with our human way of life."[47]

I would respond that we should not expect Christ's conscious experience to be exactly like ours, for He had a unique mission as Redeemer of all men, and a unique condition as the Incarnate Son of God. His humanity received additional gifts proper to His mission and divine identity. Just as grace does not destroy nature but perfects it, so the fullness of gifts of knowledge did not destroy Christ's humanity, but perfected it.

2. It is urged that the vision of God is incompatible with Christ's redemptive mission because it is in fact the end of that mission, to be attained after the Resurrection.[48] The accusation is also made that medieval

---

carnatione, ch. 4, n. 2, 8; A. Vacant, "Agnoètes," *Dictionnaire de théologie catholique*, vol. 1 (Paris, 1930), col. 596.

42. Herman Schell was the first important theologian to dissent from the common teaching. See his *Katholische Dogmatik: Kritische Ausgabe*, ed. Josef Hasenfuss and Paul-Werner Scheele (Munich: Ferdinand Schöningh, 1968–1994), vol. 3, 110–13.

43. Karl Rahner, "Dogmatic Reflections on the Knowledge and Self-Consciousness of Christ," in *Theological Investigations*, vol. 5 (Baltimore: Helicon, 1979), 193–215.

44. See Jean Galot, *Who Is Christ? A Theology of the Incarnation*, trans. M. Angeline Bouchard (Chicago: Franciscan Herald, 1981), 356.

45. See Jean Galot, "Le Christ terrestre et la vision," *Gregorianum* 67 (1986): 434; Galot, *Who Is Christ?*, 356; Thomas G. Weinandy, "Jesus' filial vision of the Father," *Pro Ecclesia* 13 (2004): 189.

46. See Galot, *Who Is Christ?*, 356.

47. Galot, *Who Is Christ?*, 357. See also Karl Rahner, "Dogmatic Reflections on the Knowledge and Self-Consciousness of Christ," 194–95.

48. See Christian Duquoc, *Christologie: Essai dogmatique*, vol. 1: *L'Homme Jésus* (Paris: Éd. du Cerf, 1968), 169; Galot, *Who Is Christ?*, 357.

theologians attributed the vision of God to Christ because of an excessive use of the "principle of perfection"[49] (attributing all possible perfections to Christ that are compatible with His mission), combined with an insufficient appreciation of the demands of Christ's mission, for which, it is held, the vision would be an impediment.

We have seen, however, that the vision of God was crucial in various ways for the fulfilling of His mission. It was necessary so that He could love each one of us in a personal and human way during His earthly life. It was necessary so that He could humanly grasp the true malice of all human sins as an offense to the Father, in order to offer perfect expiation. It was necessary for His mission of revealing the Father, which presupposes that He humanly knew the Father from the beginning. Finally, it was necessary so that He could humanly grasp the fullness of His identity as Son of God and reveal Himself as such. Any one of these reasons would be sufficient to show that it was precisely Christ's redemptive and revelatory mission that demanded the vision of God.

3. The traditional thesis, it is said, confuses the self-emptying of Christ's earthly life with His glory as the Risen Lord, attributing the fullness of the vision of God to the earlier state, when it belongs only to the latter.[50]

However, if that were the case, it could not truthfully be said that Christ "loved me and *gave Himself for me*." Since He suffered and gave Himself for each human person before attaining His post-Resurrection glory, He must have already known us in His human mind and heart.

4. It is argued that the vision of God would have made it impossible for Christ to exercise true freedom.[51]

On the contrary, greater knowledge makes possible greater freedom. Because Christ knew the unbearable price He was to pay to accomplish His mission, He could more freely choose it, without being misled by ignorance. His intimate knowledge of each human being allowed Him freely to choose to die for each one individually.

49. See Galot, *Who Is Christ?*, 348.

50. See Hans Urs von Balthasar, *Theodrama: Theological Dramatic Theory*, vol. 3, *The Dramatis Personae: The Person in Christ*, trans. Graham Harrison (San Francisco: Ignatius Press, 1988), 178; Galot, *Who Is Christ?*, 356.

51. See Karl Rahner, "Dogmatic Reflections on the Knowledge and Self-Consciousness of Christ," 201; Engelbert Gutwenger, "The Problem of Christ's Knowledge," in *Who Is Jesus of Nazareth?*, vol. 11 of *Concilium* (New York: Paulist Press, 1966), 92.

5. Often the idea of the beatific vision in Christ is ridiculed as giving Him knowledge of all the minutia of facts and all the details of scientific discoveries, which would seem absolutely foreign to our human experience.

This objection overlooks the unified nature of the vision of God, in which everything is seen in God and in its relation to God.

6. Finally, it has become a commonplace to object that Christ could not have possessed the beatific vision during His Passion because it would have been incompatible with the immense spiritual suffering He experienced.[52]

However, the nearly unanimous consensus of theologians from the thirteenth century until Pius XII held both that Christ's human soul had the vision of God, and that He suffered true spiritual suffering, without finding these two truths to be incompatible.

John Paul II commented on this mystery in his Apostolic Letter *Novo millennio ineunte*. He affirms that Christ continued to "see" the Father in His agony, and that this vision was not only not incompatible with His suffering, but made possible the deepest dimension of that suffering: Jesus' agony over the horrific mass of human sin. For "He alone, who sees the Father and rejoices fully in him, can understand completely what it means to resist the Father's love by sin."[53]

St. Thomas explains this simultaneous presence of contrary affective experiences by maintaining that while the vision of God is a unitary act of knowing in the Word, nevertheless this act reveals many different objects.[54] Consideration of God's glory in itself causes immense joy. However, consideration of God's glory offended through the sins of men is capable of causing the deepest sorrow.[55]

St. Thomas distinguishes here between the higher and lower parts of Christ's soul. The higher part considers God directly, whereas the lower part considers creatures.[56] Normally the contemplation of God in the high-

52. See Rahner, "Dogmatic Reflections on the Knowledge and Self-Consciousness of Christ," 203. See also Jean Galot, "Le Christ terrestre et la vision," *Gregorianum* 67 (1986): 435.

53. John Paul II, *Novo millennio ineunte* 26–27 (trans. from the Vatican website: http://www.vatican.va/holy_father/john_paul_ii/apost_letters/documents/hf_jp-ii_apl_20010106_novo-millennio-ineunte_en.html).

54. See Aquinas, *ST* III, q. 46, a. 8.

55. See Nicolas, Marie-Joseph, "Les mystères de la vie cachée du Christ et les hommes de l'histoire," in *Problèmes actuels de christologie*, ed. H. Bouëssé et J.-J. Latour (Bruges: Desclée de Brouwer, 1965), 96.

56. See Aquinas, *ST* I, q. 79, a. 9.

er part of our will and intellect overflows into the lower part of the soul and produces an emotion of consolation, as in the blessed in Heaven. However, during the Passion of Christ, St. Thomas holds that each part of Christ's soul and each faculty was miraculously permitted to perform its own proper function without being overpowered, as it were, by higher functions and consolations, such as the vision of God.[57]

The fact, therefore, that Christ possessed the absolute fullness of contemplation in Gethsemane does not mean that He could not suffer. Quite the contrary! St. Thomas holds that Christ's grief "surpassed all grief of every contrite heart, both because it flowed from a greater wisdom and charity, by which the pang of contrition is intensified, and because He grieved at the one time for all sins, according to Isaiah 53:4."[58]

VII. Conclusion

Christ's vision of God during His earthly life is a tenet of Catholic doctrine that has vital importance for the life of the Church. This teaching cannot simply be regarded as an archeological relic from Scholasticism that can be safely consigned to the dust heaps of history. This truth is vital for many reasons, not least because it is necessarily linked to Christ's mad and boundless love for each human person in His human heart. It is also necessarily linked to the fact that Christ died for each man *personally*, in order to atone for every concrete human sin that He knew concretely in His humanity and grieved over in all the horror of its ungrateful rejection of the infinite love of God. The weakening of the perception of this truth in the mind of Christians is deeply linked to the crisis of faith of the past half century and to the languishing of the mystical life, in which the soul corresponds through grace to the mad and boundless love of Christ, "who loved me and gave Himself for me."

57. See Aquinas, *ST* III, q. 46, aa. 6 and 8.
58. Aquinas, *ST* III, q. 46, a. 6 ad 4.

CHRISTOPHER P. KLOFFT

Making Love in the Pew

The Relational Interplay between Sexuality and Liturgy

While the term "a marriage made in heaven" usually refers to an especially compatible set of circumstances or persons suited for a relationship or project, for Catholic and Orthodox Christians, it has a more profound meaning. This is not simply a "poetic" way to express the Paschal Covenant that sets us free. Scripture abounds with nuptial references to this saving union of Christ and His people, most specifically describing life in the Kingdom of God as the "Wedding Feast of the Lamb."[1] Despite this consistent unitive imagery in Christian thought to the contrary, there has often been a certain discomfort with any sort of conflation between the intimate relationship between God and the human person (which we may oversimplify here and call "worship") and the intimate relationship between husband and wife. Unfortunately, the term "sexual" is a negatively charged term, both in past Church thinking and in social parlance, where it is invariably linked to hedonism or criminality.[2] It seems that many find the earthiness, the frankly messy humanity of specifically sexual intimacy

1. Rev 19:7–8 (NAB).

2. In regards to the Church's teaching, one need only look to the classic suspicion placed on sexual activity by many (but certainly not all) of the Fathers. Augustine, responsible for the foundation of Catholic teaching on marriage in particular, is often cited in this regard, though his suspicions are often overstated. In contemporary discourse, describing something as "sexual" is often linked with the notion of taboo, accompanied by the winking acceptance of the breaking of that taboo. This can be seen throughout advertising in secular media, as well as depictions of relationships in popular culture.

between spouses, to somehow be at odds with the "pure" worship present in the liturgy or even the personal prayer life of the individual.

Yet, this has not stopped some theologians from considering that the spousal act is in truth a form of worship,[3] and it is in *this* sense that we are "taking back" the concept of sexuality, a concept too central to the Christian essence to have semantics mar its value. As the unitive factor of complementary entities, individuals "made for each other"[4] reach their perfection in this union because it is the end for which they were made. This is, therefore, theologically most appropriate, and has been developed by others.[5] This comparison is rooted in the fundamental mystery of the Christian faith: the Incarnation. Hence, any consideration of the Christian covenant must take seriously the conjugal imagery of the Scriptures as it applies to the sacrament of marriage if such pondering is to be true to its Source. And this Word offers valuable fruit for vital reflection for us on the pattern of God's love for His people. However, I would like to reverse the order of typology here: while it is true that sexual intimacy between spouses can be a form of worship, worship, especially present in the liturgy and the form of the sacraments, is also a symbol of the sexual, physically unitive relationship between God and the individual believer.

In order to make sense of this, some definition of terms is required here. My proposal here is not intended to be merely analogical. Analogy points to a likeness, a way of knowing or understanding. It can lead one to truth, but itself does not contain the truth. Thus, we recognize the limitation of analogy. For example, the Eucharist is not an analogy of God's living gift of the divine Self to us—rather, it actually *is* so. As a simple way of considering this, we can note that any analogy ultimately breaks down after it is poked and prodded enough. If worship were understood to only be *like* the sexual relationship between God and His people, its theological value would be trivialized. Thus, since this truth is ill served by "analogy," I will instead consider it with the far richer term: *symbol*.

3. Of particular note here is the work of John S. Grabowski. See *Sex and Virtue: An Introduction to Sexual Ethics* (Washington, D.C.: the Catholic University of America Press, 2003).

4. "The man said, 'This one, at last, is bone of my bones and flesh of my flesh; This one shall be called woman, for out of her man this one has been taken.' That is why a man leaves his father and mother and clings to his wife, and the two of them become one body" (Gn 2:23–24). This is from the NAB; the NSRV concludes the verse "one flesh."

5. See especially the work of Pope John Paul II, including the *Theology of the Body*, but also

Here, too, the term "symbol" must be taken back to its Christian fullness from the abuse of colloquial trivialization. A symbol goes beyond the limits of analogy. Its Greek roots (*sym-ballein*) mean "to bring all things together" in one place or meaning. Properly speaking, a symbol contains far more than that which it signifies. It is in this way the Church understands the sacraments as symbolic.[6] Symbols are also necessarily multivalent; as such, if one were to define the specific and sole meaning of a symbol, it ceases to be a symbol properly so called. As symbols, the sacramental life is open to rich layers of understanding, layers which cannot be exhausted even by continuous reflection.

The third definition I wish to provide at the outset is what I mean by "sexual." In the fields of anthropology, psychology, sociology, and yes, moral theology, excessive ink has been spilled in articulating the precise meaning of "sex." Obviously, there cannot be a genital sexual experience between God and the person in the literal sense. However, sexual intimacy encompasses the experience of one's whole personhood as an inspirited body, as articulated at great length in the teaching of Pope John Paul II.[7] Therefore, it is possible to speak about the sexual experience of the person with God beyond the physical or genital in the affective, unitive dimensions of the person. Even the physical component cannot entirely be ignored.

Finally, one must recall the meaning of the covenantal relationship between God and His people. As the Israelites developed their understanding of the relationship begun through Abraham, it became more and more clear that the covenant was best understood in spousal terms. Yahweh is the groom and the people Israel is His bride. The language representative of this profound reality begins in Genesis, continues through Exodus, where

---

presented in *Familiaris Consortio*. There is also no shortage of commentators on these texts, including Grabowski.

6. The landmark work on this notion of symbol is Karl Rahner, "The Theology of the Symbol," in *Theological Investigations* 4 (New York: Crossroad, 1966), 221–52.

7. "This first expression of the man, 'flesh of my flesh,' also contains a reference to what makes the body truly human. Therefore it referred to what determines man as a person, that is, as a being who, even in all his corporality, is similar to God. We find ourselves, therefore, almost at the very core of the anthropological reality, the name of which is 'body,' the human body. However, as can easily be seen, this core is not only anthropological, but also essentially theological. Right from the beginning, the theology of the body is bound up with the creation of man in the image of God. It becomes, in a way, also the theology of sex, or rather the theology of masculinity and femininity, which has its starting point here in Genesis": John Paul II, *The Theology of the Body: Human Love in the Divine Plan* (Boston: Pauline Books and Media, 1997), 47.

Yahweh proposes to His people on Mt. Sinai, and reaches its richest articulation in the writings of the prophets. That the clear sexual, spousal imagery in the Song of Songs, Isaiah, Jeremiah, and Ezekiel can be startling to us is proof that we have allowed a Godless pall of guilt to overshadow this divine gift.[8] In the Christian scriptures, this understanding is further developed to represent the spousal relationship between Christ the bridegroom and his bride, the Church, the community of believers that extends beyond Israel. Perhaps the best articulation of this is found in Ephesians 5, where human marriage is directly related to the covenantal relationship.[9] Indeed, this covenant is the *only* means given to us by which we are to understand our relationship with God. If Covenant is a spousal relationship, then it makes sense that the richness of marital intimacy also exists between God and His people. It is manifestly "conjugal": literally that the Most High is "yoked together" (Latin: *con-iugum*) with His people.

Even the intimacy of this covenant relationship is itself symbolic of something more. The relationship of husband and wife, whose love overflows as a third person in the body of their child, makes sense in light of the familial, communal intimacy which *is* the Holy Trinity, an intercommunion of eternal love between the three divine Persons. While all our imagery and theological explanations are necessarily imperfect and humbled in the face of this tremendous mystery, all of our expressions of love ultimately reflect this foundational relationship, the root and heart of the experience of personified Love. Situating this mystery in the context of human marriage, it makes sense that Pope John Paul II would refer to marriage as the "primordial sacrament," the original place of relational encounter between God and man, made manifest in the one flesh union of the man and the woman.[10]

8. See, for example, any number of texts, including Gn 2, Ex 19, Hos 1–2, Ez 16, and the entirety of the Song of Songs.

9. "For no one hates his own flesh but rather nourishes and cherishes it, even as Christ does the church, because we are members of his body. 'For this reason a man shall leave [his] father and [his] mother and be joined to his wife, and the two shall become one flesh.' This is a great mystery, but I speak in reference to Christ and the church" (Eph 5:29–32).

10. "Resulting from this likeness [to God] there is also the primordial awareness of the conjugal significance of the body, pervaded by the mystery of original innocence.... Thus, in this dimension, there is constituted a primordial sacrament, understood as a sign which effectively transmits in the visible world the invisible mystery hidden from eternity in God. This is the mystery of truth and love, the mystery of the divine life in which man really shares.... It is the original innocence which initiates this participation": John Paul II, *The Theology of the Body*, 333.

Thus, all people, on account of being made in the image and likeness of God, exist in relationship with God, who is Himself "relationship" in His Trinitarian nature. It is important to recognize, however, that this fundamental relationship, present from birth, is not yet a *spousal* relationship. It is only through the sacrament of Baptism that the human person is fully incorporated into the redeemed human community. No longer merely a creature, the baptized person enters into covenantal relationship with God.[11] This also marks the formal beginning of his or her participation in the Divine Liturgy, that Wedding Feast of the Lamb in heaven celebrated vibrantly in His Spouse, the Church on earth.

When speaking of the Liturgy, it is important to note that while it finds its "source and summit" in the celebration of the Holy Eucharist,[12] Liturgy radiates this Real Presence in manifold ways, in the other Sacraments, in Scripture and liturgical prayer. Liturgy makes manifest the work of the Trinity in the living and ongoing creation, redemption, and sanctification of the world and thus is the manifestation of the relationship within the Trinity and between God and His people. It is the "evidence," if you will, that the spousal relationship not only exists, but resonates in the "real world" as witness to that union, as when a husband and wife publicly live their vows.

Because this is the case, one can discern the quality and character of this spousal relationship by looking at the quality and character of the liturgy and the fruitfulness inherent in one's "conscious, active, and fruitful participation" in it.[13] This discernment reveals the specifically marital, and ultimately sexual, depth of this multivalent symbol.

One need only recall that there is no Sacrament that does not involve some form of physical contact in its conferral. Christianity early on filled our liturgy with clearly sexual symbolism. To cite but one example: the coital triple immersion of the male-image Paschal Candle into the female-icon "womb of the Church," the baptismal font, to render it "fer-

11. "From the baptismal fonts is born the one People of God of the New Covenant … They are 'a chosen race, a royal priesthood, a holy nation, God's own people, that [they] may declare the wonderful deeds of him who called [them] out of darkness into his marvelous light'": *Catechism of the Catholic Church*, 1267–68. The passage cited is from 1 Peter, itself a citing of Exodus 19, which expresses the covenant relationship between Yahweh and Israel.

12. *Lumen Gentium* 11. See *Vatican Council II: The Conciliar and Post Conciliar Documents*, Volume 1, revised edition, ed. Austin Flannery (Collegeville: Liturgical Press, 1992).

13. *Sacrosanctum Concilium* 11 (Flannery edition).

tile" for giving "new birth" in Baptism. Modern minimalism and profound misunderstanding of incarnational liturgy has radically impoverished the Divine-human passion inherent in the Liturgy. Is it any wonder, then, that Catholics now scoff at the Church's positions on sexual sanctity, contraception, or the meaning and precious value of every human life?

One can see elements of a happy, healthy relationship in one's marital relationship with God in the same way that one can witness the elements that make up a happy, healthy relationship with one's spouse. Some further examples will demonstrate this.

Success in marriage is predicated on good communication. Perhaps most simply put, spouses must take time to talk to one another and to listen to one another. This is especially so in regard to the serious matters that come into their shared life, but the daily conversation, the sharing of thoughts, feelings, ideas, back and forth throughout one's day, also signifies the health of the relationship. The couple's ability to communicate well also relates to the place of the marital act within that relationship. A couple that communicates well will find a rightful and meaningful place for the marital act in the context of their relationship. Of course, this is not absolutely the case. While a married couple's sexual relationship may continue to exist apart from any meaningful communication, such activity hardly embodies the unifying, life-giving aspects signified by the act itself.[14] The bodies of the participants in the act speak for them, describing a unity that is supposed to exist, intended to exist, by the meaning of the act. This "language of the body," again to use Pope John Paul II's terminology, provides a way to understand how things should be.[15] In like fashion, consistent communication between the human person

14. "Therefore, because of its intrinsic nature, the conjugal act, which unites husband and wife with the closest of bonds, also makes them capable of bringing forth new life according to the laws written into their very natures as male and female. And if both essential meanings are preserved, that of union and procreation, the conjugal act fully maintains its capacity for [fostering] true mutual love and its ordination to the highest mission of parenthood, to which Man is called": Pope Paul VI, *Humanae Vitae*, 12. The translation I am using comes from Janet E. Smith, *Humanae Vitae: A Generation Later* (Washington, D.C.: the Catholic University of America Press, 1991).

15. "We now analyze the sacramentality of marriage under the aspect of sign. When we say that the language of the body also enters essentially into the structure of marriage as a sacramental sign, we refer to a long biblical tradition ... it is characteristic of the prophets' manner of expressing themselves that, presupposing the language of the body in the objective sense, they pass at the same time to its subjective meaning. That is to say, after a manner of speaking, they allow the body itself to speak. In the prophetic texts of the covenant, on the basis on the analogy of the spousal union of the married couple, the body itself 'speaks.' It speaks by means of its

and the divine Spouse is also necessary for the health of their sexual relationship. This is not merely "good advice" or a "suggestion"; rather, no authentically spousal relationship can exist apart from the constant communication between spouses, especially in the case of the human person and God.

So how does this communication occur? Primarily, it occurs through prayer. Through prayer, God speaks to the person, and in turn one listens and responds. The Liturgy is a specific and proper forum for this spousal communication. While all prayer serves as communication, there is something especially spousal about liturgical prayer. It is in the Liturgy that "all Christian prayer finds its source and goal."[16] At the risk of minimizing the prayer of the individual believer, prayer apart from the liturgy is so much "small talk" between God and the beloved; it should lead us to Liturgy, but it itself is not the same. The "serious business" of marital life is based on the mutual recognition of the conversational partners that time and space has been set apart specifically for that purpose.

One should also recall the words of St. Paul in 1 Thessalonians to "pray without ceasing."[17] The Church recognizes this need for constant communication and actually incorporates it into the Liturgy. The Liturgy of the Hours sanctifies the whole day through prayer, each of the Hours possessing its own character appropriate to the usual concerns of that time of day. In the Psalms, the one praying expresses the deepest longings, the joys and sadness of our lives, in the same manner that spouses express themselves to one another throughout their days. And even when the language of the Psalms does not speak directly to the circumstances of the one praying, he or she recognizes that the prayer still speaks on behalf of the rest of the Church. In that moment, the prayer may not be the prayer of that individual, but it *is* the prayer of someone in the Mystical Body of Christ at that point. In a similar way, the sacrament of Marriage is not solely directed towards the life of the couple. The love they share overflows outward to those with whom they come in contact. As spouses, they work to build up the community. Even when there may not be particular highs or lows to reflect on and discuss, there is always someone else in the community that needs

masculinity and femininity. It speaks in the mysterious language of the personal gift.... The texts of the prophets have great importance for understanding marriage as a covenant of persons ... and, in particular, for understanding the sacramental covenant of man and woman in the dimension of sign": John Paul II, *Theology of the Body*, 357–60.

16. *Catechism of the Catholic Church*, 1073.

17. 1 Thes 5:17 (NAB).

the spouses' prayers and work: a need to be addressed, a joy to celebrate, a concern requiring counsel and discernment. In the Divine Office, the spouses, divine and human, talk together of their needs and the needs of the whole community supported by them.

The apex of the relationship between the spousal relationship and liturgy (I hesitate to use the word "climax" here) occurs in the celebration of the Eucharist. In the celebration of the Mass, the fullness of sexual expression between God and the person becomes manifest. The whole liturgical act demonstrates consistent marital symbolism. The opening rite of the liturgy expresses the joy of being in the presence of the Beloved. In this rite, there is the recognition that this is not "normal space," but rather that one is in "sacred space," a place in which the believer prepares himself or herself for intimate contact with the Other. This also includes the penitential rite, in which the lover expresses sorrow for the offenses committed against the Spouse. This reconciliation is especially important in light of what is to come, for it is only fitting that the married couple express themselves in the way proper to them as spouses, the becoming of "one flesh,"[18] when there is no division, no pressing threat to their unity as a couple.

After the opening rite, the Liturgy of the Word once again symbolizes the conversation of the lovers, but this time with a special emphasis on the character of their relationship. Specifically, they speak of their past together, remembering both the good and the bad and how that has shaped their relationship up until the present day. They see who they are now in the events that have come before, recognizing that those events are as much a part of their continued relationship as they were in the past.

The offertory increases the intimacy of the encounter. The offering of gifts is likened to the foreplay of the couple as the human lover prepares to become one with the divine lover. In the Eucharistic prayer, these gifts are transformed, no longer what they were, but now a part of the spousal life shared between the two.

Finally, the full sexual symbolism of the liturgy is realized in the reception of the Eucharist. The believer takes Christ into his or her own body and the two become one flesh. The body of Christ becomes one with our bodies in the consummation of the spousal relationship begun in Baptism. In this encounter, the covenant is renewed. It is obviously unifying, and

18. Gen 2:24 (NAB).

it is also life giving, as is proper to the nature of the marital act itself.[19] Strengthened by the encounter with the Beloved, the baptized leaves the encounter to be Christ for those with whom he or she comes in contact. The sacramental imagery here is powerful and deliberate: the Eucharist is not some heightened state of awareness, some purely spiritual ecstasy, or even a specially regimented form of prayer. It is a specific joining of the physical with the physical, a Body with a body. Even though our sacramental theology recognizes the ability to participate in the Eucharist without actually physically consuming the Body and Blood of Christ in some circumstances, it is recognized as the exception, not the norm. The proper form for the celebration of the sacrament involves the joining of two bodies becoming one flesh. More powerful sexual imagery does not exist, and it is key to understanding the full richness of "the source and summit of the Church's life."[20]

The relationship between sex and worship is nowhere more explicit than in the Eucharist, but that is not to say that other symbolic references do not exist in the rest of the Church's sacramental life. The practice of the sacraments is not just an exercise of the spirit, or a matter of mental prayer alone. Rather, the richness of sacramental imagery includes the Church's engagement with the physical through objects made holy by their use, actions pregnant with meaning, words and music chosen to bring the participants more fully into the action, sights, and sounds that inspire the senses. These are the very same elements that elevate the marital encounter above the level of mere mechanical performance. Sacramental worship, like sexual experience, is an engagement of the whole embodied person through the senses to signify a unity that goes beyond the elements present in the encounter.

But these are just a few examples. Beyond the physical aspects of ritual already discussed above, one could fruitfully consider the sexual imagery present in all seven sacraments, further solidifying the symbolic connection between sex and worship. In the sacrament of Reconciliation, the human person recognizes the offense committed against the Beloved. The Beloved does not reject the spouse who has sinned against Him, but instead offers forgiveness and a return to the fullness of unity in the covenantal

19. *Humanae Vitae* 12 (Vatican translation).
20. *Sacrosanctum Concilium* 10 (Flannery edition).

relationship. This is recognized not only in the words spoken to the penitent but also in the actual placing of hands on him or her. Forgiveness is not just a cold, distant acceptance of the apology, but an embrace, a contact between the two covenantal partners. Similarly, in the Anointing of the Sick, the embodied nature of the person is recognized in the tender anointing of various parts of the person's body. These parts are recognized for the offenses committed against God, yet they are also the same parts by which the lover engages the beloved. The sacrament recognizes the desire for union, hindered at present by both one's sinfulness and one's illness.

Of course, theological reflection should always be aimed at fruitful growth for God's people. "Faith seeking understanding" should not remain merely professional intellection, interesting only to specialists with no lived connection in the life of the Church. So what "new fruit" might a sexual understanding of the liturgical life bring about? Is it to encourage reflection in the prurient minds of the congregation, who are far more likely to listen to a homily about sex than they are about the liturgy? Well, I can't be too quick to acknowledge that this sadly may be the case! But more importantly, these reflections encourage God's people to take seriously not only the deep relationship that is presumed when we use the word "worship," but also the meaning of being embodied creatures capable of relating to God and one another through a union of one flesh. Through this relational paradigm, the Church as a whole can move away from an emphasis wrongly placed on excessive concern for duty, obligation, and "acts of supererogation" and can instead take more seriously the expectations present in the meaning of "covenant." No one who truly loves his or her spouse considers the proper behavior of a married person to be a matter of duty or obligation; rather, we act the way we do because we love the other. Our words and actions demonstrate how important the beloved is to us. Furthermore, our loving behavior is aimed at fostering that relationship that it might grow in holiness and reach beyond ourselves, to be a transforming presence in the world towards the building up of the Kingdom. A sexual perspective on the act of worship takes this simple observation seriously.

NIKOLAJ ZUNIC

Sexual Ethics and the Purpose of Marriage

It is no mystery that traditional moral perspectives on the area of sexuality, such as the teaching of the Catholic Church, have come under fire in the last half-century, particularly in western democracies. Many practices which were once disapproved are now advocated by many as permissible, such as deviant sexual behavior and homosexual relationships. What has contributed to this general shift in our thinking about sexual ethics and the role of marriage in human life? I would like to argue in this paper that our views about sexuality are related essentially to our expressions of love and that, furthermore, love lies at the basis of a sound rationality that buttresses natural law arguments in defense of proper moral conduct. If rational arguments about the rectitude of certain sexual lifestyles are no longer persuasive today, this may be due to a disordered personal love which is adversely affecting human reason.

When we situate the topic of love in the domain of human sexuality, the term that comes first to mind that best describes this phenomenon is that of erotic love. This is the love, as Plato described it, that begins in a condition of poverty or lack and seeks to find fulfillment in an other who fills the emptiness within.[1] *Eros* is a consuming and devouring love; its basic orientation is towards the satisfaction of egocentric desires and needs. The love that human beings have for each other in the sexual realm is at its most elementary level manifested in the experience of pleasure, which is

1. See Plato, *The Symposium*, trans. Christopher Gill (London: Penguin, 1999), 203b–d, 39.

intrinsically related to the subject's body and thus can only be egocentric, in the sense that its reference-point is the ego or the self. What is missing in pure erotic love is a true, committed, selfless attachment to the other for the other's sake, what Gabriel Marcel calls hetero-centric love. Borrowing from Jacques Maritain, we can call eros an *anthropocentric love* which is a love focused solely on the good of the human being at the expense and diminution of the other as other. An anthropocentric love values self-fulfillment above everything else and claims its satisfaction in the emotional and physical pleasure it receives from one's partner. This anthropocentric love is responsible for the passion with which so many couples enter into their relationships and at the same time for the dismissal of any suggestion of the existence of fixed moral norms in the sexual life. For if I live primarily at the instigation of my anthropocentric love, a love absorbed in the pursuit of pleasure, then I do not want anything to get in the way of this project and am inclined to override any other concern or interest. This erotic love, then, can become absolute.

A purely human, all-too-human love, which is conceived as originating and culminating in the human being, becomes trapped within its own circle of activity without any real outlet for transcendence. The final end of the anthropocentric love then can only be the self-fulfillment of the human subjects and nothing beyond them. Thus the infertile couple's wish to have a child, motivated by love for each other, leads them to the fertility clinic; and the homosexual couple enters into and affirms their partnership because of the love that exists between them. Yet this love, which I am claiming is an anthropocentric love, does not hold out any form of transcendence because it is governed by an attitude of self-fullfilment that is based on a merely human foundation. In other words, there is no awareness or recognition in the expression of this love that the love could possibly have originated from outside the human subject and is destined for a transcendent end. The traditional alternative to erotic love is *agape*, the virtue of charity, but in this context of human sexuality we can describe it, once again using Maritain's terminology, as a *theocentric love* because the focus has now shifted away from the human being towards God, the source of sheer transcendence.[2] Theocentric love places the love of God above that

2. For rich discussions of the various types of love, see C. S. Lewis, *The Four Loves* (London: HarperCollins, 1960) and Dietrich von Hildebrand, *The Nature of Love*, trans. John F. Crosby with John Henry Crosby (South Bend, Indiana: St. Augustine's Press, 2009).

of the human being. Its fundamental characteristic is that of transcendence, in the sense of love surpassing the merely human scope of meaning. There is a recognition within a theocentric love that the human person is not the creator or initiator of love, but is rather the participant in this love. Theocentric love is marked by fullness and abundance and its expression is an act of giving, rather than of taking.

Theocentric love is proposed as the alternative to an anthropocentric love because it represents a true and meaningful transcendence of the human and an effective escape from the closed and stifling confines of the all-too-human. Most of the great Christian mystics and theologians—I am thinking here particularly of Bernard of Clairvaux's *De diligendo Deo* and Pope Benedict XVI's encyclical *Deus Caritas Est*—conceived of human love as originating in a selfish attitude and egoistic orientation and gradually growing into a love of God for God's sake. Eros can take us to agape and the anthropocentric love can eventually lead into the theocentric love, but the challenge at this juncture in our discussion is how precisely this transition happens. If the anthropocentric love finds its proper home in the secular humanism of modern culture, how can it be channeled towards the transcendent end of a love of God, which signals the proper end of love as such, since God is love? To arrive at an understanding of how this transition is made we need to examine closely the idea of the end or goal (*finis, telos*) as it functions in the domain of human sexuality. In other words, we need to ask the question of teleology: What is the end of human sexuality? To what purpose do human beings engage in sexual activity?

The well respected English philosopher G. E. M. Anscombe has written extensively on moral issues, but more specifically about sexual ethics. Her article "Contraception and Chastity," written in the aftermath of *Humanae Vitae*, seeks to provide clarification for and defense of Pope Paul VI's teaching concerning the moral illicitness of the use of contraceptives.[3] As a Catholic thinker, Anscombe is well aware of the natural law tradition and certainly knows how the Catholic Church views natural law, particularly in relation to theology and divine revelation. A careful reading of this paper manifests the honest attempt that Anscombe offers to furnish rational, philosophical arguments for the position that contraception is immoral.

3. G. E. M. Anscombe, "Contraception and Chastity," in *Why Humanae Vitae Was Right: A Reader*, ed. Janet E. Smith (San Francisco: Ignatius Press, 1993), 121–46.

However, it is also apparent that Anscombe vacillates in this approach and at times seems to suggest that only a properly informed Christian conscience could possibly recognize the truth of the doctrines propounded in the Catholic tradition. For instance, Anscombe begins her discussion of contraception with an extensive focus on the Church's historical reaction to contraception through the ages, stretching back to the Church fathers, such as St. Augustine, who consistently affirmed that contraception is morally wrong. The suggestion here is that only the Church has assiduously opposed contraception and other immoral sexual acts. The implication is that this way of considering the domain of sexual ethics is unique to the Church, rather than falling within the purview of human nature and human reason as such. At a certain point in the essay, Anscombe states succinctly what her understanding of natural law is and how it is to be interpreted:

> "Natural law" is simply a way of speaking about the whole of morality, used by Catholic thinkers because they believe the general precepts of morality are *laws* promulgated by God our Creator in the enlightened human understanding when it is thinking in general terms about what are good and what are bad actions. That is to say, the discoveries of reflection and reasoning when we think straight about these things *are* God's legislation to us (whether we realize this or not).[4]

Thomas Aquinas wrote that natural law is the rational creature's participation of the eternal law.[5] There is some debate about what Aquinas meant by the term "eternal law," but it is generally acknowledged that he did not mean "divine law."[6] In this delineation, Anscombe appears to suggest that

4. Anscombe, "Contraception and Chastity," 131.

5. "The natural law is nothing else than the rational creature's participation of the eternal law": Thomas Aquinas, *Summa Theologica*, trans. Fathers of the English Dominican Province, 5 vols. (Allen, Texas: Christian Classics, 1981), I-II, q. 91, a. 2.

6. See Anthony J. Lisska, "On the Revival of Natural Law: Several Books from the Last Half-Decade," *American Catholic Philosophical Quarterly*, 81 (2007): 613–38, at 622: "In discussing Aquinas' account of natural law, Kainz, Theron, and Schockenhoff, among others, need to be careful when considering eternal law and divine law. These concepts, which Aquinas keeps distinct, are neither identical nor co-extensive. 'Eternal law' is the set of divine archetypes in the divine mind; 'divine law' is a reference to revelation, that is, a direct appeal to the Scriptures. Hence, divine law is a thoroughly theological concept. Eternal law, on the other hand, is a philosophical concept used by Aquinas to tease out the relationship between human nature and the creative plan of God. But eternal law and divine law differ conceptually and ontologically." Brian Davies, by contrast, suggests that Eternal Law is identical with God himself on the supposition of the doctrine of divine simplicity, namely, that God is not distinct from his attributes. See Brian Davies, *The Thought of Thomas Aquinas* (Oxford: Clarendon Press, 1992), 154–55.

natural law is rooted in and gains its validity through divine law, which would make natural law reasoning dependent on theology and hence something that potentially could not be apprehended by reason alone.[7] When Anscombe writes that the principles of natural law are ultimately "God's legislation to us," we are reminded of her essay "Modern Moral Philosophy," in which she advances the provocative thesis that modern deontological ethics, which emphasize the place of obligation and duty in morality, are in fact remnants of a divine command ethics.[8] In other words, the foundation of all moral obligations can only be found in God and His commands; if we attempt to place this foundation anywhere else, then deontological ethics is deprived of its obligatory character. Therefore, I wish to suggest that Anscombe waffles in her understanding of moral reasoning, but especially natural law reasoning: often it is regarded as independent of theology, but it is also viewed at other moments as rooted in the life of God.

As regards the end or goal of sexual activity, Anscombe pays attention to the intention of the agent who participates in the sexual act. She carefully distinguishes between a primary and secondary intention.[9] The primary intention of an act is the intention that is intrinsic to the act itself—the basic aim of the act that is being performed. On the other hand, the secondary intention is a further intention that accompanies the immediate act, but is not constitutive of the act as such. So, in the arena of sexual congress, the primary intention of the act of sexual intercourse, if it is morally licit, is to be open to procreation, that is, to be generative, whereas the secondary intention would be the general desire to have children or to found a family. What makes the use of contraceptives morally wrong and Natural Family Planning acceptable is how the primary intention is defined in both contexts. In the case of contraception, the primary intention of the sexual act is to block all possibility of generation, whereas this is not the case when a couple restricts sexual intercourse to the naturally occurring infertile periods. If we turn our attention to the secondary intention, it is clear

7. See G. E. M. Anscombe, "Contraception and Natural Law," *New Blackfriars* 46 (1965): 517–521, at 517: "Belief in the natural law is the belief that the discoveries of reason about ethics are the promulgation of laws to the rational creature by the Creator."

8. G. E. M Anscombe, "Modern Moral Philosophy," in *The Collected Philosophical Papers of G. E. M. Anscombe, Volume 3: Ethics, Religion and Politics* (Oxford: Basil Blackwell, 1981), 26–42.

9. Anscombe, "Contraception and Chastity": 135–36. See also G. E. M. Anscombe, *Intention*, 2nd ed. (Cambridge, Massachusetts: Harvard University Press, 2000), 34–36.

that in both situations the wish is to avoid having children. It is because the secondary intentions are the same for both contexts—i.e. for the use of contraceptives and for Natural Family Planning—that many people become confused when the Church condemns contraception yet positively endorses Natural Family Planning as a vehicle for responsible parenthood. However, it is clear that the couple practicing Natural Family Planning should not restrict all of their sexual acts to the infertile periods and remain childless throughout their marriage. To refuse to procreate at all is considered to be morally wrong by the Church and sound moral reasoning.[10] Still, we need to ask ourselves where this additional obligation or duty to be open to having children comes from when the method of Natural Family Planning as such is deemed to be morally licit. The problem here is that it appears that what is necessary is some additional content for the moral norms governing sexual ethics. Expressed differently, a wider and more encompassing context of meaning is necessary in order to inform us of the proper end or purpose of the sexual act than what mere reason can deliver.

In his book *The Very Rich Hours of Jacques Maritain*, Ralph McInerny highlights a very interesting and little known fact about Maritain's views on the Church's teaching on contraception. McInerny tells us that Maritain was convinced that there was no moral difference between the use of contraceptives and practicing the Natural Family Planning method.[11] Maritain believed that both approaches aim to avoid conception from taking place; this is the basic intention of the couple, regardless of how one wishes to analyze it. This news about Maritain's views may be surprising, given his devotion to the Church, but in fact it is quite consistent with his understanding of moral philosophy and the ultimate destiny of the human being.

When we are dealing with the moral life of the human being, we need to examine the human being in his or her wholeness. This includes all of the physical, intellectual, empirical, and spiritual realities that impinge upon the

10. See G. E. M. Anscombe, "You Can have Sex without Children: Christianity and the New Offer," in *Ethics, Religion and Politics*, 82–96, at 90–91: "But a marriage in which the intention is to enjoy intercourse and always to avoid children is invalid, not merely unchaste like the case just considered. It would not make any difference if the method of avoidance were merely regular use of infertile times: marriage contracted on this policy with a woman whose infertile time was sharply defined would be no marriage at all. We are often told that St Augustine condemned the safe period. It is not true; he condemned the Manichean practice of seeking to avoid children altogether, by using infertile times, contraceptives and sterilizants; and we ought to condemn this too."

11. Ralph McInerny, *The Very Rich Hours of Jacques Maritain: A Spiritual Life* (Notre Dame, Indiana: University of Notre Dame Press, 2003), 182–84.

human being's activity to become truly happy in life. To this end, moral philosophy needs to be informed and guided by theology, because, in the moral domain, we need to consider the ultimate end of the human being. This is Maritain's well-known doctrine of *moral philosophy adequately considered.* In his book *An Essay on Christian Philosophy,* Maritain explains his position with the utmost clarity:

> Man is not in a state of pure nature, he is fallen and redeemed. Consequently, ethics, in the widest sense of the word, that is, in so far as it bears on all matters of human action, politics and economics, practical psychology, collective psychology, sociology, as well as individual morality—ethics in so far as it takes man in his concrete state, in his existential being—is not a purely philosophic discipline. Of itself it has to do with theology, either to become integrated with or at least subalternated to theology.[12]

Maritain's unambiguous point is that human morality requires the aid of theology, of supernatural grace, and of Christian faith in order for the human being to become truly happy, which is the proper end of the moral life. If morality requires the assistance of theology, if moral reasoning needs the inspiration of faith, then reason alone cannot attain the correct insights into moral truth. A different and more expansive orientation is needed to realize the kind of lives we are meant to lead.

This broad, holistic conception of human life, as Maritain entertains it, from beginning to end, from birth to death and beyond, incorporates a vision of life as on a journey towards an ultimate end that is understood as our human destiny. This includes, naturally, a teleological perspective, but also an emphasis on temporality and history, with all the change and development that this entails. A truly adequate and hence theological ethics would need to take into account the human situation in history and time in order to conceptualize more clearly how human destiny is to be defined and understood.

This is a view that John Haldane, another important contemporary Catholic philosopher, holds. In his article "Ethics, Religion, and Relativism," Haldane presents the view that the true meaning of ethics is to be found in an historical understanding of God's providential operation in creation. Haldane writes at the end of the essay:

12. Jacques Maritain, *An Essay on Christian Philosophy,* trans. Edward H. Flannery (New York: Philosophical Library, 1955), 39.

Here we have returned to the theme with which I began: the idea that morality might depend on religion.... Here the connection is between the experience of value and a transcendent teleology. It is less immediately conceptual and more phenomenological, anthropological, and metaphysical, being the dependence of an understanding of the shared human condition, with its underlying commonalities, upon an understanding of the historical and metaphysical situation in which human life is located: an understanding that calls for an author of history and agent of providence.[13]

To situate human life within the grand sweep of the divine economy should inform us that discrete moral acts, such as in the arena of human sexuality, gain their true and ultimate meaning only against the back-drop of God's designs for His creation. As the Christian tradition informs us, God is love and His providential care over his creation is guided and motivated by love. God's love for His creation is His love for human beings, which should be the inspiration for our love for each other. A genuine interpersonal love, therefore, requires an awareness of and attachment to a source of transcendence that is marked by a commitment that persists through time, this being the hallmark of God's covenantal love for humanity. These reflections lead to the view that human sexuality requires marriage as the context of its meaning. Marriage is understood in this regards as a commitment of love between a man and a woman, persisting through life, expressing an openness to the birth and education of children, and culminating in one's destiny, which is to live in friendship with God forever. The purpose of marriage is to help human beings, with respect to their sexuality, to achieve their ultimate supernatural destiny.

Examined holistically, marriage carries within itself several meanings and serves multiple objectives. As John Witte, Jr., explains, marriage possesses four dimensions of meaning: it is a contract, social estate, natural institution and spiritual association.[14] John Finnis makes the argument, furthermore, that

[m]arriage is a distinct fundamental human good because it enables the parties to it, the wife and husband, to flourish as individuals and as a couple, both by the most far-reaching form of togetherness possible for human beings and by the most

13. John Haldane, "Ethics, Religion, and Relativism," *The Review of Metaphysics* 60 (2006): 121–39, at 138–39. See also Haldane, "From law to virtue and back again: On *Veritatis Splendor*," in *Faithful Reason: Essays Catholic and philosophical* (London: Routledge, 2004), 152–63.

14. John Witte, Jr., "The Meanings of Marriage," *First Things* 126 (2002): 30–41.

radical and creative enabling of another person to flourish, namely, the bringing of that person *into existence* as conceptus, embryo, child, and eventually adult, fully able to participate in human flourishing on his or her own responsibility.[15]

The ethical aspect of marriage is unmistakable, which is evident not only in its legal standing in society, as a binding contract that has import on financial and property arrangements, but most importantly in the overall personal development of the human being. Marriage not only aids spouses to flourish, such as by providing an intimate form of friendship and thereby allowing one to avoid the hardships of loneliness, but is an essential context for the generation and the education of children. Children require the stability and the love that comes from a happy marriage in order to thrive and succeed in life. One could say, since childhood is a necessary stage of personal development for all human beings, that marriage defines the human essence, that inscribed into the very nature of the human person is the marriage bond. Gabriel Marcel has described the essence of marriage to be its intersubjective presence, the reality that human beings are united in a nexus of relationships. A marriage is a positive affirmation of life and the child who is born from spousal love incarnates this nuptial bond.[16] On this account, to be human is to manifest the mystery of communion that marriage is.

One could justifiably argue that marriage is the proper articulation of the sexual drive in human beings that aims at procreation. Karol Wojtyła/Pope John Paul II, in his book *Love and Responsibility*, describes the sexual urge, which he distinguishes from the sexual instinct, as having an existential meaning because its aim or "vector of aspiration" is the continuation of the existence of the human species.[17] In this sense, sex and marriage are bound together, being two sides of one coin, because they both deal with the very existence of the human being, the facticity of the human person and his or her destiny, or, in other words, the fundamental life-goal that the person will pursue. The meaning of human existence—not only its nature, but also its end—is embedded in human sexuality and the ethical institu-

15. John Finnis, "Marriage: A Basic and Exigent Good," *The Monist* 91 (2008): 388–406, at 389.

16. Gabriel Marcel, "The Mystery of the Family," *Homo Viator: Introduction to a Metaphysic of Hope*, trans. Emma Craufurd (New York: Harper Row, 1962), 68–97.

17. Karol Wojtyła, *Love and Responsibility*, trans. H. T. Willetts (New York: Farrar, Strauss and Giroux, 1981), 45–54

tion of marriage that governs the coming-to-be and furtherance of human life.

To shed more light on the meaning and purpose of marriage, we can consolidate some of the points that were raised earlier in this paper. If it is true that marriage has an ethical meaning, anchored in the existence of the human person as such, and if ethics, as a form of life that aims at human fulfillment, is arguably in need of a transcendent source of inspiration and guidance, understood along the lines of a theological ethics (Maritain's moral philosophy adequately considered), then the case can be made that marriage aims at a supernatural end, one that surpasses the merely temporal and natural domains of human life.

In his reflections on marriage, Jacques Maritain depicts marriage as a work of love.[18] The proper aim of a marriage is to allow for spouses to deepen their love and to grow in the perfection of charity. The education that is undergone in a marriage and family is principally a training in love, developing the love that is present in the relationships that exist and improving it to make it more perfect. Probably the best way to describe the essence of a marriage is that it is an ongoing work-in-progress in perfecting love. When a man and a woman decide to marry, they do so typically, in our world, not because they are guided by some profound sense of vocation or destiny—that is, the conviction that they are meant to be together and that God is calling them to spend the rest of their lives as a married couple—but because of something much more banal: simply because they like each other.[19]

The impulse behind marriage proposals is quite often a feeling of romantic love, a genuine attraction to the other on a personal as well as physical or sexual level, and not some elevated, spiritual meaning of vocation. This romantic love, what Maritain calls "*amour-passion*," is undeniably a form of love and acts as a stimulant to marriage, but it must be surpassed by a higher type of love, that of dilection, the love of commitment and friendship. Dilection, which Maritain also describes as "*bel amour*," aims at "the

18. Jacques Maritain, "Love and Friendship," in *Untrammeled Approaches*, trans. Bernard Doering (Notre Dame, Indiana: University of Notre Dame Press, 1997), 165–98, at 183–88.

19. See G. E. M. Anscombe, "You Can Have Sex without Children," 94–95: "upon the whole we enter upon marriage to please ourselves, not as people entering upon a vocation. . . . Christian people neither get married with a sense of *such* a vocation nor stay unmarried because they feel the lack of it; they marry because they want to, because they must. . . ."

spiritual companionship between a man and a woman," whose basic orientation is towards the welfare of the other, instead of the satisfaction of selfish needs.[20] Dilection is the "love-for-the-good-of-the-beloved," the *amor amicitiae*, as opposed to the *amor concupiscentiae*, "the love-for-the-good-of the-subject."[21] The authentic spousal love is that of dilection, which serves the good of the other and produces a spiritual and personal friendship between spouses. This process of growth in love, originating in a self-centered love, that of romantic or passionate love, and then becoming the properly spousal love of dilection, is spurred on to climb to even greater heights, to the love of "*amour fou*," the ecstatic love of complete devotion to the other which is typically found in perfect charity.[22] *Amour fou* is the love in which the individual transcends himself and ecstatically identifies with the other.[23] It is the highest, most extreme kind of love. The lover gives himself entirely to the other and a perfect union is established. The two spouses become one flesh. However, this earthly, human ecstatic love achieves its apotheosis in the love of God, the spiritual union of the human being with God.

To love God with one's entire soul and to be completely united with God is the proper essence of *amour fou*, a rare state for any human being. To be sure, it is often thought that a tension exists between the married state and the complete devotion to God, which some maintain can only be lived out in a celibate, unmarried condition. An incompatibility does exist between these two states, Maritain asserts, if in the married state the spouses are seeking to find their proper end in themselves. In this case, the human *amour fou* and the *amour fou* for God cannot be reconciled.[24] However, it is possible to be married and to love one's spouse, both spiritually and physically, that is, in developing a friendship as well as in pursuing sexual intimacy, and at the same time to love God with an *amour fou*, as is proper to the order of the perfection of charity. Maritain explains that

20. Maritain, "Love and Friendship," 184.

21. Ibid., 166.

22. The translator of Maritain's text writes that he felt it appropriate to keep the French wording for this type of love because of the many connotations attached to this expression that would be difficult to capture with one English translation. *Amour fou* can mean mad or crazy love as well as unconditional, boundless, obsessive, exclusive and ecstatic love. See Maritain, "Love and Friendship," 168, n. 6.

23. Maritain, "Love and Friendship," 168–70.

24. Ibid., 189.

this reconciliation is made possible when the spouses give up the *amour fou* that they may have for each other and focus their *amour fou* instead on God.[25] Only God should be the object of one's *amour fou*. This does not mean that spouses cease to love one another. They continue, as they should, to love each other with the love of dilection, the proper mode of spousal love. But they need to be aware and to recognize that their gift of self needs to be perfected further in the utter abandonment to God. The path that married couples enter upon when they marry is the process of the deepening and expanding of their love, which is nothing other than the surrendering of their own egocentric desires and needs and the opening up of themselves to others. These others are one's spouse and children, but the fully transcendent Other is God, the love of whom is the ultimate purpose of marriage.

25. Ibid., 190–91.

GARY CULPEPPER

A Marriage Made in Heaven

The Maritains on Spousal Love and Mystical Life

In his essay "*Amour et amitié*,"[1] Jacques Maritain provides a commentary—or better, "reflections drawn from the experience of an old man"[2]—on a text that appears in Raïssa's *Journal*,[3] an entry dated 20 April, 1924. After Jacques develops his gloss on her text—in an effort to clarify Raïssa's own original distinction between human friendship and distinct forms of conjugal love,[4] considered both in themselves and as analogical manifestations of the Life of the Trinitarian Persons—he proceeds further to propose his own distinctive views on "some problems which today preoccupy many minds."[5] Many of the questions that Jacques seeks to address here with a kind of urgency seem very remote from our minds today: questions concerning the Christian "mystical state" and its relation to "infused contemplation," or the "active life" wherein infused contemplation is present

1. The essay appears in Jacques Maritain, *Carnet de Notes* (Paris: Desclée De Brouwer, 1965), 301–54. It appears in English translation as "Love and Friendship" in *Notebooks*, trans. Joseph W. Evans (Albany, New York: Magi Books, 1984), 219–57. The translations are my own.

2. Maritain, *Carnet*, 302; Evans, 219.

3. Raïssa Maritain, *Journal de Raïssa* (Paris: Desclée De Brouwer, 1963); English: *Raïssa's Journal*, trans. Joseph W. Evans (Albany, New York: Magi Books, 1972).

4. Though "*amour*" can, perhaps, refer to that form of love that is merely passion, or romance, it refers primarily in the Maritain's usage to the mature form of love that is inseparable from "friendship," or reciprocal love for the good of the other, integrated into the state of married love.

5. Maritain, *Carnet*, 302; Evans, 219.

though "masked."[6] The heart of his concern, however, is the Christian understanding of the relation between the goodness of conjugal love, especially in its sacramental form, and Jesus' eschatological doctrine concerning the sublation of conjugal love in the loving vision of God.[7]

Jacques' distinctive perspective on this complex subject is advanced, we might recall, in that time of conciliar ferment which produced the teaching on the "universal call to holiness" in *Lumen Gentium*. He renounced as "pseudo-theology" the view that conjugal love, with its active sexual life, is *de jure* "imperfect" relative to the religious state. His theological reflections in this essay anticipate in certain respects the well-known "Theology of the Body" proposed in the early 1980s by John Paul II, and Benedict XVI's own reflections on the relation between *eros* and *agape* in Part I of his encyclical *Deus Caritas Est*. Particularly instructive for our purposes will be the attention that Benedict draws to the criticism of Christian teaching as inherently directed toward the repression of natural human sexual desire, exemplified by Friedrich Nietzsche's aphoristic claim that Christian religion "poisons" erotic love, and thereby leaves only vicious existential possibilities for *eros* in its historical wake.[8] As with the work of these two Popes, Jacques' own

6. He treats these issues in mystical theology especially in *Carnet*, Part II, 314–33; *Notebooks*, 229–42. Although I will not treat this material in depth, it should be pointed out here that Jacques follows Aquinas in his definition of the Christian "mystical state": it is that form of Christian life wherein the Gifts of the Holy Spirit (given by grace to all Christians together with the theological virtues of faith, hope, and charity) are habitually exercised, an exercise which marks the beginning of a greater ecstatic receptivity to the unifying work of the Holy Spirit when measured by the potencies of our human nature.

7. Raïssa will refer to this "sublation" as a mystical or eschatological "surpassing the limits of the heart" (*Journal*, 221; *Raïssa's Journal* 339). She presents this doctrine in connection with the New Testament image of Jesus, and hence God, as the Bridegroom, and Jesus' quotation of the command to love God with the whole of one's heart, soul, and strength (Deut. 6:5) in the context of his new teaching on the inheritance of eternal life as presented in Lk. 10:27, Mt. 22:37, and Mk. 12:28. Jesus' teaching on the status of married persons in the resurrected form of life is presented in Mt. 22:29–30 as part of his debate with the Sadducees, just before he is presented quoting Dt. 6:5 in debate with the Pharisees, who had heard of his response to the Sadducees concerning marriage and the resurrection. Raïssa does not appeal directly to Jesus' teaching on the "displacement" of the human spouse by God in the Risen life (Mt. 22:29–30), although her reflection is formally centered on this doctrine. (See *Carnet*, 313–14; *Notebooks*, 227–29.)

8. Pope Benedict XVI, *Deus Caritas Est* (Boston: Pauline Books and Media, 2006), 3, 4–5. Benedict attempts to counter Nietzsche's charge with his argument that "Corresponding to the image of a monotheistic God is monogamous marriage. Marriage based on exclusive and definitive love becomes the icon of the relationship between God and his people and vice versa. God's way of loving becomes the measure of human love. This close connection between *eros* and marriage in the Bible has practically no equivalent in extra-biblical literature": *Deus Caritas*

teaching attempts to overcome such criticism through a renewal of Christian thinking upon the subject. His own response, however, proves more complex, given his Thomistic commitment to a framework that distinguishes "natural" human potencies, desires, and ends from the graced elevation of these potencies and desires to the supernatural end of Trinitarian life. In effect, his Thomistic analysis generates a distinct problem that requires a distinctly Thomistic solution, a problem, however, that gives greater precision to the question of the relation of the goodness of conjugal love and its eschatological fulfillment in the beatific vision of God. In particular, Jacques argues that there exists a certain existential form of erotic, conjugal love—one that featured prominently in his own married life—that must be renounced as a condition for entrance into the eschatological perfection of loving union with God. His doctrine as a whole, however, clears a path toward overcoming not only Nietzsche's view that Christianity is a form of hatred for the body, but also his view that erotic love itself, whether it have a human or God as its object, is an impediment to the desire of the will for a fullness of life.[9]

In her journal entry, Raïssa proposed this distinction between *amour* and *amitié*:

> The essence of love [*amour*] is in the communication of oneself, with the fullness of joy and delight in the possession of the beloved. The essence of friendship [*amitié*] is in a benevolence prepared to sacrifice oneself for the friend. God loves us with the love of friendship by providing for all our needs, and by dying for us upon the Cross. God loves us with love [*amour*] by making us participate in His nature by grace—by making the sanctified soul His dwelling...."[10]

In Jacques' gloss, he clarifies first that Raïssa locates these two loves, *amour* and *amitié*, and their distinction, within the unity of the love that Aquinas would identify as reciprocal love-for-the-good-of-the-beloved, or *amor amicitiae* (cf. *ST* II-II, q. 23, a. 1). The most significant feature of this distinction, according to Jacques, has to do not with the degrees of "intensity" of

---

Est, 11, 16–17. Benedict does not explore, however, like the Maritains, the question of the relation between erotic spousal love and Jesus' teaching on the perfection of erotic love in the resurrection, according to the teaching presented in Mt. 22:29–30.

9. "Love of *one* is a barbarism: for it is practiced at the expense of all others. Love of God likewise": Friedrich Nietzsche, *Beyond Good and Evil*, trans. R. J. Hollingdale (New York: Penguin Books, 1990), 90.

10. Raïssa Maritain, *Journal*, 149; *Raïssa's Journal*, 162–63.

the respective loves, but their "ontological quality," specifically, their proper power to "ecstasize" the person in a relation of union with the beloved. The difference between these loves rests ultimately on the greater unifying power, not intensity, of *eros,* specifically when integrated into the love that is friendship. According to Jacques, the person who loves with the love of friendship (*agape-philia*) offers oneself "indirectly" to the beloved through the gift of what "one has," whereas in the love that is *amour* (*eros-agape*), one offers oneself "directly" to the beloved in an exclusive and unreserved gift of the totality of one's very person, the gift of what one "is." This is a subtle distinction, as the gift of oneself to another in friendship can attain, as Raïssa points out, to that height of "intensity" which involves laying down one's life for the other, as Jesus does upon the cross. How can one give more than one's own life to another, or, alternately, from what perspective can the gift of one's own life to another be understood to be "merely" the gift of what one "has"?

Jacques' effort to clarify further the structure of love as *eros-agape* requires him to focus especially upon the power of human "spirit" acting within the embodied structure of its erotic love for the other, engaged at the peak of its own natural powers to love. A brief primer in human forms of love follows. Merely animal sexual desire for the other, constituted by covetous desire to possess the other as an object of sensual pleasure, is declared to fall short of love constituted by "spirit." The passion of romantic infatuation is the human gateway to "spousal love" at the level of the imagination, that is, as an initial awakening to the possibility of *eros-agape* within the human person as *embodied* spirit, but which, on its own, apart from a necessary purification, is mere "illusion" in its unstable hovering between a purely covetous desire and genuine concern for the other. A process of purification within the relation mediated by the passion of romantic love is necessary for the arrival of an authentically human form of *eros-agape* constituted by the power of "spirit."

Here Jacques introduces a novel distinction, based on Raïssa's text, between two existential forms of authentic conjugal love, *bel amour* and *amour fou.*[11] *Bel amour* is, according to Maritain, "the essence of conjugal love," combining the two ends of marriage, friendship and procreation through

11. One might translate these as "fair or beautiful love" and "mad, boundless love" respectively (Evans uses the latter in his translation), although I will leave them untranslated.

sexual union, in a unity of reciprocal love wherein covetousness is sublated by genuine concern for the integral good of the other.[12] The second form of conjugal love, *amour fou*, is contained, by way of anticipation, in *bel amour*, and is activated, in rare instances admittedly, as conjugal love's "absolute form," a love that "in all truth and reality is, in the order of the ontological perfections of nature, the summit of love between Man and Woman."[13] In *amour fou*, love's own unique "paradox" and "magic" are engaged, insofar as each lover, remaining ontologically a person, offers himself or herself so completely to the other that each becomes a "part which no longer exists except through and in this Whole which is his [or her] Whole."[14]

A couple of points should be raised about this discovery of *amour fou* as the perfection of human nature "as such" (that is, considered in abstraction from its existence in a state of sin, a vocation to supernatural life in the Trinity, etc.). First, Jacques points out that Raïssa's own insights into *amour fou* are derived, in their first instance, not from reflection upon conjugal love, but from the uncreated Love of God for man and the consequent gift of unrestricted human love for God and the neighbor in charity. It is the Persons of the Trinity who subsist both "in themselves" and "toward the others" in "the fullness of joy and delight in the possession of the beloved," and this without shadow or trace of covetousness in their unity of Life. Jacques, it seems, reads this perfect Love back into the structure of human nature, as a kind of Trinitarian image, when he specifies that *amour fou* arises as something "beyond" or "in excess" (*en surcroît*) of human nature, though "in response to a radical velleity inscribed in the human being."[15] This is not a "two-story" account of the relation of human nature and divine grace. Rather, it is the insight into the interdependence of the potencies of human nature and the actualizing power of divine grace that yields the inherent ambiguity of *amour fou* considered from the phenomenological point of view:

> It would be to ignore the grandeurs of our nature to believe that this creature loved with the love of *amour fou* becomes an idol for the lover, and is *necessarily* loved by him more than God. But it would be to ignore the miseries of our nature to believe that she *cannot* be loved more than God by him who loves her with *amour fou*, and *cannot* become an idol for him.[16]

12. Maritain, *Carnet*, 335; *Notebooks*, 244.
13. Maritain, *Carnet*, 307; *Notebooks*, 223–24.
14. Maritain, *Carnet*, 307; *Notebooks*, 224.
15. Maritain, *Carnet*, 336; *Notebooks*, 244.
16. Maritain, *Carnet*, 308; *Notebooks*, 224.

Accordingly, *amour fou* can be actualized both within conjugal life (or in sexual life generally) as a sinful, idolatrous love, or within a conjugal life lived in charity as a path to holiness. Clarity on this potentially confusing point requires recalling a corollary, introduced above, to the distinction Maritain makes between friendship and conjugal love, and *amour fou* in particular. The latter is greater according to its ecstatic power, that is, its power to deliver oneself from oneself into a "Whole" beyond the singular self, but *amour fou* is not necessarily, of itself, a greater love according to what Maritain calls "intensity." There are then, within love, two measures, "intensity" and "ecstatic power," and each belongs non-competitively to its own ontological domain. In this sense, it is possible to speak of loving God more greatly according to "intensity" (under the love of friendship, or the indirect gift of what one has to Him) and loving the created spouse, in this life, more greatly according to *amour fou,* in place of offering this specific form of love to God.

What is of consequence here for the larger argument, concerning conjugal love in the mode of *amour fou* as a perfection of human nature as such, is that the action of uncreated divine love does not displace embodied *bel amour* or even *amour fou* for the spouse, but creates the space for an exclusive love between embodied creatures that the uncovetous divine love positively wills for their happiness and well-being. For Maritain, there is a profound humanism in the sacrament of marriage, manifest in the actuality of an *amour fou* that terminates in the creature in a way that "excludes" spousal love for God; this is not idolatrous, however, precisely because in the institution of the sacrament, God "excludes himself" in his desire that the married man and woman enjoy this love together as embodied spirits in its exclusivity and as a path to holiness.[17]

To this point, Maritain has described a love that, again, he claims is the ontological perfection of human nature as such, lived in the charity of friendship with God and neighbor, and exercised in the love for the spouse as a non-idolatrous *amour fou.* But it is one thing to speak of this love according to the abstraction of human nature "as such"; how is one to understand the perfection of human nature as it exists in God's concrete providential economy, wherein God elects and sends the man Jesus to exist as

17. Maritain makes it clear that outwardly expressed *amour fou* for the spouse and God cannot exist simultaneously. This point will be developed further below.

the perfect embodiment of the human vocation to union with divine love? What about Jesus' teaching that, in the Kingdom of Heaven, there does not exist the state of taking and receiving in marriage (Mt 22:29–30)? Does Jesus mean here simply that there is no sexual reproduction, because the desire for more life is satisfied, while *amour fou* between creatures survives? Or does Jesus mean that in this Kingdom, God becomes our "all in all" (1 Cor 15:23–28), and the self is "ecstasized" in direct and immediate *amour fou* for God and not the spousal other? Does this later teaching not take back, at the final instant, everything that is said about the goodness of embodied love and, in the final analysis, "poison" eros with a heavenly Kingdom where *everyone* is a celibate, according to the flesh, in mystical, spousal union with God?

Maritain made no claims to have traveled *in patria* and to have returned with a report of the love that he found there. Rather, his explorations into this matter are based on his understanding of Aquinas' theology of the Gifts of the Holy Spirit, given freely as an anticipation of the love that will exist in the heavenly Kingdom. Maritain believed that these Gifts, when received as an *habitual* determination of one's existential state, are the beginning of the mystical life, that is, a foretaste of the Risen or eschatological existential state. He believed further that Raïssa was a recipient of these habitual Gifts. In the "typical" unfolding of Christian married love, the theological virtues of faith, hope, and charity heal the natural human capacities and loves, and this healing is also an elevation insofar as these capacities are ordered to a life of holiness—a divinized life—in the mutual exercise of *bel amour* or *amour fou* between the spouses. Following Aquinas, Maritain understands that the theological virtues are in themselves imperfect, and that the perfect gift of divine Love, that which for Aquinas is determinative of the reality of beatitude as participation in the interpersonal life of the Trinity, is given in the seven Gifts of the Holy Spirit as habitual modes of one's existential state. Prior to the establishment of the Gifts as habitual, the Christian lives in an existential state wherein God is active, through the theological virtues, in the human exercise of the capacities for knowing, loving, and feeling as proportioned to our created humanity. This form of Christian life is compatible with the ongoing existence of *eros-agape*, or conjugal love, expressed as *amour fou* for the created spouse, for God wills providentially the existence of such loves as the embodied sacrament and sign of uncreated divine love on earth.

The vocation to the mystical life, through the grace of the habitual presence of the Gifts, marks the initial stages of the eschatological form of life lived already now prior to one's death.[18] In other words, it marks the beginning of a form of life lived radically "beyond" the capacities for knowing, loving, and feeling given in the structures of our created natures, a life ultimately specified by the divinizing power of the loving vision of God in glory. In the vision of God that specifies the eschatological or Risen life, God is "all in all," and this form of life, Jacques makes clear, is incompatible with the possibility of finding oneself as "part" of any "Whole" other than God. The eschatological life is nothing other than being taken into the eternal, uncreated *amour fou* that is the relations or Persons of the Trinity, the One God.

Entrance into the mystical state of Christian life, then, is possible, not only for religious, but for married persons as well, without the dissolution of the sacramental conjugal bond and way of life. What must be renounced, on Jacques' account, is that *specific* form of conjugal love in which the bond is effected as *amour fou*. The reality of conjugal love will continue, according to God's providence, as a conjugal love, *bel amour*, in which embodied sexual love remains integral to the bond.[19] In this way, Maritain affirms that in the most intimate contact possible with uncreated divine love on earth—the mystical state—God wills the joy of embodied spousal love between his creatures.

This is a profoundly liminal earthly existential state, one wherein a glimpse of the reality of perfect, embodied spiritual joy is given through participation in the "uncovetous possession" of God and all things in God.[20] This appeal to the uncovetous nature of divine love is especially

18. An explanatory note should be added to this account of the mystical life. All Christians, Jacques makes clear, enter into divine glory through an act of personal *amour fou* for God in death, an act that can vary according to intensity. He specifies further that this act of *amour fou* for God is always already present by God's grace through the whole of the Christian's life, though it remains "buried in the unconscious" and reveals itself, if at all, only in momentary "flashes." The "mystic" is simply one for whom this act begins, in an habitual and conscious mode, prior to the moment of death (Maritain, *Carnet*, 318–19; *Notebooks*, 232–33).

19. Jacques' treatment of the question of chastity, in the sense of the adoption of celibate relations in such a marriage, will be taken up further below. The point here is that sexual relations are not said to be an obstacle to entrance into the mystical life.

20. In accord with Raïssa's text, and the analogical use of *amour fou* to characterize uncreated divine love, Jacques emphasizes that the love which involves "possession" of God and all things in God is a participation in the fullness of divine love, which is radically without need, and in this sense, "uncovetous" (Maritain, *Carnet*, 310–11; *Notebooks*, 225–27).

illuminated, I think, by C. S. Lewis' understanding of such love as a "supernatural Appreciative love" in God and for all things in God, characterized by that form of appreciation that arises when knowledge and love of the other is in no way mediated by unfulfilled eros within oneself.[21] This pure appreciation for the other is not, for Maritain, to be understood as the poisoning of embodied love, a negation of the goodness of the embodied other, but the very sign and reality of the fulfillment of *amour fou* for the other in a non-erotic mode, non-erotic precisely because the perfection of the bond is elevated to a fullness wherein there remains only the joy of appreciative regard for God and the created other. In the mystical state, as an anticipation of the heavenly, the ecstasizing self-gift of *amour fou* in the bond of marriage is taken up or elevated in a more comprehensive act of self-ecstasization in God Himself, in the *ad intra* life of the Trinitarian persons and the *ad extra* action of His creative and redemptive gifts. This prepares one for entrance into the eternal form of love wherein eros, body and soul, is fulfilled on the other side of death as perfect act, perfect rest, perfect participation in life-affirming praise of Life Itself. The elevation of *eros* by Christian charity, and the Gifts of the Holy Spirit, can be seen, in the light of Maritain's analysis, not as a form of nihilism or denial of the body, but rather as the most profound act of affirmation of spousal love. The false ascetic denial of the body in this life is always, on Maritain's terms, an act of pride, a rejection of God's gift of creation through an act of willing a perfection of charity prior to the providentially appointed end of one's earthly existence or its anticipation in the call to mystical life on earth. Maritian's reflection upon the perfection of spousal love in *amour fou*, sublated ultimately in *amour fou* for God (whether in death or in that "death" which is the call to the mystical state) is a resource for a more profound understanding of the sacrament of marriage as a "command" to pursue the joy of natural embodied spiritual life until heaven, or its mystical anticipations, calls one to its ultimate perfection in self-ecstasizing love for God, wherein all creatures will be loved with a love of pure contemplative appreciation in their praise of the Creator.[22]

21. C. S. Lewis, *The Four Loves* (New York: Harcourt, Brace, 1988), 10–30, and especially 139–40.

22. Jacques' comments upon the place of celibacy in marriage (Maritain, *Carnet*, 349–52; *Notebooks*, 253–56) should be understood to arise out of the freedom of those spouses who begin to relate to one another in this relation of uncovetous appreciation for the other.

Maritain's distinction between *bel amour* and *amour fou* within marriage is both novel and central to the problematic concerning the renunciation of the latter in the call to mystical or eschatological union with God. This obtains whether treating of the "ordinary" case of renouncing such love at the moment of one's death, or in the "extraordinary" case of renunciation of such love within the context of married life as a mystical anticipation of the moment of one's death. The existence of *amour fou* within Christian marriage, as an existential state of finding one's identity within the "paradox" of a part/Whole interpersonal relation with another creature, will strike many, initially if not ultimately, as a form of idolatry. Maritain attempts to defend his view against this charge through an appeal to the "magnanimity" of divine Providence, insofar as this *amour fou* between creatures, in which mystical union with God remains "buried," is preparatory for the perfect ecstatic act of finding one's identity in God alone in the beatific vision.

According to this "ordinary" operation of divine Providence, God providentially wills the joy and delight of human *eros*, body and soul, for his creatures in their dwelling upon the earth, a delight which is enhanced rather than poisoned by the healing power of divine grace and the gift of uncreated Love to the creature as *eros-agape*. The joy and delight of ecstatic union with the created spouse cannot, however, have the last word in a providential order governed by the gift of uncreated Love—a supereminent unity of *eros-agape* and *agape-philia*—poured out on humanity in the Cross of Christ. The Christian life calls for renunciation of this (penultimate, preparatory) good—the perfection of human natural love as such—before the infinite good of ecstatic union with God in the beatific vision. Does this renunciation signal that agape ultimately, at the final hour, "poisons" *eros* and the joys of bodily love and existence?

Independent of one's evaluation of Maritain's other claims, it is not at all the case that such a conclusion follows from Maritain's analysis. Further, it seems difficult to imagine an account that, while remaining within the framework of the New Testament teaching on marriage and resurrection, affirms more fully the good of spousal love as the prime analogy for union with God according to our human nature. Maritain's account of *eros-agape* does, of course, stand in opposition to Nietzsche's atheistic efforts to affirm the goodness and joy of earthly existence. But the opposition does not have to do with Christian failure to discover joy and delight in creaturely relations of love, but rather to have discovered a greater life-affirming joy in God. This joy transforms erotic love for a creature not merely into ecstatic *amour fou*, but ultimately into a love of pure appreciation of the other, a joy that transcends the delight of exclusive possession of a creature. Nietzsche might also recognize here his own rejection, not of the earth, but of the exclusivity of erotic love as adequate to the fulfillment of the life-affirming will to power. Maritain's doctrine satisfies both of Nietzsche's demands: divine providence affirms *amour fou* for the spouse over himself under the conditions of the earth as we know it in a divine affirmation of the goodness of the earth, *and* the joy of this love is sublated, renounced and preserved, in the eschatological form of appreciative love for the other, body and soul, in heaven: an uncovetous, ecstacizing *eros*. The condition for this transformation is the "jealous magnanimity" of God: the jealousy of God's claim to be ultimately loved with *amour fou* alone is the magnanimity which sets creatures free to love others with the highest love, the love of pure appreciation in the uncovetous love of the uncreated Persons.

JAMES V. SCHALL, SJ

On the Fact of "Many Good Marriages"

Statistically speaking few institutions among men are subject to so many social servitudes varying with time and the areas of civilization, to so many accidents, hazards and miseries, to so many habits of egoism and of rudeness, nay of lie or of pretense, and exposed to so many failures as marriage. This is not surprising, since the state of marriage is the condition of the very great majority of human beings. The fact remains that there are actually many good marriages, in which human nature attains a real happiness proportionate to the here-below, and through which, in causing God to create immortal souls and new human persons to come into the world, man and woman accomplish the work of propagation commanded by Him to our race in such a manner that it is truly for them and for their children what it is in the purpose of God—the great and primordial earthly blessing.

—Jacques Maritain, "Love and Friendship," *Notebooks.*[1]

I

To begin these reflections on Maritain and friendship, I cited his passage that prepares us to see, on a descriptive basis, that marriages often fail. But still, when they succeed, they constitute that "happy ending" to which all the great romantic tales aspire and with which they conclude. The juxtaposition of what succeeds and what fails is paradoxical. The marriage form

1. Jacques Maritain, *Notebooks,* trans. by Joseph Evans (Albany, New York: Magi Books, 1984), 245.

of friendship, though it goes back to the early Fathers, has recently become almost standard among many theologians as the only proper way to talk of God's relation to His creatures. The perfection of Aristotle's notion of the highest kind of friendship, that which consists in living together in a lifetime in the exchanges of all goods, particularly the highest ones, seems best carried out in what Christians understand to be a marriage of a man and a woman. The Christian idea adds a more precise notion of everlastingness to human love, something that even in the natural order seems intrinsic to it.

Yet, what Christian thought and practice have understood to be the essence of marriage increasingly, as statistics show, appears to be little observed, appreciated, or agreed with. Every form of sexual liaison is declared equal. Marriage has no "privileged" legal or public position because of its intrinsic uniqueness. One might almost say, to recall among other sources John Paul II's many discussions of it, that never have we had a nobler and more beautiful understanding of what marriage is at its best. At the same time, the institution seems almost dying for wont of those who gracefully live it till death do them part in the presence of their children and their children's children, as Scripture itself hopes they may do.

Millions of quiet abortions occur at all stages of pregnancy both among unmarried and married, in almost any country in the world. It is, we are told, a "right" and a matter of good "public" policy. Early stage abortions with a pill make the act much less visible, but they have the same result as late stage abortions with a knife. Meantime, we read of rapid population decline in the most "advanced" countries. Children not only are not born; they are not wanted. We also see the reappearance of religious polygamy. Widespread, easy divorce is common, as is concubinage, living-ins and outs, and all sorts of arrangements that not even the experts know how accurately to describe.

We have homosexuals and lesbians who suddenly tell us that they want to be "married" permanently, just like the marrieds used to do. To most of us, this arrangement seems like the last thing they would desire or agree to want, let alone faithfully practice. How many "gay divorces" follow "gay marriages?" In such "marriages," they even want children that their own processes cannot beget. Among the same homosexuals, there remains wide-spread and seemingly senseless shifting of "partners." I even saw an article advocating the legitimizing of bestiality. Another article sought to lower the age limits on sex with minors. Pedophilia, though in the news almost daily, seems unworthy even to mention, as do oral sex and other such mostly inexpressible topics.

Scientists, in the name of seeking a cure or a human "improvement" through their own methods, propose ways to bypass begetting via cloning and other anti-erotic procedures. Intercourse, let alone marriage, seems unnecessary even to keep the race going. Sex becomes sterile. State family or educational agencies claim competence to bring up the child however begotten. We have sperm and ova banks. In vitro fertilization is a regular business. We speak of designer babies who look and have intelligence like anyone but their parents. We talk of expanding our life span so we do not need many babies; we will just keep the aged going on and on. Euthanasia is likewise coming to be a favored option.

Most of these things we know, or should know, but it is worthwhile to repeat them together as they belong to the same core idea. First born females in many societies are routinely killed, as are children diagnosed before birth as potentially deformed. We no longer see many retarded children in the streets as they have already been eliminated. Not a few consider the very having of disabled or deformed children or even families with several normal brothers and sisters to be in violation of what is called "social justice." It is said to be a poor use of scarce resources. Learned professors in famous universities propose that the law allow the legal killing of unwanted or deformed babies up to a year or two after birth. From another angle, more than one or two babies are said to be a burden on the planet. In fact, not a few think human beings themselves over-tax the planet. The earth, it seems, would be doing just fine if only we humans were not running freely about on it, eating, using oil, begetting, and things like that.

The situation is actually worse than we want to admit. Leon Kass told the graduating class at St. John's College in 2007 that such scientific means are always proposed in the name of "improving" mankind. They are rarely identified as what they are. "To conquer infertility or to improve the genetic make up of our children," Kass said, "we are becoming comfortable with turning procreation into manufacture, looking upon our children less as gifts to be treasured, more as products to be perfected." We have a debate among us about whether external enemies are more dangerous than internal ones. Both are dangerous, of course. The external enemies, particularly in Islam, call our public moral situation, often said to represent "progress," degrading, which it is. The popes make the same sort of analysis.

"The greatest moral challenges headed our way do not, in fact, come from hate-filled fanatics threatening death and destruction," Kass continues.

> They come rather from well meaning scientists and technologists offering life, pleasure and enhancement.... Human nature itself lies on the operating table, ready for alteration, for eugenic and psychic "enhancement," for wholesale redesign. In leading laboratories, new creators are confidently amassing their powers and quietly honing their skills, while on the streets their evangelists are zealously prophesying a post-human future. For anyone who cares about preserving our humanity, the time has come to pay attention.[2]

Benedict XVI said as much in the Regensburg Address in 2006.

The medical profession and the scientists associated with it no longer think there is such a thing as human nature that limits their experimental activities. They try to do what they are asked to do. We are to be "redesigned" in the image of the designers, which has no source of design but their own wills and the desires of those wanting to be refashioned. This is almost exactly what C. S. Lewis predicted would happen in *The Abolition of Man*. What we know as man is being eliminated and replaced by a scientifically planned being of whatever shape or structure we can produce.

To make matters even more astonishing for the modern world, when Jacques and Raïssa Maritain, the subjects of our reflections, spoke of marriage, they addressed it also in the context of their own vows of celibacy within marriage, a rare but not unknown relationship within the history of Christianity. For many this non-practice of marital relationships seems to be the most outlandish aberration of all. This notion of celibacy is difficult enough to understand. But celibacy within marriage, except in the sense of the conditions of mutual exclusivity on which any marriage is based, seems incomprehensible to us today. The Maritains spoke from within a tradition of spiritual and even mystical perfection. But they spoke only for themselves. Their view of marriage as such was that depicted in the central line of classical and Christian thought.

Our theologians and popes, however, speak ever more frequently of the "nuptial" relation of man to God. This image of God is not based on *intellectus* and *Verbum* or on causality, but on the face-to-face fidelity that is at the

2. Leon Kass, Commencement Address, St. John's College, Maryland, May 13, 2007, http://alumni.stjohnscollege.edu/news/8277.

heart of weddings and marriages. Fergus Kerr, in *Twentieth-Century Catholic Theologians,* writes: "While the standard neo-scholastic theology course was dealing with the relationship between creature and Creator in terms of primary and secondary causality and the like, Henri de Lubac was already introducing the high theology of the epithalamic relationship between the believer and Christ which would flower in the writings of Hans Urs von Balthasar and Pope John Paul II."[3] This image of the erotic relationship is so powerful that we see most everyone trying to imitate it in conditions in which it cannot exist. The very value of the analogy of the relation of God to the world depends on getting the essence of marriage and love correct in the first place.

The Church, meanwhile, as the chief minority voice on this topic in the modern world, has pretty well conclusively spelled out what the marriage of a man to a woman should be. One might say on this basis that the Church is the last defender of the romantic as well as of the familial. Marriage is natural. It is that institution in which the highest human things of love, friendship, and fertility can occur in the most fitting manner. Man and woman are both human beings; both are gifts, with the same transcendent destiny. But they are different and irreplaceable to each other and to their children. This difference is itself a great good.

Man and woman are intended to join together in their love that can perfect themselves and others. This love is what binds them, the source of their immediate happiness. The binding love is also vital to children in their very well-being. It has its exclusivity. Out of this love, not out of scientific engineering, children are born as gifts, not "products," to use Kass' acid phrase. Children require a home, a stable relation between their parents. Indeed, using the often confusing terms of "rights," children have a "right" to a father and a mother, the father and mother that begot them. This is true even if, from natural events (death) or human disorder (divorce, promiscuity), they do not have them. The not having present what should be there is a lack that has its effect.

Even though the parental relation may and does fail in many particular circumstances, what ought to be present remains as the governing princi-

3. Fergus Kerr, *Twentieth-Century Catholic Theologians: From Neoscholasticism to Nuptial Mysticism* (Oxford: Blackwell, 2007), 83. Joseph Ratzinger's use of this same imagery is found on 199–202.

ple by which we understand what is needed and wanted in society. A failed family, as it were, does not prove the superiority of some other arrangement. Rather it proves the family's superiority. What is put into effect to replace the failed marriage or family is never superior to what is intended by marriage in the first place. Maritain's calling our attention to the difficulty in practice of living a married life is a reminder of the effects of sin. The remedy for failures is not science but a return to what love and marriage are. This latter is what is most missing in the public order. The effort to replace marriage or alter its essence produces not improvements but rather ever greater aberrations.

II

The "fact" of good marriages, alongside the "fact" of failed ones, makes it clear that this institution, what it really is, stands quite close to the center of our understanding of human nature. Good marriages take us to the heart of things, to the place of order, truth, love, passion, and responsibility in our lives. Modern political and economic thought has too often, to its detriment, ignored, or downplayed, or even attempted to replace the family. Much of the reason for the rise of big government in modern times, what has often too easily justified it, has been a direct result of failed marriages. From Plato on, we know that a delicate relation exists between our personal lives and the form and condition of the polity in which we live. Disordered forms of government follow and reinforce forms of personal failures.

It can be argued, then, that the way to restore government and politics to its proper limits is to restore or reinvigorate the family. The first step in restoring the family, however, is to think rightly about love itself in its proper human and divine manifestations. In the end, the love that ought to be at the center of marriage points to the love that is at the heart of creation, itself a reflection of the divinity. Once we know what "creation" is, it is not an accident to learn that the begetting of children is called "pro-creation." Looked on from another angle, however, the family is the neutron bomb of our social and political existence. When it blows up, the results are catastrophic for our relations with each other.

In these matters, Jacques Maritain has much to tell us. The Appendix to Maritain's *Notebooks* contains two explanatory diagrams of the material presented in the chapter on love and friendship. "Those who do me the honor of reading me," Maritain wrote, "know that I have an immoderate liking for synoptic tables and schemas."[4] He rightly sensed that what he has been saying in this chapter was "sufficiently complex" to need sketching out in organized form. The first table, on which I wish to comment here, is about the "analogical notion of love," while the second is about "the perfection of charity." Love begins with man and works its way through loveable things to God; charity begins with God and works its way to man.

Maritain's considerations go from the most fleeting sensual acts of pleasure to the mystical encounter with God. All of these experiences fall under the general heading of love and its many ramifications and distinctions. Love, as such, does not depend on making the proper distinctions, though truth does. It is not, in the end, a healthy thing to deal with love without also thinking about it. The power to think and the power to love, after all, belong to the same being and neither can function properly without the other. Truth takes us to what is worthy of being loved; love takes us to the thing actually loved.

Since many writers during and after Maritain's time, from C. S. Lewis, to Joseph Pieper, to Benedict XVI himself in *Deus Caritas Est*, have looked at these same terms—*Eros, amicitia, agape, storge, mania*—I would like to make some comments on Maritain's usage. Behind these discussions are the great philosophical and theological questions of our love for each other and for God, as well as for God's love of us. Love is said to be "blind," and it often is. Love is also said to bind, and should if that is what it is. But the purpose of love is to see clearly and rejoice in what is loved and therefore to bind ourselves to what is worthy. Both mind and heart "see." Both mind and heart strive to keep what they see in what they love.

I find Maritain's oft-used term "mad, boundless love" to be a rather awkward-sounding phrase. The original French is *amour fou. Fou* has every meaning from mad or insane to foolish. The word "mad" when added to love is not pejorative and seeks to stress the intensity of the emotion in reaction to its object. Each of the words in the translated phrase, however, has a valid history and meaning, though the word "boundless" does not seem to be in the original French except perhaps by implication. That is, a "bounded" as opposed to a "binding" love does not get at its most exalted, freeing, or ecstatic sense.

4. Maritain, *Notebooks*, 305.

The title of Pieper's masterful commentary on Plato's *Phaedrus,* itself one of the classic dialogues on love and friendship, along with the *Symposium,* was precisely *Enthusiasm and the Divine Madness.* "Enthusiasm," in one sense, means being "full of the gods." *Mania,* or madness, means, not insanity, but our uninhibited response to the reality of the divinity. When we encounter or react to it, as Plato says in the *Laws,* we do so by "singing, sacrificing, and dancing." Maritain thus has no hesitation of speaking of the "mad, boundless love" (*amour fou*) that we have for God. He can do this more easily because intimations of this sort of love exist in our relation to every thing we love, especially persons. But the marital form of this love is the one that seems to make his point most graphically.

The writers who follow Leo Strauss, again in commenting on Plato, speak of something they call the "erotic love of philosophy." This is the highest natural vocation of the rational animal. The phrase combines *Eros* and *nous.* Its relation to the love of what is beautiful, to marital love, is not accidental, as we see in the *Symposium.* The love of anything beautiful leads us upwards to what is itself beautiful. The proper analogate for "philosophical *Eros"* has to be the *Eros* found in the relation of a particular man and woman. This is what Diotima explains to her pupil Socrates. This very usage implies that the search for truth itself has behind it an unsettling, perhaps "mad," drive that can only be compared to erotic love. On first encountering it, we are taken out of ourselves because of what we unexpectedly have come across, what we previously did not know existed.

Moreover, "philosophical *Eros*" implies that truth and love have to do with objects who are persons, who can respond. Logically, no lover can help wondering if he is loved in return. Something reciprocal is expected here. Unrequited love, not surprisingly, is a cause of a great sadness in our souls. Reciprocity is precisely what distinguishes the love of benevolence from the love of friendship in Aristotle's own understanding of this matter. Truth, as it were, occasions the reality of a want of what is not ourselves into our very being. To know is to be the other, the thing known. Love looks to our seeing and willing the good of another as other. We want to know the truth of the other who is; we want to will the good of another for his own sake. Yet it is we who wish it and no love is satisfied without a return. It cannot be otherwise.

III

The first of Maritain's schemas is entitled "On the notion of love towards human beings." But the second part of this same first schema adds the "love towards God." The word "analogically" is used to say that the love of God is something like and something different from the love of one another. The experience of any true love, especially marital love, naturally finds itself in its very reality pointed to the cause of what love is in the first place. We know that we experience it. We also know that we are participating in something greater than, but inclusive of, our experience. Without our actual experience, we would not wonder about its reality and its reaches. The so-called "totally Other" of God does not make the separation of God and the world incomprehensible. Love is not an equivocal word when used of man and God.

Basically, if we love anybody, we cannot fail to know at least something of the love of God. God is always in the line of, but beyond, any finite love. Indeed, the notion of love as charity will imply that the graced love with which we love is a more than human love. The proper objects of human love are all directly created to love God above all things. We cannot love anyone who is not created with this destiny as his own end. The love of one another is also overshadowed by this divine love. It includes all those who love what God loves. This is the basis of the love of one another and indicates why the love of one another cannot be a substitute for love of God.

The "love toward human beings" in contrast to love "towards God" is said, at the bottom of the first page, to be an "object of direct knowledge in our experience." Thus, when we read through Maritain's description, it is to identify and point out something we directly know or at least ought already to know in our own lives. We do not have to have it revealed to us though we might need it pointed out to us how we already have it. This pointing out is why we study philosophy. "Philosophical *Eros*" describes the eagerness we have for knowing truth through knowing one another in conversation.

The schema is divided into two large parts entitled 1) "Disinterested love" (*amor amicitiae, agape*) and "love of covetousness" (*amor concupiscentiae, epithumia*). Evidently, the Latin *amor* is the Greek *Eros*. "Disinterested love" in its turn is divided into 1) "Love" (*Eros-agape*) gift of what one is" and 2) "Friendship" (*agape-philia*) gift of what one has." These "gifts" are both said to be based on "disinterested love." The word "disinterested" presumably is designed to distinguish it from "interested" love. In principle, it is difficult to see how any love can be anything but interested. It would be simply impossible to will the good of another without in any sense being oneself interested in the loved one. On the other hand, the point that Maritain is making is simply that the first and primary object of love is the good of the other.

When Aristotle distinguished friendships of utility, pleasure, and those of the highest things, he did not necessarily mean that there was something wrong with any of these relations. They all had a proper place and identified something worthy, something better done when they were present. In fact, precisely by calling them kinds of friendship, Aristotle meant to distinguish them from the relations of justice that were not as such friendship, even though they were good and necessary relationships.

The word "concupiscence" has a more pejorative meaning than Aristotle's friendship of utility. The latter falls within the range of things that are good. Things of utility to us are meant to supply what we need to live or live well. It is true that there is an emphasis on our needs rather than on the object that supplies the needs, but there is nothing unhealthy as such in a "passion" to enjoy a good meal or wine. There can be excess or defect here, as in all the moral virtues. Both the classical and Christian thinkers were aware of the ease with which human beings could elevate what they want out of proportion to what was right. But this difficulty was really another sort of problem from that of whether the passions were in themselves good things.

The love of covetousness means that I love the object for the pleasure or good that other gives me. But it really does give me a needed good. Imaginary food will not help me if I am hungry or even just wanting something to chew on. It can be a purely animal passion; but, as we are bodily beings, when called "passion," it can also rise to be a valid component of both friendship and the love that is *agape* in the proper kind of relationship. Thus, in the love of man and woman, this aspect will have a different modality than in other relations of friendship. Indeed, strictly speaking, passion, always called *eros* or *epithumia,* can only exist in this relation.

Maritain says that we can distinguish what he calls "*bel amour*" (more or less sketched as gift of oneself) and, in its perfection, "mad, boundless love" (full gift of oneself). These distinctions are still philosophical ones.

But he recognizes that the experiences that we have in the natural order do point across the divide between man and God, to the love we can have for God. Thus, we can have a "mad, boundless love for God," a "friendship for God," and a "desire and joy of possessing God." These are distinguished and we can have all three at once. These responses are to the reality of God and hence there is an analogy at work. We do not want to say that our relation to God is exactly like that we experience in relation to others of our kind. What we do wish to say is that what we experience is real enough. It teaches us something about what is more than ourselves, that something more lies behind what we are.

In *Deus Caritas Est,* Benedict also discussed the question of *Eros* and *agape.* It is noteworthy that the word *Eros* is seldom used in the New Testament. The word used most often for love is rather *agape.* Benedict related these as "ascending" love, from creature to God, and descending love, from God to creature. Both ultimately had the same source and hence were not contradictory. *Eros* is the Greek word. It does signify the going out to the beautiful, to the object that is not oneself. *Agape* is rather the love that goes out. It constitutes, in the case of God, the very being of the creature who is to be loved. In addition, it has the idea of sacrificial love. What is new in the New Testament is not merely to love one another, but to love one another "as I have loved you," that is, to death.

Clearly, this approach takes us into the Incarnation and the redemption. This meaning then brings up the question of forgiveness and the ability to suffer in the place of another. The "greater love than this is when a man lays down his life for his friends" is at play here.

C. S. Lewis distinguishes *philia* from *agape* and *Eros.* Aquinas, when he came to speak of the love of God, spoke of it in terms of *amicitia,* of friendship. Evidently, there is a friendship that is not an *Eros* in the proper sense. The relation of most people to each other is, once beyond justice, that of friendship, not *amor.* This is not to say that there cannot be a relation that is both *amor* and *amicitia.* Aristotle himself says that this is possible between man and wife. This is what constitutes the marital relation as one of especial importance within the human community. But this importance is enhanced by the special result of erotic love in children and all that entails. The very health of a family depends on the erotic and friendly relation of parents to each other. This is the foundation of the stability of the family and the security of the children.

Maritain calls the love of God charity. He uses the Latin word *amicitia*, not the Greek word *philia*. This becomes more important when we realize that the problem that the ancient philosophers had with the First Mover or God was precisely that this God lacked any direct relation to or interest in the human creature. This situation could not be remedied until we had a concept of a God who had what the Greek god lacked, namely, the otherness of friendship, a lack Aristotle noted in passing. The doctrine of the Trinity is thus directly related to how we define our relation to God. Is there or is there not reciprocity? Christ says in the Gospel of John that He no longer calls us servants but friends. The reason He gives for this change is that He tells us all the things that the Father has told hm. Aristotle had said that the highest act of friendship is the exchange of the highest things, indeed all things, between friends. Aquinas' use of *amicitia* as the basis of charity or the love of God thus reveals a profound truth and radical innovation in our relationship to God.

In Maritain's schema, *Eros* and *amicitia* are kept separate with *amour* holding the higher position. Maritain, however, uses the word *agape* in both contexts. One implication would be that there could be, even in the natural order, a relationship in which *Eros* and *amicitia* belong together in harmony. This would be the marriage relationship, as Aristotle himself had noted. Maritain seems to consider that the love called *philia* or friendship is lesser in intensity than the love that is *Eros-agape*. This association would correspond to the theological ideas that picture man's relation to God under the nuptial relationship. Christ loves His Church as His bride. The joy and delight that follow from what is good and beautiful are present and can be desired as such, but properly they follow from our first seeking the end itself.

IV

Joseph Pieper says that the love that is *Eros* is face-to-face, while the love that is friendship is side-by-side. Several recent philosophers from Buber to Levinas to von Balthasar have taken up the many strands of Scripture, both Old and New Testament, in which we are said to seek the "face" of God, that we long to see Him "face to face." This approach begins to take on added significance when we factor in the resurrection of the body. Joseph Ratzinger has discussed this in his book *Eschatology, Death and Eter-*

nal Live, as well as in *Spe Salvi*. What is at stake, of course, is whether the ultimate reaches of love include the precise kind of beings we are, with bodies and souls, which in principle can be the only real object of love, the complete person.

When it comes to applying the notion of "mad, boundless love" to God, we have to recall several things. The "mad, boundless love" here refers to the lovers' reaction to what, not itself, is worthy of the highest love. This is what Maritain was trying to express with the phrase, *amour fou*. Pieper will say that this kind of love is what takes us outside of ourselves, to be forgetful of self; even the word "alienated" from ourselves is sometimes used. The notion of "philosophic *Eros*" points in the same direction. In Plato's great imagery in the *Laws*, we are told that God alone is "serious." Our human affairs are really "unserious." We are the "playthings" or "toys" of the gods. These words are not used to insult us, but to point to what alone is serious.

What is interesting, in conclusion, about reading Maritain on these matters is his abiding concern with mystical and contemplative love of God. We need saints who spend their time with God, praising God, being absorbed in God. Who needs this? As Pieper said, the whole social order depends on those who spend time with God. That is to say, someone must keep the end present among us. That end is to be loved as something that, while keeping us to be ourselves (we are not Buddhists), directs our attention to what is loved.

Maritain spent a good deal of time on political and social philosophy, on art, on psychology, on diplomacy even. His excursus of the contemplative and mystical life as being so important should not escape us. We live in a time when almost the only thing we talk of is politics, this world, our own wants and needs. Christianity was in large part responsible for this turning to the world in which a man's eternal status was determined also by his practical love of his neighbor. But this same world can easily itself become, as it has become, the real god we look to. This world becomes the only kingdom and, as *Spe Salvi*, shows so well, it is not enough.

Maritain knew of the "fact of many good marriages," their importance not only in themselves but in what, by being themselves, they teach us about God. Maritain's life-witness, even in his own marriage, was to the contemplative order, to the love of God that is called "*amour fou.*" His schema allows us to acknowledge that we can also love God with the love with which He has loved us. This would be the perfection of love as it is directed to the highest object, the inner life of the divinity itself. The words used to describe this experience—*amour fou, Eros, mania, philia, agape, raptus*—each brings out something of the experience in man that arises when he beholds the God that is Trinity.

Maritain distinguishes *Eros-agape* from *agape-philia*. As I mentioned previously, the former is the more important concept. It implies that the love that is *Eros* itself can be heightened by the love that is *agape*, that is, the "gift of what one is." The logic of this wording would mean that the highest gift that we can ultimately give to God, something we could not simply do by ourselves (hence charity), is to give ourselves back to God. The emphasis, however, is not on us but on God. But we also love God with the love called "*agape-philia*. This is defined as the "gift of what one has." The *what it is* that we are was initially a gift of God to us. What we have is what we do or acquire. We turn back, give back what we are and have, as Ignatius of Loyola said, "*Quidquid habeo vel possidio, mihi lartitus es.*"

CONTRIBUTORS

MONTAGUE BROWN is professor of philosophy at Saint Anselm College, where he is also Director of the Institute for Saint Anselm Studies and Editor of *The Saint Anselm Journal*. He is the author of *The Romance of Reason, The Quest for Moral Foundations, The Restoration of Reason: The Eclipse and Recovery of Truth, Goodness, and Beauty*, and *Freedom, Philosophy, and Faith: The Transformative Role of Judeo-Christian Freedom in Western Thought*.

JOHN J. CONLEY, SJ, is the Henry J. Knott Chair of Philosophy and Theology at Loyola University Maryland. His research interests include ethics, aesthetics, and early modern philosophy. Recent publications include *The Suspicion of Virtue: Women Philosophers in Neoclassical France* (Cornell University Press) and *Adoration and Annihilation: The Convent Philosophy of Port-Royal* (University of Notre Dame Press).

BRYAN CROSS received a B.S. in cellular and molecular biology from the University of Michigan, a M.Div. from Covenant Theological Seminary, and a Ph.D. in philosophy in December, 2012, from Saint Louis University. His dissertation is titled "Alasdair MacIntyre on the Practice of Philosophy" and focuses on the implications of MacIntyre's philosophy regarding our understanding of both the pedagogy and practice of philosophy. He has taught philosophy at Saint Louis University, Lindenwood University, and Kenrick-Glennon Seminary. He presently lives in Saint Louis, Missouri, with his wife Carol and two daughters.

GARY CULPEPPER is associate professor of theology at Providence College in Providence, Rhode Island. He teaches courses at the undergraduate and graduate level in the thought of St. Thomas Aquinas, contemporary Christian theology, and the history and methods of Christian theology. He is a member of Evangelicals and Catholics Together and the Jewish-Catholic Theological Exchange. His primary area of research is the history of the transmission of the doctrines of God and Christ from their patristic and medieval forms into the present, with particular attention to the work of St. Thomas Aquinas and his present-day interpreters. He is married to his wife Katherine, and is grateful for the gift of their two daughters, Marie and Anne.

BROOKE WILLIAMS DEELY is the author of two scholarly monographs in history and philosophy, *Jacques Maritain: Antimodern or Ultramodern?* and *History and Semiotics.* She has also authored essays on Maritain, as well as in the fields of semiotics and women's studies. Several of her essays have been translated and published abroad. She is co-editor of an anthology, of a book series in semiotics, and guest co-editor of a Special Issue on History of the international journal *Semiotica.* She has taught at the University of New Mexico, University of Delaware, Loras College, Indiana University, and, since 2000, the University of St. Thomas, Houston, in the Honors Program, Philosophy Department, Master of Liberal Arts Program, and Study Abroad Program, for which she taught a course on the Maritains in France. She directed the Women, Culture, and Society Program from 2009–2012.

JOHN MARSON DUNAWAY is professor of French and interdisciplinary studies at Mercer University in Macon, Georgia. He was presented the Jacques Maritain Scholarship Award by the American Maritain Association in 2007 and is a former Vice-President of the association. His publications have centered on French religious writers, notably Maritain, Simone Weil, and the Catholic novelists. His translation of Vladimir Volkoff's 2004 novel, *L'Hôte du Pape/The Pope's Guest,* will appear next year at Mercer University Press.

LAWRENCE FEINGOLD converted to Catholicism in 1989 together with his wife, while engaged in realist marble sculpture in Pietrasanta, Italy. He studied philosophy and theology at the Pontifical University of the Holy Cross in Rome from 1990 to 1999, earning a doctorate in Dogmatic Theology, summa cum laude, with a dissertation entitled *The Natural Desire to See God According to St. Thomas Aquinas and His Interpreters* (2nd edition: Ave Maria, Florida: Sapientia Press, 2010). From 2006 to 2012 he was an assistant professor of theology in the Institute for Pastoral Theology of Ave Maria University. Since 2012, he has been an associate professor of theology and philosophy at Kenrick-Glennon Seminary in St. Louis. Recent books are *The Mystery of Israel and the Church* in three volumes: Vol. 1, *Figure and Fulfillment*; Vol. 2, *Things New and Old*; Vol. 3, *The Messianic Kingdom of Israel* (St. Louis: The Miriam Press, 2010).

PETER FELDMEIER holds the Murray/Bacik Endowed Chair in Catholic Studies at the University of Toledo. He received his Ph.D. in Christian spirituality from the Graduate Theological Union in Berkeley in 1996 and has written extensively in Catholic systematic theology, comparative theology, and Christian spirituality. His most recent books are *The Assurance of God: A Response to Atheism and a Reason for Faith* (Liguori, 2013), *Encounters in Faith: Christianity in Interreligious Dialogue* (Anselm, 2011), and *The Path of Wisdom: A Christian Commentary on the Dhammapada* (Peeters/Eerdmans, 2011). He was also "The Word" Columnist for *America Magazine* in 2011–2012.

DANIEL B. GALLAGHER, a priest of the Diocese of Gaylord, works in the Office of Latin Letters at the Vatican Secretariat of State. He taught philosophy at Sacred Heart Major Seminary and is the editor of the *Values in Italian Philosophy* series. A regular contributor to the *Philosophy and Popular Culture* series and *The Berkshire Review*, he has also published in *First Things, Josephinum Journal of Theology, Fellowship of Catholic Scholars Quarterly, Sacred Architecture Journal, Maritain Studies, New Oxford Review*, and other scholarly journals and books. His main interests lie in metaphysics and aesthetics, and particularly in the overlapping issues of classical, medieval, and modern theories of beauty and art.

JAMES G. HANINK is professor of philosophy at Loyola Marymount University (Los Angeles). He contributes to publications of the American Maritain Association, most recently "Does the Philosophy of Nature Need the Intuition of Being? If So, What Is It?" in *Reading the Cosmos: Nature, Science, and Wisdom*, ed. Giuseppe Butera (2011). For a contribution to the Canadian Jacques Maritain Association, see his "The Metaphysics of Moral Evil: Context, Truth and Character," in *Études Maritainiennes / Maritain Studies*, XXVI. Hanink is active in University Faculty for Life. See, for example, his "Jacques Maritain and the Embryo: A Master's Muddle," in

Life and Learning XV. He and his wife Elizabeth have five children and four grandchildren.

HERBERT E. HARTMANN received his philosophical education at the University of Toronto from 1972 through 1979. While there, he studied with Father Weisheipl, Father Owens, and Professors K. Schmitz, L.E. Lynch, Alan Bloom, and Anton C. Pegis. Dr. Pegis had chosen him to be one of three inaugural professors at the Center for Thomistic Studies at the University of St. Thomas in Houston. Following the death of his father in 1979, he relocated from Houston to Chicago to manage and oversee the family business, but he continued to teach full-time and part-time for thirteen years at Loyola University of Chicago. He has been teaching full-time since 1993: Thomas Aquinas College (1993–2005); Southern Catholic College (2005–2010); and Our Lady of Thornwood Seminary (2010–2012). He is presently a Clinical Professor of Philosophy in the School of Philosophy at Catholic University of America.

DONALD J. KEEFE, SJ, entered the New York Province of the Society of Jesus in 1953, having received an LLB from Georgetown University Law Center. He received the S.T.D. degree from the Pontifical Gregorian University in 1967. Study during this period led to the publication of *Thomism and the Ontological Theology of Paul Tillich* (Leiden: Brill, 1971). In 1991 he published in two volumes the primary statement of his methodological approach in theology, *Covenantal Theology: The Eucharistic Order of History*, and later a revised edition in a single volume with Appendix (Novato, California: The Presidio Press, 1996). Among some forty-five articles he has published, a helpful illustration of Keefe's approach may be found in his "Authority in the Church: An Essay in the Theology of History," *Communio* 7 (Winter, 1980): 343–63. A further treatment of the issues discussed in the present contribution may be found in "Liberation and the Church: The Illusion and the Reality," *The Center Journal* 1 (Winter, 1981): 45–64, and in "The Relation of Nuptial Symbolism to Eucharistic Realism," *The Pacific Journal of Theology*, II/21 (1999): 88–119.

CHRISTOPHER P. KLOFFT received his Doctorate of Sacred Theology from The Catholic University of America. He is currently assistant professor of theology at Assumption College in Worcester, Massachusetts. His fields of specialization include sexual ethics, gender, marriage, moral development, and the intersection of morality with culture and politics. He is the author of *Living the Love Story: Catholic Morality in the Modern World*, published by Alba House (2008) and is presently preparing a work highlighting the crisis of culture resulting from an inadequate anthropology of sexuality.

CATHERINE M.A. MCCAULIFF received her Ph.D. in medieval studies at the University of Toronto. She previously received an A.B. *cum laude* from Bryn Mawr College and later a J.D. from the University of Chicago. She now teaches European Union law, European Legal History, Agency, Partnerships LLCs, First Amendment and Comparative Law and Religion, among other offerings, at Seton Hall University School of Law. Professor McCauliff is writing a book on Maritain as a European facing some of the most important issues of his (and our) time: 1) the need to respect human rights across the globe, 2) the commitment of Europe to an identity marked by peace, unity, justice and economic fairness, and 3) the recognition of religious freedom for all peoples and persons, just as she expanded her essay published here for an article in the *Seton Hall Law Review*.

JOHN F. MILLARD received his B.A. from Boston College and his M.A. and Ph.D. from the University of Toronto. He now teaches at The Blessed John XXIII National Seminary, where he is the Director of the Pre-Theology Program. Dr. Millard has for many years been a regular participant in and supporter of the American Maritain Association.

CHRISTOPHER S. MORRISSEY is associate professor of philosophy at Redeemer Pacific College, the Catholic liberal arts college at Trinity Western University in Langley, British Columbia, where he also teaches courses in the Latin language and in Greek and Roman history. He studied Greek and Latin at the University of British Columbia and has taught courses in these languages and in other classical subjects at Simon Fraser University. Morrissey specializes in philosophical theology and his recent focus has been on its genesis in the monotheistic speculations of Hesiod and Plato, as suggested by Eric Voegelin's philosophy of history. Morrissey's book of Hesiod's poetry has been published by Talonbooks. He has also published book chapters and journal articles on the philosophy of Thomas Aquinas and his commentatorial tradition, which includes John Poinsot ("John of St. Thomas"), from whom we may trace a foundational doctrine of signs for the interdisciplinary field of semiotics.

BERNADETTE E. O'CONNOR is professor of philosophy at the University of the Incarnate Word in San Antonio, Texas. Her research interests are in Thomistic metaphysics, Heideggerian *Seinsdenken*, and the contributions psychoanalytic thought, feminist studies, and cultural studies can make to the development of the natural law. She has other publications forthcoming from the American Maritain Association.

FRANCISCO PLAZA is associate professor of political science at Palm Beach Atlantic University and Chair of its department of history and political science. Prior to his current academic position, Plaza founded the first liberal arts program in Venezuela and served as Representative of Venezuela to the Organization of American States. A graduate of The Catholic University of America, his doctoral dissertation, "The Spirit of Truth in the Forces of Freedom," explores the political thought of Yves R. Simon. His most recent book, *El Silencio de la Democracia* (Caracas: El Nacional, 2011), identifies the challenges to democratic stability in Latin America in light of the totalitarian drive of emerging mass political movements. This book also belongs to Plaza's broader research project, which looks to retrieve the unspoken foundational strengths of the liberal-democratic order from the perspective of personalism, as developed by such authors as John Paul II, Maritain, Guardini, Voegelin, and Millan-Puelles.

JONATHAN J. SANFORD is professor of philosophy and Assistant Vice President of Academic Affairs at Franciscan University of Steubenville. He is the editor, with Michael Gorman, of *Categories: Historical and Systematic Essays* (CUA Press, 2004), and a book in Wiley-Blackwell's Philosophy and Popular Culture series, *Spider-Man and Philosophy: The Web of Inquiry* (2012). He is the author of a number of articles and book chapters addressing metaphysical and ethical questions from an Aristotelian-Thomistic perspective. His latest manuscript, *Before Virtue: A Critical Reflection on the Contemporary Virtue Ethics Movement* is currently under press review. He has been a member of the American Maritain Association since 2008.

JAMES V. SCHALL, SJ, is a professor in the department of government at Georgetown University. His books include *The Modern Age*, *The Mind That Is Catholic*, *At the Limits of Political Philosophy*, *Another Sort of Learning*, *On the Unseriousness of Human Affairs*, and *Schall on Chesterton*.

GLENN STATILE is currently an associate professor at St. John's University in New York City. He specializes in the history and philosophy of science, science and religion, aesthetics, and philosophy of religion. He has published widely in such journals as *The Philosophical Forum*, *Aitia-Humanities Magazine*, and the *Fellowship of Catholic Scholars Quarterly*. He is the editor of *The Tests of Time* published by Princeton University Press as well as *The Journey of Metaphysics* published by Pearson, now in its 5th edition. He is also the author of *Polymathics Investigations* and two books on Descartes. He resides in Astoria, New York, with his wife Agnes.

WILLIAM SWEET is professor of philosophy at St. Francis Xavier University, in Nova Scotia, Canada. He is a past president of the Canadian Philosophical Association, president of the Istituto Internazionale Jacques Maritain (Rome), president of the World Union of Catholic Philosophical Societies, and a member of the Steering Committee of the Fédération Internationale des Sociétés de Philosophie. Among his recent books are *Responses to the Enlightenment: An Exchange on Foundations, Faith, and Community* (2012, with Hendrik Hart), *Migrating Texts and Traditions* (2012), and *Ideas Under Fire* (2012, with J. Lavery and L. Groarke). He is also editor and translator of Maritain's *Natural Law: Reflections on Theory and Practice* (2001) and Maritain's *Lectures on Natural Law* (Notre Dame, forthcoming).

JOSÉ YULO teaches courses on philosophy, western civilization, United States history, and public speaking, utilizing a modified form of the ancient Socratic method. He has a Doctorate in Education from the University of San Francisco, with an emphasis on the philosophy of education. He also holds a Master's degree in political communication from Emerson College in Boston, as well as a Bachelor's degree in the classical liberal arts from St. John's College in Annapolis, Maryland. Originally from Manila in the Philippines, his research interests lie in Greek philosophy, the histories of Greek and Roman politics and warfare, and the literature of J. R. R. Tolkien.

NIKOLAJ ZUNIC is an associate professor of philosophy at St. Jerome's University in Waterloo, Ontario, Canada. He earned his BA at the University of Toronto and his MA and PhD at the Institute of Philosophy of the Catholic University of Leuven, Belgium. In his research, he focuses on philosophical anthropology, metaphysics, modern and contemporary philosophy, particularly in the German philosophical tradition, and 20th-century personalism, with figures such as Martin Buber, Gabriel Marcel, Jacques Maritain, and Max Scheler. He has published articles in various academic journals, such as *American Catholic Philosophical Quarterly*, *The Heythrop Journal* and *Maritain Studies*. He is also the editor of the AMA volume *Distinctions of Being: Philosophical Approaches to Reality*, just published by Catholic University of America Press (2013).

INDEX OF NAMES

PUBLICATIONS OF THE AMERICAN MARITAIN ASSOCIATION

GENERAL EDITORS

Anthony O. Simon (1990–2004)

Michael Torre (2009–2013)

Jacques Maritain: The Man and His Metaphysics

Edited by John F. X. Knasas, 1988

ISBN 978-0-268-01205-2, (out of print)

Distributed by the University of Notre Dame Press

Freedom in the Modern World: Jacques Maritain, Yves R. Simon, Mortimer J. Adler

Edited by Michael D. Torre, 1989, Second Printing, 1990

ISBN 978-0-268-00978-6

Distributed by the University of Notre Dame Press

From Twilight to Dawn: The Cultural Vision of Jacques Maritain

Edited by Peter A. Redpath, 1990

ISBN 978-0-268-00979-3

Distributed by the University of Notre Dame Press

The Future of Thomism

Edited by Deal W. Hudson and Dennis Wm. Moran, 1992

ISBN 978-0-268-00986-1

Distributed by the University of Notre Dame Press

Jacques Maritain and the Jews

Edited by Robert Royal, 1994

ISBN 978-0-268-01193-2

Distributed by the University of Notre Dame Press

Freedom, Virtue, and the Common Good
Edited by Curtis L. Hancock and Anthony O. Simon, 1995
ISBN 978-0-268-00991-0
Distributed by the University of Notre Dame Press

Postmodernism and Christian Philosophy
Edited by Roman T. Ciapolo, 1997
ISBN 978-0-8132-0881-7
Distributed by the Catholic University of America Press

The Common Things: Essays on Thomism and Education
Edited by Daniel McInerny, 1999
ISBN 978-0-9669226-0-8
Distributed by the Catholic University of America Press

The Failure of Modernism: The Cartesian Legacy and Contemporary Pluralism
Edited by Brendan Sweetman, 1999
ISBN 978-0-9669226-1-5
Distributed by the Catholic University of America Press

Beauty, Art, and the Polis
Edited by Alice Ramos, 2000
ISBN 978-0-9669226-2-2
Distributed by the Catholic University of America Press

Reassessing the Liberal State: Reading Maritain's Man and the State
Edited by Timothy Fuller and John P. Hittinger, 2001
ISBN 978-0-9669226-3-9
Distributed by the Catholic University of America Press

Faith, Scholarship, and Culture in the 21st Century
Edited by Alice Ramos, and Marie I. George, 2002
ISBN 978-0-9669226-5-3
Distributed by the Catholic University of America Press

Jacques Maritain and the Many Ways of Knowing
Edited by Douglas A. Ollivant, 2002
ISBN 978-0-9669226-4-6
Distributed by the Catholic University of America Press

Truth Matters: Essays in Honor of Jacques Maritain
Edited by John G. Trapani, Jr., 2004
ISBN 978-0-9669226-6-0
Distributed by the Catholic University of America Press

The Human Person and a Culture of Freedom
Edited by Peter A. Pagan Aguiar and Terese Auer, O.P., 2009
ISBN 978-0-9669226-7-7
Distributed by the Catholic University of America Press

Maritain and America
Edited by Christopher M. Cullen, S.J. and
Joseph Allan Clair, 2009
ISBN 978-0-9669226-8-4
Distributed by the Catholic University of America Press

The Renewal of Civilization:
Essays in Honor of Jacques Maritain
Edited by Gavin T. Colvert, 2010
ISBN 978-0-9669226-9-1
Distributed by the Catholic University of America Press

The Vocation of the Catholic Philosopher:
From Maritain to John Paul II
Edited by John P. Hittinger, 2010
ISBN 978-0-9827119-0-3
Distributed by the Catholic University of America Press

Reading the Cosmos: Nature, Science, and Wisdom
Edited by Giuseppe Butera, 2011
ISBN 978-0-9827119-1-0
Distributed by the Catholic University of America Press

Distinctions of Being: Philosophical Approaches to Reality
Edited by Nikolaj Zunic, 2013
ISBN 978-0-9827119-2-7
Distributed by the Catholic University of America Press

Love and Friendship: Maritain and the Tradition
Edited by Montague Brown, 2013
ISBN 978-0-9827119-3-4
Distributed by the Catholic University of America Press

CPSIA information can be obtained at www.ICGtesting.com
Printed in the USA
BVOW08s0337120913

330951BV00001B/18/P

9 780982 711934